The Other Shakespeare

The Two Gentlemen of Verona

The Other Shakespeare

Unexpurgated Edition

The Two Gentlemen of Verona

---

by William T. Betken

BARDAVON BOOKS
Rhinebeck, New York

First Edition, 1982

Library of Congress Cataloging in Publication Data

Shakespeare, William, 1564-1616.
    The other Shakespeare—the Two gentlemen of Verona.

    Bibliography: p.
    1. Betken, William T., 1924-   II. Title.
PR2838.A2B4   1982   822.3'3   81-52512
ISBN 0-941672-00-X (Clothbound)   AACR2
ISBN 0-941672-01-8 (Paperback)

Valentine Publishing & Drama Company
PO Box 461, Rhinebeck NY 12572

TABLE OF CONTENTS

PROLOGUE

I love Shakespeare.

And I am frustrated and heartsick that actors everywhere mouth their lines without understanding most of them, and that audiences everywhere listen to these lines with even less understanding—while all pretend otherwise.

It is my purpose here to take just one of Shakespeare's plays, *The Two Gentlemen of Verona*, refute the absurd interpretation of it by even the most eminent of scholars, and, finally, to replace such misinterpretation with something far closer to the play's original Elizabethan meaning.

Furthermore, virtually every refutation and every new meaning proposed here is underpinned by reference to the accepted literature of the past several hundred years as well as to Shakespeare's other works. This means that for the sake of scholastic validity the reference notes are rather copious. Realizing that many readers and students may not be interested in the detailed process of scholastic validation, these notes form one of four separate sections of this work—*Notes*.

The main section, of course, is the play itself in its original form other than the usual modernizing of punctuation, spelling, and verse-prose alignment. This is titled *Original*.

Another section, designed for the general reader, has the self-explanatory title of *Comments*.

The final section, appearing parallel with the *Original*, is a line by line rendering of the original from Elizabethan English to modern American English. This section—*Modern* —is technically speaking an adaptation, not a version. Its purpose is precisely that of a libretto translating from one language to another.

Lest the word "translation" be met with horror by purists, it is nothing new at all. Any edition of Shakespeare with footnotes—which is to say all editions—is presenting a partial translation. Since I found it necessary for scholarly validation to offer so many notes on the meaning of words and lines, the very exposition of such meaning was becoming self-defeating; it is bad enough that readers of any edition must jump back and forth between footnotes and text, but to multiply this problem, even with the best of intentions, was unacceptable. So I simply carried the process to its only logical conclusion, which was to in effect make a note on each and every word of the play, in modern American English, and then put them all together in a modern libretto.

Instead then of jumping to footnotes for explanations or meanings, the general reader may refer to the *Modern* text paralleling the *Original*. Where doubt or additional curiosity still exists the reader may then refer to the *Notes* themselves. To this end the meaning of a given *Modern* line, with few exceptions, compares to its physically parallel line of the *Original*. No attempt has been made to alter or "improve" Shakespeare in the slightest—only to adhere faithfully to the original meaning line by line. Further discussion of this point can be found in the *Induction* which follows.

It is recommended that the reader first read the *Original* text to refresh his (or her) memory or, if new to the play, to get the feel and sweep of it. He then obviously has a variety of approaches on the second reading—*Comments* and/or *Modern* text, and/or *Notes* —depending on his interests and inclination. To fully understand the bawdy sections, however, he will want to refer to the glossary at the end of the book if not also the *Notes*.

Although more detail regarding the bawdy will be found in the *Induction*, it should be noted here that understanding much of Shakespeare depends on an understanding of the bawdy he employs. Recent findings of modern scholars in this area of Shakespearean study are revealing whole new meanings to many of his lines and allusions. It is incredible— and should not have been—that some of the most common bawdy terms have to this day remained unnoticed; *wit*, for example, meaning male or female pudend, is rife in Elizabethan plays and is used in this bawdy sense by Shakespeare alone dozens of times. Of course all bawdy terms then had to be couched in double entendre to accommodate the censor and the church, both of which in turn had to accommodate a very permissive queen. While this particular edition is unexpurgated, a young people's version, suitably revised and shortened, is planned.

Finally, it should be emphasized that *The Two Gentlemen of Verona* is regarded as one of the least of Shakespeare's plays. It has been generally thought of as the most immature, carelessly written, awkwardly constructed, and inane by most scholars, some even attributing it to non-Shakespearean hands. If I feel sorry for the bard's being generally unappreciated in full because he is so sorely misunderstood, it is only natural that I feel especially sorry for his genius being unappreciated in this, the "ugly duckling" of his plays.

And now it's curtain time.

New understanding of Shakespeare must in the last analysis be supported by something other than personal deduction or opinion.

To begin with, the greatest departure here from all previous editions is in the assignment of bawdy meanings to certain words. So many such conjectures are indicated here for the first time that they add up to a significant expansion of what is called Shakespearean bawdy.

The last is a misnomer; there is only an Elizabethan bawdy, which of course Shakespeare shared. Thus, just for one example, almost all of the bawdy terms used in this play can be found with the same bawdy usage in *Ralph Roister Doister*, a play by Nicholas Udall some fifty years before *The Two Gentlemen of Verona*. However, the support used herein is limited to Shakespeare's own works for added validity. A minimum of two such uses, each from different plays, are offered in the glossary. The expression *et al* after the citations of bawdy cross-references indicates that Shakespeare uses the term frequently.

As modern students of Shakespeare know, Eric Partridge's *Shakespeare's Bawdy* is the only major contribution to the bard's bawdy ever, and he is the first to truly recognize the extent of it. He was and is, however, primarily a lexicographer, especially of slang and "underground" English, and he subsequently applied this knowledge to Shakespeare's writings.

Kökeritz, for one, has criticized his book: "Despite its sensational title this glossary of obscene allusions in Shakespeare's plays and poems has little new to offer; it is a casual piece of work, obviously carried out in great haste and very incomplete. Nevertheless it has some value, mainly because of the detailed picture it provides of Elizabethan broadmindedness. This is, indeed, its redeeming feature." This edition joins, although more mildly, in that assessment.

Partridge has an unscholarly habit of assigning a bawdy meaning on the basis of only an isolated instance with the to be expected result that in a few cases he is simply wrong, being perhaps overly eager to see bawdy where it does not exist. In many other instances he is in the right bawdy, but in the wrong interpretation. But this aside, his work stands as a major milestone in what is bound to become a new evaluation of Shakespearean, and for that matter Elizabethan drama.

This edition is particularly indebted to Partridge, but not for the expected reason. Although his work is cited frequently here it is almost always as additional reference to the self-imposed support criteria already referred to.

The indebtedness of this edition to Partridge rests in his having made the study of Shakespeare's bawdy respectable. His well known glossary probably would not have been widely accepted were it not for his reputation as a lexicographer.

In this volume all bawdy terms are asterisked in the notes and found in the glossary with supportive cross-references to similar usage in the other plays.

The only other recent milestone in considering Shakespeare anew is Helge Kökeritz' *Shakespeare's Pronunciation*. It is a sincere, scholarly, and thorough study of the way the Elizabethans "probably" pronounced their words. Unfortunately the work is so fastidiously detailed and weighed down with the jargon of orthoepy and orthography (the study of pronunciation and spelling, in other words) that it never gained the widespread attention it deserves.

This edition however is very indebted to that work. New meanings and confirmation of old ones arise from knowledge of probable Elizabethan pronunciations and spellings. Thus *lease* was pronounced *leash*, explaining Shakespeare's double entendres with these two words. Similarly, *sleep* and *slip, suit* and *shoot, read* and *rid, raising-raisin-reason, ship-shape-sheep*—to mention just a few—all had identical or nearly so pronunciations. Kökeritz, like Partridge, has discovered new bawdy meanings based on his own findings, and he is also frequently cited in this edition.

Of the many editions extant of *The Two Gentlemen of Verona* only two—the *Arden Shakespeare* (1969) and the new *Cambridge* edition (1921)—stand far beyond all others in their exhaustive detail and thoughtful interpretations. Precisely because of this they required the most refutation, accounting for the frequency with which they are cited here.

Of course the source material of all other references are to be found in the appended bibliography. To avoid cumbersomeness only the last name (e.g., Bond, Malone, Theobald) of the author is given at the point of citation; accommodating this is the arrangement of the bibliography alphabetically by last name. Distinguishments between multiple works of the same author are noted.

The majority of notes on word meanings are far more extensive than and differ from all standard editions. This is so primarily to allow a reading of the *Original* completely independent of the *Modern*, and secondarily to render meanings in American rather than British English. Word groups have also been considerably expanded beyond the usual for easier referring back to the *Original* text (e.g., *learn me* — teach me, instead of the usual *learn* – teach). Also, the objective here is that of specificity and accuracy of meaning, whereas meanings in the *Modern* are somewhat compromised to accommodate meter, rhyme, and above all "fluidity"— immediate understanding—of the meaning.

Writing what is essentially a *Modern* adaptation was of course the most laborious effort of all. After many approaches were tried it was decided to use only two criteria— *meaning* and the *fluidity* of that meaning in terms of modern American English. It seemed to be the most valid road to an optimum compromise, and compromise is all it ever can be, between original meaning and modern understanding.

Within that guideline faithfulness to the original meaning was always given preference over modern meaning whenever something had to give. Thus the "style" of the modernization may often appear stodgy, sometimes perhaps stilted. This was aggravated by the attempt to have the meaning of one line identical with that of its "companion" line—i.e., not allow the easier overall equating of a group of lines with their counterparts. That difficulty was increased by the limitations of retaining the same meter, and occasionally rhyme, in the *Modern*. The only exceptions to these standards are stretches of prose bawdy where converting into "modern bawdy" and keeping the humorous flavor required that certain liberties be taken.

No attempt was made to "improve" on Shakespeare or to be clever, innovative, or poetic. Modern slang or allusions, often tempting, were disdained to avoid an unwanted "modernization" of place, time, and characters. Similarly words and concepts such as *master, servant, mistress* Silvia, *Sir* Valentine, were retained. Every decision had its exceptions: normally *thou, hath, wouldst* were replaced with *you, has, would,* just as *shall* and *will* were interchanged, yet well known and often quoted lines are largely untouched; *alas*, as some other words, has, with exceptions, been replaced because of its modern connotation of humorous exaggeration. These are merely a few of the line-by-line considerations that had to be made. There is really no way to appreciate the problems of the process except to try one's own hand at it after setting one's own criteria.

The whole purpose of this edition is limited to bringing this play back to its original Elizabethan life insofar as that can be done through modern meaning. To this end there are several facets of Shakespearean study deliberately omitted or not emphasized as being more of a cluttering hindrance than a revealing help.

Accordingly extensive discussion of the folio printing of the play, of original dearth of stage directions, of scene headings, of performances, etc., is omitted except to note here that this play may have been far more popular than formerly thought. Fact #1, three plays, and only three, in the 1623 (first) printing have a glaring similarity in format which is not explained away by their having had the same transcriber (Ralph Crane) in common; Fact #2, two of them, *The Merry Wives of Windsor* and *The Winter's Tale*, were still being performed at that time; and Fact #3, a non-fact, nobody knows whether this third play of that group, *The Two Gentlemen of Verona*, was or was not still being performed at or about that time. Based on these considerations any unprejudiced conclusion would be the probability that such performances, some thirty years after its debut, did occur, which in turn would suggest that this play was exceptionally popular. But all of the scholars addressing this riddle, prejudiced by their own judgment that this is a "poor" play, assume, simply assume, that the play was an Elizabethan turkey and try to explain away the riddle with an assortment of theories that are as wild as they are weak.

Also, there is no discussion here of the so-called "source material", which can be helpful to a serious scholar, but is useless to the general reader. Unfortunately, there is a breed of scholars which delights in finding a line, character, or event in one play that is similar to another such item in one of Shakespeare's other plays; and they truly become ecstatic if they find a similarity in mythology or some obscure literature. But the heralded "discovery" is never followed by a statement as to how it is significant. There is however, an implication that the bard was a kind of bookworm who wrote his plays in a library of an ivory tower without benefit of life's experience, and this could not be further from the truth.

This edition stipulates to Shakespeare's utilization of ideas from both reading and experiencing, but no Elizabethan playwright, no playwright, approaches Shakespeare in the transformation of basic ideas into brilliant drama. If "source material" reveals anything at all it is that a piece of coal can be transformed into a diamond.

Finally, no pseudo-intellectual psychoanalysis of the characters will be found here. Or will there be the slightest suggestion that Shakespeare "meant" something other than he said, or that he is "really" exploring, presumably between the lines, some philosophical concept, or that the play is "in truth", unbeknownst of course to the audience, a disguised allegory. Shakespeare is nothing if he is not plain and straightforward.

Plain and straightforward is what this book, in its own way, hopes to be.

* * *

THE TWO GENTLEMEN OF VERONA

CHARACTERS

DUKE OF MILAN, father of SILVIA
VALENTINE and
PROTEUS, Gentlemen of Verona
ANTONIO, father of PROTEUS
THURIO, a foolish rival to VALENTINE
EGLAMOUR, agent for SILVIA in her escape
SPEED, a clownish servant to VALENTINE
LAUNCE, servant to PROTEUS
PANTHINO, servant to ANTONIO
HOST, with whom JULIA lodges in Milan
OUTLAWS
JULIA, a lady of Verona, beloved by PROTEUS
SILVIA, beloved by VALENTINE
LUCETTA, waiting woman to JULIA
Servants, Musicians.

TIME

Sixteenth century.

PLACE

Italy: in Verona, in Milan, and a Forest.

All names above were pronounced in Shakespeare's time for all practical acting purposes the same as modern American or British English. Only four offer possible problems, and should be pronounced as follows: Prótyus, Thúryo, Égglamore, and Lawnce. These are rough approximations of the more detailed pronunciation treatment given in Helge Kökeritz' *Shakespeare's Names: A Pronouncing Dictionary,*" Yale University Press, 1959. No significant differences arise even when a trisyllabic treatment occasionally occurs in the text.

MODERN

ACT I

SCENE 1 — *An open Plaza in Verona.*

Enter VALENTINE *and* PROTEUS.

VAL.   You can't persuade me, Proteus, my friend.
Home-staying youths end up with homebred brains.
If youthful passion did not chain your days
To watching ev'ry move of her, your love,
I would be asking you to join with me;
To see the wonders of the world abroad
Instead of like some slugworm living home,
Waste all your youth with pointless idleness.
But since you're rapt with love, enjoy it well,
Even as I will, when I fall in love's spell.

PRO.   Must you now go? Then, Valentine, adieu!
Do think of me when, if by chance, you see
Some rare noteworthy object in your travels.
And make a wish that I were there to share
Your happiness; and when things may go wrong,
If danger should envelop you,
Entrust your troubles to my holy prayers,
For I will pray for you, my Valentine.

COMMENTS

The Two Gentlemen of Verona was one of the first plays Shakespeare wrote. English drama at the time, not having fully come into its own, was still borrowing from the long established Italian dramatic form; and this play was largely in that mode and mold. In this tradition, which started in ancient Rome, the play opens almost predictably in an Italian public square; and the customary boy-meets-girl action, lively intrigues, and impertinent servants of the Roman playwrights Plautus and Terence are all here.

Always the craftsman, Shakespeare has in the first two lines at-

ORIGINAL

ACT I

SCENE 1 — *An open Place in Verona.*

Enter VALENTINE *and* PROTEUS.

VAL.   Cease to persuade, my loving Proteus;
Home-keeping youth have ever homely wits;
Wer't not affection chains thy tender days
To the sweet glances of thy honor'd love,
I rather would entreat thy company,
To see the wonders of the world abroad;
Than, living dully sluggariz'd at home
Wear out thy youth with shapeless idleness.
But, since thou lov'st, love still, and thrive
                    therein,
Even as I would, when I to love begin.
    PRO.   Wilt thou be gone? Sweet Valentine, adieu!
Think on thy Proteus, when thou, haply, see'st
Some rare noteworthy object in thy travel.
Wish me partaker in thy happiness,
When thou dost meet good hap; and in thy danger,
If ever danger do environ thee,
Commend thy grievance to my holy prayers,
For I will be thy beadsman, Valentine.

---

tained audience attention with an imperative, established the principals as close friends, one is named *Proteus*, and the other is going
abroad, not to mention a lecture on youth and wittily setting the
tone of the play.

NOTES

homely — homespun (it is used in its "ugly" sense later, Act II);
tender — young; *shapeless* — purposeless; *love still* — continue to
love; *haply* —by chance; *noteworthy object* — i.e., tourist sight,

monument; *good hap* — good chance, luck; *grievance* — grief, troubles; *beadsman* — one who, usually for payment, says prayers for another (not dissimilar from a professional mourner).

MODERN

VAL. You'd use some book of love to pray for me?

PRO. Upon some book I love, I'll pray for you.

VAL. That is some shallow story of deep love,
The youth who swam a mile each night to love.

PRO. That's a deep story of a deeper love:
For he was deeper than his shoes in love.

VAL. It's true; for you are over boots in love,
And yet you did not even cross a brook.

PRO. O'er boots? Hey, I'm the *boot* of some dumb joke.

VAL. No, you will get no boot out of this.

PRO.   What?

COMMENTS

The reference to Hero and Leander (see *Notes*) was not something beyond the ken of the largely illiterate audience. Like other allusions to classical mythology, it appears throughout Shakespeare's and other plays of the time. It must be remembered that schooling then—including the bard's—consisted almost entirely of the three "R's" plus Latin, Greek, history, literature and mythology. Indeed, even the tradesmen and their apprentices, as Harrison notes, "had already received an education in rhetoric and the classics which would dumfound most modern high-school boys."

This impregnation of the educated minority brushed off on the unschooled masses. By the same process illiterate and ill literate Americans have no trouble associating balcony—or upper story—love scenes with Romeo and Juliet, or beauty with Venus, or handsomeness with Adonis.

After *Valentine's* mocking pun on love-making by long distance swimming, the playwright stretches his pun on *boots* as a bridge to a larger mockery of love itself, rendered in double entendre.

ORIGINAL

VAL.   And on a love-book pray for my success?
PRO.   Upon some book I love, I'll pray for thee.
VAL.   That's on some shallow story of deep love.
How young Leander cross'd the Hellespont.
PRO.   That's a deep story of a deeper love;
For he was more than over shoes in love.
VAL.   'T is true; for you are over boots in love,
And yet you never swom the Hellespont.
PRO.   Over the boots? nay, give me not the
        boots.
VAL.   No, I will not, for it boots thee not.
PRO.   What?

NOTES

some book of love — this line suggests that *Valentine* is point-ing to a book in *Proteus'* hand.

Leander — "Hero and Leander" are legendary lovers who lived on opposite sides of the Hellespont, a three-quarter mile wide water strait between Greece and Turkey. The youth Leander regularly swam the strait at night to be with his fair Hero until one night the light she always set to guide him went out. As a result he drowned, and in her grief Hero followed him to a watery grave.

'T is true; for — some scholars believe that the word *for* here is a misprint in the original manuscript—that the word should be *and* or *but*. However, with the interpretation given here (see *Modern*) the word *for* makes perfect sense; i.e., *Valentine* is saying, " 'T is true (that Leander must have been very deeply in love); *for* you are over boots (deeply, like Leander) in love, and yet you never swom the Hellespont."

give me not the boots — don't make fun of me; *boots thee not* —gains you nothing.

MODERN

VAL.   To be in love, where scorns are thanks
            for groans,
And heartbreak met with sneers; one moment's worth
            of fun
Fades quickly into weeks of worried nights;
Though maybe won, perhaps a hapless gain;
If lost—that's one less hurt to overcome;
You act the fool because you lose your head,
Or else, you lose your head in foolish acts.

PRO.   So, beating 'round the bush you call me
            fool.

VAL.   Since there's no beating sense into you, yes.

PRO.   It's love that you are mocking; I'm not love.

VAL.   Love is your master, for he masters you;
And he that is made captive by a fool,
Should not, I think, be certified as wise.

———————————

COMMENTS

Valentine's comments on love mark the first time in the play that a character consciously uses bawdy (see *Notes*); and since Valentine is a "straight" character the conscious bawdy here is not humorous; rather, it gives an earthy emphasis to the cynicism of his thoughts on love.

Indeed, he is reflecting the very tell-it-like-it-is worldliness of every Elizabethan in the audience. He talks glibly of the disillusionment love brings, the *twenty watchful . . . nights* of worry over pregnancy after the *one fading moment's mirth*, which at best buys folly, and at worst is destroyed by its own folly.

ORIGINAL

VAL.   To be in love, where scorn is bought
with groans;
Coy looks with heart-sore sighs; one fading moment's
mirth,
With twenty watchful, weary, tedious nights:
If haply won, perhaps a hapless gain;
If lost, why then a grievous labor won;
However, but a folly bought with wit,
Or else a wit by folly vanquished.

PRO.   So, by your circumstance, you call me fool.

VAL.   So, by your circumstance, I fear, you'll
prove.

PRO.   'T is love you cavil at; I am not love.

VAL.   Love is your master, for he masters you;
And he that is so yoked by a fool,
Methinks should not be chronicled for wise.

NOTES

groans — the unpleasant, not the ecstatic, pains of love-making. (Partridge designates it as a bawdy term meaning the pain of losing virginity and cites a use in Hamlet. It is not, and nowhere does Shakespeare use it as a bawdy term; in Hamlet, as elsewhere, it is simply synonymous with hurting, suffering, pain.

coy — contemptuous.

haply — a triple play on the root word "hap": (1) *haply* — perhaps (but in the specific sense of perchance); (2) *perhaps* — perhaps; (3) *hapless* — unhappy.

however — either way.

*wit — (1) mental faculties in general (not necessarily cleverness); (2) bawdy term for the male or female organ. (*The asterisk, and hereafter, denotes that cross references to other Shakespearean bawdy uses of the word will be found in the *Glossary*.)

circumstance — first usage, circumlocution; second usage, condition or state (circumstances one finds oneself in).

MODERN

PRO.   Yet writers say, as cankerworms will eat
The sweetest flower's bud, so love itself
Will feed upon the finest heads of all.

VAL.   And writers say, as the most forward bud
Is eaten by the worms before it swells,
Even so by love the young and tender head
Is turned to folly; with'ring in the bud,
Losing his lushness even in his prime,
And all the promise of his future hopes;
But why do I waste time to counsel you,
Devoted as you are to blind desire?
Once more, "Adieu"; my father's at the dock
Expecting me, so he can see me off.

PRO.   I'll go that far with you, friend Valentine.

VAL.   Thanks, Proteus, no; and now I've got to
leave.

In Milan let me hear from you by letters
Of how your love life goes, and whate'er else
Should happen here while I, your friend, am gone;
And likewise I'll write you from time to time.

PRO.   Then best of luck and happiness in Milan!

VAL.   The same to you at home! And so, farewell.

Exit VALENTINE.

COMMENTS

Valentine's comments on love end with a powerful simile alluding to venereal disease (see *Notes*). The words are so graphic as to preclude its being a simile of *wit* in the "mentality" sense.

Here then is a man after the Elizabethans' heart. A solid, sensible fellow with his two feet on the ground. He is much too smart to ever get involved deeply in love, let alone marriage. But, of course, as everyone knows, he has not fallen in love—yet.

ORIGINAL

PRO.   Yet writers say, as in the sweetest bud
The eating canker dwells, so eating love
Inhabits in the finest wits of all.
　　　VAL.   And writers say, as the most forward bud
Is eaten by the canker ere it blow,
Even so by love the young and tender wit
Is turn'ed to folly; blasting in the bud
Losing his verdure even in the prime,
And all the fair effects of future hopes;
But wherefore waste I time to counsel thee?
That art a votary to fond desire?
Once more adieu; my father at the road
Expects my coming, there to see me shipp'd.
　　　PRO.   And thither will I bring thee, Valentine.
　　　VAL.   Sweet Proteus, no; now let us take our
　　　　　　　leave.
To Milan let me hear from thee by letter,
Of thy success in love, and what news else
Betideth here in absence of thy friend;
And I likewise will visit thee with mine.
　　　PRO.   All happiness bechance to thee in Milan!
　　　VAL.   As much to you at home! and so, farewell.
　　　　　　　Exit VALENTINE.

NOTES

　　canker — the non-horticultural meaning here is in the context
of early onset venereal disease; "*canker*, An eating, spreading sore
or ulcer." (Oxford English Dictionary, hereafter O.E.D.)
　　inhabits — dwells; *blow* — swell, puff up; *blasting* — wither-
ing; *verdure* — flourishing or lush condition; *votary* — devotee;
fond — foolish; *road* — marina; *shipp'd* — shipped off, embarked;
bring — accompany; *Milan* — pronounced Mee'lan; *betideth* —
befall, happen; *visit thee with mine* — send you my letters (visit
vicariously).

MODERN

PRO.   He goes to hunt for honor; I seek love.
He leaves his friends to bring them honor back;
I leave myself, my friends, and all for love.
You, Julia, you have turned me inside out,
Made me neglect my books, lose track of time,
Reject advice, and set the world at nought;
My mind with brooding's weak, heart sick with thought.

Enter SPEED.

SPEED. Sir Proteus, bless you; have you seen my master?
PRO.   He just departed now, to sail to Milan.
SPEED. Twenty to one then he shipped out already;
And I'm a dumb lost sheep for missing him.
PRO.   Yes, sheep will often stray, both if and when
The shepherd—like your master—is away.
SPEED. Do you conclude my master is a shepherd then, and I a sheep?
PRO.   I do.

COMMENTS

Since *Speed's* entrance must be delayed so that he "misses" catching up with *Valentine*, the playwright uses this brief span to establish the intensity of *Proteus'* infatuation with *Julia*. And if there is any question as to why *Speed* dallies rather than run after his master, it is soon resolved when it develops that he has a little remuneration due him from *Proteus*.

ORIGINAL

PRO.   He after honor hunts, I after love;
He leaves his friends to dignify them more;
I leave myself, my friends, and all for love.
Thou, Julia, thou has metamorphos'd me;
Made me neglect my studies, lose my time,
War with good counsel, set the world at nought;
Made wit with musing weak, heart sick with thought.

Enter SPEED.

SPEED.   Sir Proteus, save you; Saw you my master?
PRO.   But now he parted hence, to embark for
Milan.
SPEED.   Twenty to one then he is shipp'd already;
And I have play'd the sheep in losing him.
PRO.   Indeed a sheep doth very often stray,
An if the shepherd be awhile away.
SPEED.   You conclude that my master is a shep-
herd then, and I a sheep?
PRO.   I do.

———————

NOTES

friends — loved ones (including family); *leave myself* —
neglect myself; *war with good counsel* — refuse to take well intended
advice; *made wit with musing weak* — made (my) mind weak from
(my) brooding (pedantic purists "correct" *made* to *make*); *thought*
— pining thought.
    parted — departed; *sheep* — rural, and accordingly many low-
er class people of the day—and some yet—pronounced it "ship"
(which *Speed* undoubtedly does, adding a comic touch).

MODERN

SPEED. Why then my hard horns are his hard horns, whether I am awake or . . . go to bed.

PRO. That answer answers to the description of a horny sheep.

SPEED. And proves me still a sheep?

PRO. True, and your master a shepherd.

SPEED. No—That I can make a logical case against.

PRO. It may be hard, but I'll prove it in a different manner.

SPEED. Well, the shepherd seeks the sheep, and not the sheep the shepherd; but I seek my master, and my master seeks not me. Therefore, I am no sheep.

PRO. The sheep for fodder follow the shepherd; the shepherd for food follows not the sheep; you for wages follow your master, your master for wages follows not you. Therefore, you are a sheep.

SPEED. Another proof like that will make me cry ba-a-a-a.

COMMENTS

Speed, the impertinent servant and clown, a virtually requisite character type for this Italianate comedy, temporarily suspends the action of the plot with an extended mockery of *Proteus*. It is an episode of bawdy which, like those to follow, offers relief and variety, in an almost vaudevillian style, to the play. While it need not be tied into the plot, the author nevertheless uses it to reveal that *Proteus'* love affair is still in its Beatrice and Dante phase.

NOTES

*horns — (1) of sheep, and (2) male erections; more than one commentator has suggested the other bawdy meaning of "cuckoldry," but how that is supposed to apply to unmarried men always remains unexplained.

ORIGINAL

SPEED. Why, then my horns are his horns, whether I wake or sleep.

PRO.   A silly answer, and fitting well a sheep.

SPEED. This proves me still a sheep.

PRO.   True; and thy master a shepherd.

SPEED. Nay, that I can deny by a circumstance.

PRO.   It shall go hard but I'll prove it by another.

SPEED. The shepherd seeks the sheep, and not the sheep the shepherd; but I seek my master, and my master seeks not me; therefore, I am no sheep.

PRO.   The sheep for fodder follow the shepherd, the shepherd for food follows not the sheep; thou for wages followest thy master, thy master for wages follows not thee; therefore thou art a sheep.

SPEED. Such another proof will make me cry baa.

---

wake — be or stay awake; the construction of nighttime revelry has been offered here based on a single use in Shakespeare (Hamlet, Act I, Scene 4) where the king stays awake to carouse; that line from Hamlet, along with a few other examples of staying awake to carouse, is used by the O.E.D. to support a meaning "with unfavourable implication: to sit up late for pleasure or revelry; to turn night into day."; yet, in all of O.E.D.'s examples wakefulness and revelry are purely associative since how and when does most carousing occur if not by being or remaining awake at night—one might as well argue that to light candles or illuminate has an "unfavourable implication".

sleep — also means to have sexual intercourse (as today—to sleep with).

answer — also means the sexual response of the male to a female, or (usually in jest or mockery) to another male or beast; a male-female socket conceptualization.

circumstance — first usage, arguing a logical case for something; second usage, *another* (circumstance), i.e., another pertinent detail.

*hard — erection of penis or clitoris.

Perhaps because the society was agrarian bawdy references to animals abound in Elizabethan plays. Nor was it as mild as barnyard humor. *Speed* here sets up a joke based on the double entendre of (1) his metaphorical horns belonging to his master-shepherd while awake, and (2) his real "horns" as well when he "sleeps". Although homosexuality was certainly acknowledged then, this is not the allusion here; it is rather an allusion, in jest here, to homosexual acts between normal individuals which were not unexpected to occasionally occur between masters and servants, or any two closely associated humans.

Proteus responds unwittingly with the bawdy answer of "answer", compounding it with *fitting well a sheep.*

Speed then sets up a new twist of humor with *a circumstance,*

MODERN

PRO.   Now, listen here! Did you give my letter to Julia?

SPEED. Yes, sir. I a poor black sheep, gave your letter to her, a rich white sheep; and she, the she sheep, upon reading your writing, gave me, the he sheep, a righting . . . and a big nothing for my writhing.

PRO.   That's a lot of meat all in one place.

SPEED. If something is overweight . . . I know of a reducing plan—

PRO.   Now you're getting yourself in too deep. I'm on the verge of giving you a big piece of—

SPEED. —No, sir! You needn't pay me a whole gold piece for delivering your letter.

PRO.   I was trying to pin you down and—

SPEED. —From a big piece to a pin? Handle it time in and time out, it's still three times too small for carrying a message to *your* lover.

by which he means a circumlocutory pseudo-syllogism which was so popular then (and still, being for example a mainstay of Abbott and Costello's comedy).

Proteus, again naively (see *circumstance* in word list above), offers to prove that *Speed* is a sheep by something else, which something else *shall go hard.*

Then they are off and running—at the mouth. In a kind of Elizabethan version of Peter Piper Picked a Peck of Pickled Peppers, *Speed* trills *shepherd seeks the sheep*—pronouncing it "ship," of course—followed by *Proteus* with the sheep *for fodder follow.* And it ends with what was probably a realistic *baa* from Speed.

The pervasion of "animality" through Elizabethan humor was surely on the mind of the eminent Shakespearean scholar Alexander Pope when (1725) he spoke of "the gross taste of the age". But grossness is relative. Rural American humor has always been replete with expressions such as "stump-broken calves".

ORIGINAL

PRO.   But dost thou hear? gav'st thou my letter to Julia?

SPEED.   Ay, sir; I, a lost mutton, gave your letter to her, a laced mutton; and she, a laced mutton, gave me, a lost mutton, nothing for my labor!

PRO.   Here's too small a pasture for such a store of muttons.

SPEED.   If the ground be overcharged, you were best stick her.

PRO.   Nay, in that you are astray; 't were best pound you.

SPEED.   Nay, sir, less than a pound shall serve me for carrying your letter.

PRO.   You mistake; I mean the pound, a pinfold.

SPEED.   From a pound to a pin? fold it over and over, 't is threefold too little for carrying a letter to your lover.

COMMENTS

The bawdy term *"nothing"* sets the stage for one of Shakespeare's elaborate jokes, one that begins at the expense of *Proteus* and ends at the expense of *Speed*. In keeping with the custom of the day, *Speed* not only expected to be paid by *Proteus* for delivering the letter, but also to be tipped by the recipient. Another custom then was that ladies of means compensated young men for any other services rendered. *Speed*, then, is furious at receiving "nothing" but "nothing" (see *Notes*) for his labor, and the remainder of the scene is built upon this.

NOTES

*mutton — also means human flesh; not so much a bawdy term as slang; also cf. Partridge at "mutton," which is denoted as female flesh, but usage suggests male flesh as well—viz. here where *Speed* calls himself a *lost mutton*.

laced mutton — common term for prostitute. Knight thinks the "caught sheep" meaning of *laced mutton* applies here since otherwise *Proteus* would be angry; but why "caught" when the more common meanings of "corseted" or "adorned with lace" will do; and why even those meanings when *laced* sounded so much like *lost* then (cf. Kökeritz) that with but a proper improper gesture *Speed* could telegraph "prostitute" to the audience while *Proteus* thought he was merely saying "lost mutton".

*lost — also means sexually spent.

*nothing — the zero shape or "O", i.e., the female pudend.

labor — i.e., of love.

*pasture — also means female pubic hair.

store — quantity, stock.

overcharged — overburdened, carrying too much weight, i.e., (1) too many sheep for a small pasture, and (2) too much mutton (*Speed*) for another small **pasture*.

stick — ? . . . generally regarded as a double entendre of (1) *stick*, to slaughter, and (2) *stick*, sexually attack: Shakespeare, however, never used the word in the exact sense of "slaughter" elsewhere and rarely, even, as a transitive verb; while the commentators are probably correct in the bawdy interpretation, this edition rejects their readings of "slaughter" since *Speed* would then be saying *you were best* "slaughter" *her*; it is likely that *Speed* has switched from double entendre of *overcharged* to single entendre of *stick*, and that this is all too clear to *Proteus*, motivating the latter to say *Nay, in that you are astray* and adding the force of *'T were best pound you*.

astray — also a play on *a stray*.

pound — first usage, impound, confine (many commentators interpret an additional play here on "beat, pummel" to account for *Speed's* reaction of *Nay*, but Shakespeare never used *pound* as a verb except with the meaning of "impound, confine"; *Speed's Nay* results from his mock inferring that *Proteus* means a pound of genitalia); second usage, unit of money; third usage, animal (like dog-) pound; fourth usage, unit of weight.

pinfold — pen for animals; *pin* — anything very small, with a probable play here on an ornamental codpiece stickpin (cf. V-3 of The White Devil by John Webster, published 1612—" [He's the one standing over there] /In a blew bonnet, and a paire of breeches/With a great codpeece. Ha, ha, ha,/ Looke you his codpeece is stucke full of pinnes/ With pearles o'th head of them. Doe not you know him?")

fold — then had the meaning more of "enfold," which use still exists, as in a bird "folding" its wings; *Speed* appears to be referring to the practice of enfolding the male organ in the cloth of a codpiece; and of course *threefold* is a harmless play on *fold*.

A likely scenario then of this exchange is that while straight man *Proteus* hears comic *Speed* say, "I, a lost mutton, gave your letter to her, a 'lost' mutton; and she, a 'lost' mutton, gave me, a lost mutton, nothing for my labor!" The audience, however, attuned to the roguish *Speed*, is hearing in effect, "I, a black sheep, gave your letter to her, a whore; and she, a whore, gave me, a very spent sheep, *nothing* for all my effort."

The audience is ready then for the allusion of *pasture*. (Since "here" and "hair" were pronounced alike then there is a possible bawdy play on *Here's*.) Relating *ground* to *pasture*, and *overcharged* to *too small*, *Speed* offers some unasked for advice, *best stick her*, and *Proteus* replies in mild distaste with *best pound you*. *Speed*, glancing pointedly and perhaps turning to the spectators with coy surprise, says *Nay* . . . thanks but no thanks. Then, playing on the *pin* of *pinfold*, *Speed* at first looks bewilderedly to the audience at this sudden weight-size change from *pound* to *pin* and then looks back, with the best of excuses to do so, at the ornamental stickpin in *Proteus'* codpiece; such pins were then the last word in gentlemanly fashion, and the one or more that *Proteus* undoubtedly had on would have instantly commanded the attention of the entire theater.

Then, with the whole house so transfixed, *Speed* with insulting belittlement, so to speak, renders the appraisal that it is in no way enough to take care of *your love*. The rapt silence of the audience must at this point have been split with a roar, for everyone—except *Proteus*—knows that *Speed* knows, very much knows, whereof he speaks.

MODERN

PRO.   But . . . what did she say?

SPEED. Aye.

PRO.   Nod, aye; that's—noddy.

SPEED. No, I mean, sir—I say she did nod, and you ask me if she did nod, and I say, Aye.

PRO.   And that set together is—noddy.

SPEED. Now you have taken the pains to set it together, you can take it for your pains.

PRO.   Payin's?—No, no, you will have it for bearing the letter.

SPEED. Well, I perceive that I'm obliged to bear . . . with you.

PRO.   What do you mean, bear with me?

SPEED. Indeed, sir, the letter, naturally, having nothing but the word, noddy, for my pains.

PRO.   I'll be damned, but you have a quick wit.

SPEED. And yet it can't catch up with your slow purse.

PRO.   Come on now, get to the point. What did she say?

SPEED. Open your purse so that the money and the point are both delivered at the same time.

PRO.   Well, sir, here is for your pains. Now what did she say?

ORIGINAL

PRO.   But what said she?

SPEED.   Aye.

PRO.   Nod, aye; why that's noddy.

SPEED. You mistook, sir; I say she did nod; and you ask me if she did nod; and I say, Aye.

PRO.   And that set together is—noddy.

SPEED. Now you have taken the pains to set it together, take it for your pains.

PRO.   No, no, you shall have it for bearing the letter.

SPEED. Well, I perceive I must be fain to bear with you.

PRO.   Why, sir, how do you bear with me?

SPEED. Marry, sir, the letter very orderly; having nothing but the word, noddy, for my pains.

PRO.   Beshrew me, but you have a quick wit.

SPEED. And yet it cannot overtake your slow purse.

PRO.   Come, come, open the matter in brief; what said she?

SPEED. Open your purse, that the money, and the matter, may be both at once delivered.

PRO.   Well, sir, here is for your pains; what said she?

NOTES

I — here is one of Shakespeare's shorter lines that has mystified scholars, so they changed the original to where virtually all editions now read *Aye* (or *Ay*); and by way of further demystification various superfluities were added such as *Did she nod?* and the stage direction (SPEED *nods.*). Yet no one makes sense of the line.

Although "Aye" was spelled "I" then (justifying the orthographic change) *Proteus* does not regard this as a receptive response by *Julia*, which should be his normal reaction to an affirmative. His to be expected response of *Aye what?* or perhaps *What more said she?* is instead a response showing that *Proteus*, no less than the scholars, is mystified.

The key here is that *Speed* apparently delivers only one solitary *nod*. Several "nods," or "nodding," would have reinforced the *Aye* to mean that *Julia* was in some way receptive to the letter. Furthermore one meaning of a singular, solitary *nod* then was a "beckoning". So when *Proteus* asks *But what said she?* all that *Speed* seems to have done was to look gleefully at the audience and hark back to his amorous triumph by throwing back his head in a prostitute's beckoning and delivering, primarily to the audience, a suggestive *Aye*.

MODERN

SPEED. Truly, sir, I think you'll hardly win her.

PRO.   Why? Could you perceive as much from her?

SPEED. Sir, I could perceive nothing at all from her; no, not so much as a silver piece *for delivering your letter*; and if she was tight with me, who doesn't have much, I'm afraid she'll really be tight with you, who has so very much. Give her no sweetmeat, only nutmeats, for she's a very tightwad.

PRO.   You mean that she said nothing?

SPEED. Not even so much as *Take this for your pains*. Well, sir, at least I can testify to your generosity; considering the tip you gave me, I will thank you . . . to

Proteus' response is a bewildered, meaningless *noddy* (which nonce adjective, expectedly, has been examined by many for "hidden" meanings). *Proteus* probably pronounced the word nod-I (cf. Kökeritz) which is deliberately misinterpreted by *Speed* as "not aye". Then *Speed* engages in a little word fun, based on the similar sounds of *nod* and "not," for the sole purpose of giving himself another opportunity to deliver his beckoning *Aye*.

take it — also means to submit sexually, the phrase always referring to the passive partner; *fain* — obliged.

bear — also means to be the "underneath" sexual partner; *Marry* — Indeed!

orderly — naturally, properly, i.e., "of course".

Beshrew me — a mild expletive.

Come . . . brief — "Get to the subject."

Speed, irritated with *Proteus'* obtuseness, tells him the equivalent of "stuff it". *Proteus* misinterprets *pains* to mean "payings," and *Speed* in his turn puts the same construction on *you shall have it* as he meant in his *take it*, and a quip on *bear* ensues.

ORIGINAL

SPEED. Truly, sir, I think you'll hardly win her.

PRO.   Why? Couldst thou perceive so much from her?

SPEED. Sir, I could perceive nothing at all from her; no, not so much as a ducat for delivering your letter; and being so hard to me that brought your mind, I fear she'll prove as hard to you in telling your mind. Give her no token but stones; for she's as hard as steel.

PRO.   What, said she nothing?

SPEED. No, not so much as—Take this for thy pains. To testify your bounty, I thank you, you have testern'd me; in requital whereof, henceforth carry your hereafter carry your letter yourself. And so, sir, I'll remember you to my master.

PRO.   Get out—go keep your ship from being wrecked;

With you aboard it will not sink, for Fate
Is saving you for hanging back on shore.
I must now send some better messenger;
I fear my Julia would ignore my notes,
If she's kept posted by the likes of you.

Exeunt.

COMMENTS

The scene ends in a question mark of *Did Speed really?* But no one is too concerned over the answer since the *Speed-Proteus* repartee is really for laughs.

Ever the dramatist, Shakespeare, even in his bawdy scenes, always carefully builds to a climax. His bawdy, although sometimes coming close, is never just a string of one-liners. There is here a warp of financial pains interwoven with a woof of sexual pains threading its way from what was nothing for his *labor* to what climaxes with nothing for his *pains.*

Yet *Speed* is too resiliently impertinent to come across as a born loser. Also, this is more than the universal humor of seeing a hoity-toity gentleman made a fool of or the dowager slipping on a banana peel. This is as well the universality of the saucy white maid, insulting black butler, or frustrated working man, all still very much alive in our cartoons, television, and songs such as "You Can Take This Job And Shove It".

. . . The Elizabethan lyrics of which end this scene.

NOTES

hardly — possible play on bawdy meaning of *hard; perceive* — a play on the two meanings then of both perceive and receive; *brought your mind* — brought her your sentiments.

tell(ing) — also bawdy meaning of the male role in coition, apparently from similar pronunciation then to *tail.*

letters yourself; and so, sir, I'll commend you to my master.

      PRO.   Go, go, be gone, to save your ship from wreck;
Which cannot perish, having thee aboard,
Being destin'd to a drier death on shore:—
I must go send some better messenger;
I fear my Julia would not deign my lines,
Receiving them from such a worthless post.

Exeunt.

---

    mind. — also means male organ (also cf. *wit*).

    stones — also means testicles.

    as hard as steel — the exact nuance may be elusive, but the basic meaning is clear; it could be a play on *as* (like) "*hardest tail,*" with *tail* being the male organ (or possibly the female organ if Partridge is correct that it also then meant what it does today, with which this edition disagrees); another meaning could be *as* (like) "*hardest stale*" (where "stale" then meant prostitute) although Kökeritz, while admitting the possibility, feels that "steel" and "stale" were not pronounced alike; conflict between *Speed's* earlier "belittlement" and these constructions, if any, comes under the heading of comic license; it is obvious, however, that this phrase could use some refinement.

    Speed's remuneration from *Proteus* is apparently unsatisfactory. He pointedly does not thank *Proteus* and lets everyone know that he had at least expected a *ducat*. Bemoaning how *hard* she was to him financially, he adds—in wishful thinking—his belief that *she'll prove as hard to Proteus* sexually. He finishes derisively, and perhaps with a groan, by insisting that she is a *hard* woman.

    Take this . . . pains, of course, is the climactic line of the bawdy episode, although one would never know it from the literature. No commentator comments on *Proteus'* line, which, lacking motivation, is the playwright's setup for the punch line, no comment on how this flows naturally to the rest of *Speed's* speech, and, ergo, no comment on any meaning here whatsoever.

    Speed is probably quoting the paramour's very own words; even more, he is probably doing it in sexually fraught falsetto . . . and perhaps with well timed wriggle, groan, and flip of the coin

Proteus gave him—being the *this* of *Take this*. The line is nothing less than a quadruple entendre on *pains*. Here is a play on the physical pains of sex with a "hard" woman, the pains of no payin's from the lady for his sexual favors—not to mention delivering the letter, the pains of underpayment from *Proteus*, but, above all, the pains he inflicts on *Proteus* with the very suggestion that he may have had an affair with his beloved. The audience, although in on the joke right along, must have gasped slightly before it roared at *Speed's* recklessly bold insult, veritably putting his head in the lion's jaw.

   testern'd — tester, testern, testorn, and teston were variable spellings of old coins of small value.

   Being destined . . . — alludes to an old proverb to the effect that anyone destined to be hanged will never die from drowning.

    not deign my lines — not bother to read my letters.

    *post — postman, messenger; also the male organ.

    The rest is a wind down of the scene. *Proteus* does not believe —as the audience surely now does—that *Speed* has done anything more than insult him, but this is enough, of course, to infuriate him; and *Speed* only adds fuel with his final insults. As *Speed* exits flipping the coin, *Proteus* follows, berating him.

    And it is perhaps fitting at this point to flip to a page in the New Cambridge edition and read—"But Speed is a poor stick, without character, and he has not a single witty thing to say from beginning to end."

MODERN

ACT I

SCENE 2 — *Garden of* JULIA'S *House.*

Enter JULIA *and* LUCETTA.

JUL.   Lucetta, tell me, now that we're alone,
Should I allow myself to fall in love?

LUC.   Yes, ma'am, so long as you don't get . . . in
trouble.

JUL.   Of all the many fine young gentlemen,
Who every day contrive to speak with me,
In your opinion, which is my best choice?

LUC.   Run down the list; I'll tell you what I think,
Based on my . . . limited experience.

JUL.   What do you think of handsome Eglamour?

LUC.   Now there's a knight who's elegant and
fine;
But, were I you, he never would be mine.

JUL.   What do you think of rich Mercatio?

LUC.   Well of his wealth; but of himself—so-so.

JUL.   What do you think of gentle Proteus?

LUC.   Oh, Lord! How handsome men make fools
of us!

JUL.   Say now! What makes your eyes roll at his
name?

LUC.   I could not help myself—I blush for shame,
That I, the lowly servant that I am,
Should find such fault with splendid gentlemen.

NOTES

stumble not — morally, i.e., become pregnant; *fair resort* —
fine group; *with parle encounter me* — solicitously speak to me;

ORIGINAL

ACT I

SCENE 2 — *Garden of* JULIA'S *House.*

Enter JULIA *and* LUCETTA.

JUL.　　But say, Lucetta, now we are alone,
Would'st thou then counsel me to fall in love?

LUC.　　Ay, madam; so you stumble not unheed-
　　　　fully.

JUL.　　Of all the fair resort of gentlemen,
That every day with parle encounter me,
In thy opinion, which is worthiest love?

LUC.　　Please you, repeat their names, I'll show
　　　　my mind,
According to my shallow simple skill.

JUL.　　What think'st thou of the fair sir Eglamour?

LUC.　　As of a knight well-spoken, neat and fine;
But, were I you, he never should be mine.

JUL.　　What think'st thou of the rich Mercatio?

LUC.　　Well of his wealth; but of himself, so so.

JUL.　　What think'st thou of the gentle Proteus?

LUC.　　Lord, Lord! to see what folly reigns in us!

JUL.　　How now! what means this passion at his
　　　　name?

LUC.　　Pardon, dear madam; 't is a passing shame,
That I, unworthy body as I am,
Should censure thus on lovely gentlemen.

---

neat — elegant; *passion at* — emotionally react to; *passing* — surpassing, excessive; *censure thus on* — find fault with.

MODERN

JUL.   Why not with Proteus, as with all the rest?
LUC.   Because of many good ones he's the best.
JUL.   Your reason?
LUC.   I have no more than just a woman's reason;
I think he's best . . . because I think he's best.
JUL.   Do you suggest I love him with . . .
       abandon?
LUC.   Yes, if you're sure he'll not abandon you.
JUL.   Why, he of all the rest has never moved
       me.
LUC.   Yet he of all the rest, I think, most loves
       you.
JUL.   His lack of speaking shows his love is small.
LUC.   The fire that's sheltered most, burns best
       of all.
JUL.   They do not love, who do not show their
       love.
LUC.   Oh, they love least who boast about their
       love.
JUL.   I'd like to read his mind.
LUC.   Then read this letter, madam.
JUL.   *To Julia* — Who's it from?
LUC.   The letter will show that.
JUL.   Who gave this note to you?
LUC.   Sir Valentine's page; and sent, I think, from
       Proteus;
He meant to have seen you, but I, being there instead,
Received it . . . in your name. Or so it could be said.

NOTES

never mov'd me — all the editors, either parroting the most respected of all Shakespearean glossarists, C. T. Onions, or each other, annotate this as "never courted me" or "never proposed to me"; in fairness to Onions he never cited this passage in his defini-

ORIGINAL

JUL.	Why not on Proteus, as of all the rest?
LUC.	Then thus: of many good I think him best.
JUL.	Your reason?
LUC.	I have no other but a woman's reason;

I think him so—because I think him so.

JUL.	And would'st thou have me cast my love on him?
LUC.	Ay, if you thought your love not cast away.
JUL.	Why, he of all the rest hath never mov'd me.
LUC.	Yet he of all the rest, I think, best loves ye.
JUL.	His little speaking shows his love but small.
LUC.	Fire that's closest kept burns most of all.
JUL.	They do not love that do not show their love.
LUC.	O, they love least that let men know their love.
JUL.	I would I knew his mind.
LUC.	Peruse this paper, madam.
JUL.	*To Julia*—Say from whom?
LUC.	That the contents will show.
JUL.	Say, say; who gave it thee?
LUC.	Sir Valentine's page; and sent, I think from Proteus;

He would have given it you, but I, being in the way,
Did in your name receive it; pardon the fault, I pray.

----

tions of *move*, and in fairness to his readers he was seriously remiss in not doing so; there are dozens of instances in Shakespeare (cf. Schmidt, et al) where *move* is used in the modern sense of to move one's feelings or emotions; it is a sad commentary on the end product of four centuries of Shakespearean scholars when a note such as this is needed to show that a note on *move* was not needed in the first place—that all Shakespeare meant by *move* was *move*; the importance of correcting this ubiquitous error will be seen in the following:—

Tannenbaum, in his critique of the New Cambridge edition, finds a contradiction between *Proteus'* proclaimed love affair with *Julia* at the opening of the play and *Julia's* saying here that *he . . . never mov'd me.* Mr. Tannenbaum apparently does not understand young men; *Proteus*, having fallen in love with *Julia*, self-confidently assumes that he will win her love, although everyone knows from *Speed's Truly, sir, I think you'll hardly win her* that there is not yet any going "affair". Or does Tannenbaum understand young women; *Julia* herself explains that *maids, in modesty, say "no" to that which they would have the proferrer construe "ay"*; indeed, she is so much in love with *Proteus* that she is afraid it will show, and so she protests (a little too much) that *he . . . never mov'd me*, and so it is also that she just as coyly asks her maid's advice about *Eglamour* and *Mercatio* before getting around to whom she really has on her mind, *Proteus*. (Exactly as in Romeo and Juliet I – 5 where Juliet inquires about other young men of her nurse before finally asking about Romeo.) It is a delicate rendering of *Julia's* feelings; and it is an example of how Shakespeare could write just as well with a quill tipped in tint as he could with a sword dipped in blood.

being in the way — happening to be around.

Another "problem" with many scholars is that of whether or not *Speed* knew he gave *Proteus'* letter to *Julia's* maid rather than *Julia* herself. One school, critical, deems it an awkward oversight of the playwright not to have made this clear; the other, kinder, holds that the point is unimportant. Both are wrong.

There is no question but that *Speed* thinks he has delivered the letter to *Proteus'* "lover". And, having only *Speed's* version, the audience thinks likewise. *Lucetta*, being a waiting woman to *Julia*, not a house maid, would in dress, speech and youth be similar enough to her mistress to be "mistook" for the latter (especially in a comedy where a girl is disguised as a boy). Indeed, the whole humor of the previous scene lies in the impression given the audience that *Speed* has slept with *Proteus'* beloved.

Now, in this scene, *Lucetta* must have broken up the house when she announced, with sufficient coquettishness, that she was the one who intercepted the letter—*Did in your name receive it; pardon the fault, I pray.* The audience finally learns what really happened . . . and why *Speed* received nothing—except nothing—for his payin's. This joke on *Proteus* becoming instead a joke on *Speed* is a deft stroke of an imaginative playwright, and it was as self-evident to the audience then as it is obscure to the scholars today.

Shakespeare has also been criticized for the problematical use by *Proteus* of *Speed*, who after all is *Valentine's* servant, to deliver the letter; why not his own servant, *Launce*? Using *Speed* is a necessity here for verisimilitude; *Proteus'* servant would have had met *Julia* and *Lucetta*, and with no mistaken identity there is no joke. Also, it would have been as theatrically cumbersome as it was unnecessary for the playwright to account for *Launce's* unavailability to *Proteus*, especially when *Launce* had not yet been introduced onstage. Besides, the bard was writing for an audience, and they understood the action perfectly well—even if the commentators down through the years have not.

MODERN

JUL.   As sure as I am chaste, you are a pander!
And do you dare to deal in dirty words?
And plot to undermine my innocence?
I'm sure to pander is a noble calling,
For one who is ignoble, such as you.
There, take the letter; see that it's returned;
Or else, return no more into my sight.
      LUC.   I foster love—and what? I get abuse.
      JUL.   Will you be gone?
      LUC.   . . . So you may dream and muse.

Exit LUCETTA.

JUL.   And yet, I wish that I had read the letter;
It would embarrass me to call her back
And beg her now for what I just did scold her.
What fool is she!—She knows I'm ladylike,
And could not lower myself to read it through!
Since ladies modestly say *No* to that
Which they would really like to answer *Yes*.
Oh, my! How frustrating, this foolish love
That, like a cranky babe, will scratch its nurse,
Then suddenly will quiet down and coo.
How boorishly I sent Lucetta out,
When truthfully I wanted her to stay.

NOTES

broker — go-between, pander. The Riverside edition comments on *Lucetta's* interception of *Proteus'* note:
"*this paper*: i.e. the letter which in I.i. Speed has assured Proteus he delivered personally to Julia. Another instance of confused plotting, unless lines 39 – 40 [*He . . . way/Did . . . pray.*] are interpreted to mean that Lucetta deceived Speed by pretending to be Julia, an interpretation which the word *broker* in line 41 makes unlikely."
Of course *Lucetta* deceived him, and for more than one reason, the

ORIGINAL

JUL.   Now, by my modesty, a goodly broker!
Dare you presume to harbor wanton lines?
To whisper and conspire against my youth?
Now, trust me, 't is an office of great worth,
And you an officer fit for the place.
There, take the paper, see it be returned;
Or else return no more into my sight.
    LUC.   To plead for love deserves more fee than
        hate.
JUL.   Will you be gone?
LUC.   That you may ruminate.

Exit LUCETTA.

JUL.   And yet, I would I had o'erlook'd the letter.
It were a shame to call her back again,
And pray her to a fault for which I chid her.
What fool is she, that knows I am a maid,
And would not force the letter to my view!
Since maids, in modesty, say *No* to that
Which they would have the profferer construe *Ay.*
Fie, fie! how wayward is this foolish love,
That like a testy babe, will scratch the nurse,
And presently all humbled, kiss the rod!
How churlishly I chid Lucetta hence,
When willingly I would have had her here!

————————

second one being that of uncontrollable nosiness regarding the content of the letter. Note her coy *sent, I think, from Proteus*; she does not "think", she knows. Moreover, since *Julia* is unaware of the deception, her use of *broker* is not at all "unlikely".

Having noted this from The Riverside Shakespeare, edited by G. Blakemore Evans, perspective should be maintained by further noting that in its superb concept and equally superb execution no finer one-editor edition of Shakespeare's works—American or British—exists today.

youth—inexperience, i.e., innocence; *office* — position, occu-
pation; *fee* — reward; *ruminate* — lose oneself in deep thought;
had o'erlook'd — had read; *a shame* — shameful; *pray her* — beg

MODERN

How angrily I knit my brows and frowned,
While inward joy was making my heart smile!
And now I'm forced to call Lucetta back
And ask forgiveness for my foolishness: —
Yoo-hoo! Lucetta!

Reenter LUCETTA.

LUC.   You call, your ladyship?
JUL.   Is't near dinner-time?
LUC.   I wish it were;
That you might hungrily eat up your meat,
And not eat out your maid.
JUL.   What was that you
Picked up so furtively?
LUC.   Nothing.
JUL.   Why did you stoop then?
LUC.   To pick a paper up that I let fall.
JUL.   And is that paper nothing?
LUC.   Nothing concerning me.
JUL.   Then let it lie for those whom it concerns.
LUC.   It will not lie about what it concerns,
Unless a liar should interpret it.

NOTES

kill your stomach — kill your hunger; it was also a play on the
additional meaning then for *stomach* — anger (cf. the verb form today, as in "She cannot stomach him").

meat and *maid* — the Signet edition sees a pun here on

her; *to a fault* — to commit a wrong; *chid* — chided, scolded; *maid* — maiden, i.e., decent young lady; *presently* — immediately; *kiss the rod* — submit (an expression from a proverb).

ORIGINAL

How angerly I taught my brow to frown,
When inward joy enforc'd my heart to smile!
My penance is, to call Lucetta back,
And ask remission for my folly past: —
What ho! Lucetta!

Reenter LUCETTA.

LUC.   What would your ladyship?
JUL.   Is't near dinner-time?
LUC.   I would it were;
That you might kill your stomach on your meat,
And not upon your maid.
JUL.   What is 't that you
Took up so gingerly?
LUC.   Nothing.
JUL.   Why didst thou stoop then?
LUC.   To take a paper up that I let fall.
JUL.   And is that paper nothing?
LUC.   Nothing concerning me.
JUL.   Then let it lie for those that it concerns.
LUC.   Madam, it will not lie where it concerns,
Unless it have a false interpreter.

———————

"mate"; a harmless play on similar sounds, yes (*meat* was then pronounced *mate*), but a pun, no.
lie for those that it concerns — lie for those whom it concerns.
lie where it concerns — lie (prevaricate) about what it concerns.

MODERN

JUL.   One of your lovers wrote to you in rhyme.

LUC.   So I might sing it, madam, to a tune,
Give me a bar, with pitch, that you can hold—

JUL.   No longer, I assure you, than is needed;
And sing it to the tune of *Light o' Love.*

LUC.   It is too heavy for so light a tune.

JUL.   Heavy? Perhaps it's somewhat downbeat
then.

LUC.   It could be upbeat if you bellowed it.

JUL.   Then why don't you?

LUC.   I cannot reach so high.

JUL.   Let's see this song . . . What's this, you
rascal you?

LUC.   Keep tra-la-la-ing it until the end.
And yet, I really do not like this tune.

JUL.   You do not?

LUC.   No, madam, it's too sharp.

JUL.   You, rascal, are too saucy.

LUC.   No—now you are too flat,
And jar the harmony with decibels;
Somehow your singing lacks a certain tenor.

JUL.   What tenor could outmouth a voice so
base?

LUC.   I'd love play'ng second bass with Proteus.

———————

NOTES

note — also means the male organ.

set — (1) to music (2) to cause erection.

toys — allusive here to *Lucetta's* toyings with bawdy words; it
is associative with sex but is no more a bawdy term than, say,
"sport" or "diversion" (although Partridge, q.v., feels otherwise.)

Light o' Love — a popular song of the day, the melody of which
has come down to us but the words of which have been unfortunately lost; *belike* — perhaps.

ORIGINAL

JUL.   Some love of yours hath writ to you in
            rhyme.

LUC.   That I might sing it, madam, to a tune,
Give me a note; your ladyship can set.

JUL.   As little by such toys as may be possible;
Best sing it to the tune of *Light o' Love.*

LUC.   It is too heavy for so light a tune.

JUL.   Heavy? belike it hath some burthen then.

LUC.   Ay, and melodious were it, would you sing
            it.

JUL.   And why not you?

LUC.   I cannot reach so high.

JUL.   Let's see your song;—How now, minion?

LUC.   Keep tune there still, so you will sing it out;
And yet, methinks, I do not like this tune.

JUL.   You do not?

LUC.   No, madam, 't is too sharp.

JUL.   You, minion, are too saucy.

LUC.   Nay, now you are too flat,
And mar the concord with too harsh a descant;
There wanteth but a mean to fill your song.

JUL.   The mean is drown'd with your unruly base.

LUC.   Indeed, I bid the base for Proteus.

---

*_burthen_ — old spelling of burden which here has the meaning
of the part (usually the bass) of a singer accompanying the lead
singer in a song; it also means the weight of the male body in coitus.

*_sing_ — also means, at second usage, fellatio.

minion — equivalent, when used appellatively, to the modern
"dear", but sometimes with sarcasm or, as here, petulance (i.e.,
"dearie"); _keep tune_ — keep pitch, i.e., keep singing; _concord_ —
harmony of the song; _descant_ — the lead or soprano voice of the
song.

mean — the tenor and/or alto, or middle pitched voices, in a singing group; also a play on "man" here; *base* — old spelling of "bass", with an obvious pun.

bid the base — an expression from a popular game of the day where, in one version, a player whose turn had come to be "it" would confront the other players, all of whom poised themselves "on the mark"; "it", with an element of surprise, suddenly shouted a name, thereby starting a race in which the challenged one tried to catch the challenger before the latter reached a predesignated point —the "base"; thus *Lucetta* was impishly suggesting that she would like to race, and of course be "caught" by, *Proteus*.

The previously cited Tannenbaum also writes regarding *Julia*: "['Some love of yours hath writ to you in rhyme'] is contradicted by line 35 ['To Julia—say, from whom'] which proves that she knows that the letter is for her. Clearly, this scene was partially rewritten and the contradictions have not been removed."

Mr. Tannenbaum misses the point, which is that this "contradiction" is the whole point of the light and harmless bawdy that follows.

The saucy *Lucetta* is not going to play along with *Julia's* pretense; she all but waves the letter under *Julia's* nose, teasingly withdrawing it at the last moment. If *Julia* wants to play games, then

MODERN

JUL.   This babble—I will put an end to it.

Tears letter.

Such fuss about a vow of love!—
Get out of here; and let the papers lie;
You'd like to finger them to anger me.

LUC.   She won't admit it's hers; but she would love
To be so angered with another letter.

Exit LUCETTA.

JUL.   I wish I could be angered so with this!

Picks up some pieces of letter.

Oh, hateful hands, to tear such loving words!

fine, *Lucetta* will play games too—her own. If *Julia* wants to pretend the letter is a *rhyme* written to *Lucetta*, then fine, *Lucetta* will pretend that too and proposes they *sing it . . . to a tune*. With a knowing smirk toward the audience she bawdily asks for a *note* which *Julia* can *set*. Being forced now to play the game *Luceita's* way, *Julia* replies, which reply leads *Lucetta* to say *it is too heavy*. *Lucetta* then gets an opening to suggest that *Julia sing it*.

With *Lucetta's I cannot reach so high*, *Julia* senses she is being made a fool of, and desperately wanting to see the letter as well, she asks to *see your song*. But *Lucetta* snatches it away . . . until *you will sing it out*. Finally, after *it* (is too sharp), *Lucetta* ends the bawdy by switching the reference point to *you* (are too flat); and she then comes to *Julia's* real problem, which is that she needs a "man" to fill her song. *Julia* becomes angry with this pun, and *Lucetta* goes in for the kill by, in her own inimitable way, laying bare *Julia's* innermost secret, mentioning her beloved by name— *Proteus*. *Julia* explodes, snatches and tears the letter, and, once again, contradictorily dismisses *Lucetta*.

Yes, Mr. Tannenbaum, you are absolutely right. Mr. Shakespeare is telling us that back in his day young people in love were contradictory. What else is new?

ORIGINAL

JUL.   This babble shall not henceforth trouble me.
Here is a coil with protestation!—

Tears the letter.

Get you gone; and let the papers lie;
You would be fing'ring them, to anger me.
    LUC.   She makes it strange; but she would be best
            pleas'd
To be so anger'd with another letter.

Exit LUCETTA.

    JUL.   Nay, would I were so angered with the
            same!
O hateful hands, to tear such loving words!

Injurious wasps!—to feed on such sweet honey,
And kill the bees that yield it with your stings!
I'll kiss each separate paper for amends.
Look, here it says—*kind Julia:*—unkind Julia!
And in revenge of your ingratitude
I throw your name down on these bruising stones,
Trampling contemptuously on your disdain.
And here it says—*love wounded Proteus:*—
Poor wounded name! My bosom, like a bed,
Will lodge you, till your wound be th'roughly healed;
And so I nurse it with a healing kiss.

NOTES

a coil with protestation — (such) a fuss over a vow of love; *makes it strange* — pretends it is not her letter.

JUL. Nay, would I were so anger'd with the same! — controversy exists as to whether this line originally belonged to *Lucetta.* Staunton argued that in *Julia's* "mouth . . . it seems senseless and absurd," and implied a printing error. More recently the Arden edition rebutted this suggesting that *Lucetta* spoke the preceding line in a "half-aside, which can be overheard," adding, "Julia means that she wishes the letter still existed for her to get angry over, or perhaps that she wishes her true emotion was the anger she pretended."

The original script does not indicate any aside or exit for *Lu-*

MODERN

But more than once was—*Proteus*—written down.
Be calm, good wind, blow not a word away,
Till I have found each letter in the letter,
Except my own name: which let whirlwinds bear
Up to a rugged, overhanging cliff,
And throw it straight into the raging sea!
Oh, here in one line is his name two times—
Poor forlorn Proteus, poor impassioned Proteus,

Injurious wasps! to feed on such sweet honey,
And kill the bees, that yield it, with your stings!
I'll kiss each several paper for amends.
Look, here is writ—*kind Julia:*—unkind Julia!
As in revenge of thy ingratitude,
I throw thy name against the bruising stones,
Trampling contemptuously on thy disdain.
And here is writ—*love wounded Proteus:*—
Poor wounded name! my bosom, as a bed,
Shall lodge thee, till thy wound be throughly heal'd;
And thus I search it with a sovereign kiss.

---

cetta. However, she probably did not exit before the line, in which
case Arden's "half-aside" would be probably half right—i.e., *Lucetta*
exits mumbling . . . *she would be best pleas'd to be so anger'd with
another letter*, which *Julia* is meant to, and does, hear.

Furthermore, *Julia's* meaning is not "senseless and absurd".
She simply wishes that she were not so helplessly in love that she is
totally unable to get angry at this or any letter from *Proteus*.

wasps — i.e., her fingers, but the allusion is entomologically
true except that wasps kill with their mandibles, not stings; *each
several paper* — each separate paper; *as in revenge* — as if in
revenge; *search* — probe into, i.e., thusly clean out (the "wound");
sovereign — effectively healing.

ORIGINAL

But twice, or thrice, was—*Proteus*—written down:
Be calm, good wind, blow not a word away,
Till I have found each letter in the letter.
Except mine own name: that some whirlwind bear
Unto a ragged, fearful, hanging rock,
And throw it thence into the raging sea!
Lo, here in one line is his name twice writ—
Poor forlorn Proteus, passionate Proteus,

To the sweet Julia; that I'll tear away;
And yet I will not, since so prettily
He couples it to his own plaintive names;
And so I'll fold them one upon the other;
Now kiss, embrace, disport, do what you will.

Reenter LUCETTA.

LUC.   Madam, dinner is ready, and your father
        waits.
JUL.   Well, let us go.
LUC.   What, will these papers lie in telltale view?
JUL.   If they so worry you, then pick them up.
LUC.   No! I got you worked up for laying them
        down.
Yet lying here the poor things will catch cold.
JUL.   You seem to have a mother's love for them.
LUC.   Well, madam, you see what you want to
        see.
I see things too, although you think I'm blind.
JUL.   Come on now, let us go.

Exeunt.

COMMENTS

Here is a sensitively written scene that builds from the very beginning on the most subtle of gradations, and never stops building.

At the very outset *Julia* wheedles, or thinks she is, *Lucetta* into talking about *Proteus*. Even her adjectives build from the *fair* so and so, to the *rich* so and so, and, ah, to the *gentle Proteus*. When confronted with the very thing she secretly wished for—a letter of love—she panics and protests loudly, hoping that *Lucetta* cannot hear the beating of her heart. Then, alone, she secretly confesses her true feelings and calls *Lucetta* back. A mental tug of war between them, with a banter of bawdy (see *Notes*), ensues. But this time *Lucetta* does not spare her feelings; gazing right into *Julia's* heart of hearts she reveals her secret love—*Proteus*. She is angrily dismissed while *Julia* and the letter both go to pieces.

To the sweet Julia; that I'll tear away;
And yet I will not, sith so prettily
He couples it to his complaining names;
Thus will I fold them one upon another;
Now kiss, embrace, contend, do what you will.

Reenter LUCETTA.

LUC.   Madam, dinner is ready, and your father
        stays.
JUL.   Well, let us go.
LUC.   What, shall these papers lie like tell-tales
        here?
JUL.   If you respect them, best to take them up.
LUC.   Nay, I was taken up for laying them down.
Yet here they shall not lie, for catching cold.
JUL.   I see you have a month's mind to them.
LUC.   Ay, madam, you may say what sights you
        see;
I see things too, although you judge I wink.
JUL.   Come, come, will 't please you go?

Exeunt.

––––––––––

What follows is not a soliloquy in which an ingenue emotes
but, rather, a virtual ballet. The movement leaps from the lines. She
is not alone on the stage; she is there with those poor, torn
fragments of that lovelorn letter. She swoops a few of them up,
whisks them to her lips—*I'll kiss each several paper for amends.*
And they come to life—*Look, here is writ*—KIND JULIA. Throwing
the piece down —*unkind Julia!*—she tramples it *contemptuously.*

And, here is writ—LOVE WOUNDED PROTEUS. With a ten-
derness she softly tucks "Proteus" in her bosom, then lowering her
head, kissing the paper—*And thus I search it with a sovereign kiss.*
Again she stoops, looking for other pieces of paper—*But twice, or
thrice, was*—PROTEUS—*written down.*

Each little piece of paper comes into an existence all its own,
until the ultimate personification when she *folds* two forlorn fragments, *one upon another*, and makes them dance before the eyes of
a hypnotized audience.

The theater is hushed. All attention is on the flapping paper pieces, like disembodied marionettes, as *Julia* whispers in ecstasy— *now kiss, embrace . . . contend . . . . . . do what you will . . . .* and just then, from offstage—with at least a figurative belch— *Reenter* LUCETTA with a bellowing roar—*Madam, dinner is ready . . .*

That is the end of that—and Scene 2.

NOTES

ragged, fearful, hanging rock — rugged, dreadful, overhang-ing cliff; *passionate* — impassioned; *sith* — since; *complaining* — self-pitying; *contend* — engage, wrestle; *stays* — waits; *tell-tales* — exposed secrets; *respect* — are concerned with; *taken up for* — taken to task for; *for catching* — for fear of catching; *month's mind to* — single-minded about (from the church observance of prayers to be said one month after a death—perhaps from the bereaved's meditating "single-mindedly" about the deceased); *wink* — close my eyes.

MODERN

ACT I

SCENE 3 — *A Room in* ANTONIO'S *House.*

Enter ANTONIO *and* PANTHINO.

ANT.   Tell me, Panthino, what grave talk was that,
Which made my brother keep you in the courtyard?

PAN.   About his nephew, Proteus, your son.

ANT.   Why, what of him?

PAN.   He wondered why your lordship
Allows your son to spend his youth at home;
While other men, of lesser noble station,
Send off their sons abroad to seek success—
Some to the wars, to try their fortune there;
Some to explore those islands far away;
For any, or for all these enterprises,
He said that Proteus, your son, was fit,
And asked that I try to prevail on you,
To let him spend his time no more at home,
Which would be detrimental when he's older,
Not having ever traveled in his youth.

ANT.   You needn't try convincing me of that,
For all this month I've thought a lot of it.
I have considered well how time has flown;
And how he cannot be a rounded man,
If he has not been tested in the world.
Experience is by diligence achieved,

COMMENTS

The purpose of Scene 3 is to thicken the plot. Until now there has been no dramatic conflict; there is no excitement in learning that *Valentine* is going abroad and *Proteus* is head *over boots* in

ORIGINAL

ACT I

SCENE 3 — *A Room in* ANTONIO'S *House.*

Enter ANTONIO *and* PANTHINO.

ANT.   Tell me, Panthino, what sad talk was that,
Wherewith my brother held you in the cloister?
PAN.   'T was of his nephew Proteus, your son.
ANT.   Why, what of him?
PAN.   He wonder'd that your lordship
Would suffer him to spend his youth at home;
While other men, of slender reputation,
Put forth their sons to seek preferment out:
Some, to the wars, to try their fortune there;
Some, to discover islands far away;
For any, or for all these exercises,
He said that Proteus, your son, was meet;
And did request me to importune you,
To let him spend his time no more at home,
Which would be great impeachment to his age,
In having known no travel in his youth.
ANT.   Nor need'st thou much importune me to
                    that
Whereon this month I have been hammering.
I have consider'd well his loss of time;
And how he cannot be a perfect man,
Not being try'd and tutor'd in the world:
Experience is by industry achiev'd,

---

love. But now, in the opening lines, the audience hears the unhappy
news in store for *Proteus*, even before he does. Not only must he
leave his *Julia*, but immediately. Interest is piqued—How will *Proteus* react? And after he has reacted, will he really agree to go to
Milan?

NOTES

sad — serious; *cloister* — an enclosed place or space (O.E.D.);
suffer — allow; *reputation* — status; *preferment* — advancement;
out — abroad; *discover* — explore; *exercises* — activities; *meet* —

MODERN

And then refined by the swift course of time.
So, tell me, where would it be best to send him?
    PAN.   I think your lordship is not unaware
That his companion, the young Valentine,
Attends the noblest man of Milan's court.
    ANT.   I'm well aware.
    PAN.   It would be good for you to send him there.
There he'll engage in tilts and tournaments,
Hear charming talk, and meet with noblemen;
And be a part of all that's going on,
In keeping with his youth and nobleness.
    ANT.   I like your thinking; you've advised me
            well;
Indeed, to show you just how well I liked it,
I'm go'ng to make announcement of it now;
And I intend to waste no time at all
In sending him to Milan's royal court.
    PAN.   Tomorrow, if it suits you, Don Alphonso,
Along with other gentlemen of note,
Are trav'ling to present themselves at court,
And offering their service to the Duke.
    ANT.   Good company; let Proteus go with them,
And—Look who's here!—Now we can break the news.

Enter PROTEUS.

    PRO.   Sweet love! Sweet lines! Sweet life!
In her own hand, and written from her heart;
Here is her vow of love, her honor's pledge;
Oh, that our fathers would approve our love,

prepared, ripe; *importune* — try to persuade; *impeachment to his age* — handicap or detriment when he is older; *hammering* — pondering; *his loss of time* — how time is flying for him; *perfect* — accomplished, mature.

ORIGINAL

And perfected by the swift course of time:
Then, tell me, whither were I best to send him?
    PAN.   I think your lordship is not ignorant,
How his companion, youthful Valentine,
Attends the emperor in his royal court.
    ANT.   I know it well.
    PAN.   'T were good, I think, your lordship sent
        him thither:
There shall be practice tilts and tournaments,
Hear sweet discourse, converse with noblemen;
And be in eye of every exercise,
Worthy his youth and nobleness of birth.
    ANT.   I like thy counsel; well hast thou advis'd:
And, that thou mayst perceive how well I like it,
The execution of it shall make known:
Even with the speediest expedition,
I will despatch him to the emperor's court.
    PAN.   Tomorrow, may it please you, Don
        Alphonso,
With other gentlemen of good esteem,
Are journeying to salute the emperor,
And to commend their service to his will.
    ANT.   Good company; with them shall *Proteus* go:
And—in good time. —Now will we break with him.
           Enter PROTEUS.
    PRO.   Sweet love! sweet lines! sweet life!
Here is her hand, the agent of her heart;
Here is her oath for love, her honor's pawn:
O, that our fathers would applaud our loves,

NOTES

attends — serves.

Emperor — becomes the "duke" of Milan later in the play. This is offered as evidence of rewriting by some commentators. In any case the actors in actual performance would perhaps have settled on one royal title to the exclusion of the other; and with either choice the script, if not always the meter, "works".

The non-interchangeability of emperor/duke (and later Padua/Milan) does strongly suggest a rewrite. The bard himself may have done so for, say, a revival production of the play, which could also explain the "massed-entry" scene headings (cf. *Induction*). Great strides being made today in bibliographical approaches to the text (cf. Hinman et al) may eventually solve many such riddles. More understanding of bawdy entendre, too, may make "correct" many of what are now considered minor collator/compositor/proofreader

MODERN

To seal our happiness with their consent!
Oh, heavenly Julia!

    ANT.   Well now, what letter are you reading
            there?

    PRO.   May't please you sir, it's just a word or two
Of greetings sent to me from Valentine,
Delivered by a friend who came from him.

    ANT.   Let's see the letter; let me see the news.

    PRO.   There is no news, my Lord; just that he
            writes
How happily he lives, how well he's treated,
And highly favored by the duke, himself,
And wishing I were there to share his joy.

    ANT.   And how then do you feel about his wish?

    PRO.   I'm one who's in accordance with your
            will,
Regardless of how friendly is his wish.

errors as well as editorial emendations and choices between quarto and folio readings.

your lordship — if your lordship; *practice* — participate in; *sweet discourse* — pleasant conversation; *converse* — meet; *in eye of* — able to witness, i.e., be in the center of; *salute* — present themselves; *commend* — offer; *in good time* — propitious timing; *break with* — break the news to; *her hand, the agent of* — her handwriting, the representative (messenger) of; *pawn* — pledge; *applaud* — approve.

With *Proteus'* entrance the audience first learns that *Julia* is now sending love letters to him. The abruptness of this revelation has been criticized with the suggestion that a previous scene has been deleted. Actually, after *Julia's* torn-letter scene, it should surprise no one.

ORIGINAL

To seal our happiness with their consents!
O, heavenly Julia!
    ANT.   How now? what letter are you reading
             there?
    PRO.   May 't please your lordship, 't is a word or
             two
Of commendation sent from Valentine,
Deliver'd by a friend that came from him.
    ANT.   Lend me the letter; let me see what news.
    PRO.   There is no news, my lord; but that he
             writes
How happily he lives, how well-belov'd,
And daily graced by the emperor;
Wishing me with him, partner of his fortune.
    ANT.   And how stand you affected to his wish?
    PRO.   As one relying on your lordship's will,
And not depending on his friendly wish.

ANT.   What I would will's in keeping with his
           wish.
Don't be surprised if I'm so quick to act;
For what I say, I say, and that's the end.
I am resolved that you will spend some time
With Valentinus in the duke's own court;
Whatever money he may now receive,
The same allowance you will have from me.
Tomorrow be in readiness to go—
And no excuses, please—my mind is set.

NOTES

commendation — greetings; *graced* — favored; *partner of his fortune* — sharer of his happiness; *affected to* — affected by, i.e.,

MODERN

PRO.   My lord, I can't be ready all that soon;
Please think about it for a day or two.
ANT.   Whatever you may need can follow you.
And now no more; tomorrow you shall go—
Come on, Panthino; you will be the one
To expedite him on his way.

           Exeunt ANTONIO *and* PANTHINO.

PRO.   I've stayed away from fire for fear of
           burning,
And now I fall into the sea and drown;
I did not show my father Julia's letter
For fear he'd be a hind'rance to my love;
And so, resulting from my own white lie,
He's *really* now a hind'rance to my love.

ANT.   My will is something sorted with his wish:
Muse not that I thus suddenly proceed;
For what I will, I will, and there an end.
I am resolv'd that thou shalt spend some time
With Valentinus in the emperor's court;
What maintenance he from his friends receives,
Like exhibition thou shalt have from me.
Tomorrow be in readiness to go:
Excuse it not, for I am peremptory.

———————————

feel about; *sorted with* — of the same sort as; *muse not* — marvel
not, do not be surprised; *maintenance* and *exhibition* — monetary
allowance; *friends* — relatives; *excuse it not* — make no excuses;
peremptory — resolved.

ORIGINAL

PRO.   My lord, I cannot be so soon provided;
Please you, deliberate a day or two.
ANT.   Look, what thou want'st shall be sent after
        thee:
No more of stay; tomorrow thou must go.
Come on, Panthino; you shall be employ'd
To hasten on his expedition.
        Exeunt ANTONIO *and* PANTHINO.
PRO.   Thus have I shunn'd the fire, for fear of
        burning;
And drench'd me in the sea, where I am drown'd:
I fear'd to show my father Julia's letter,
Lest he should take exceptions to my love;
And with the vantage of mine own excuse
Hath he excepted most against my love.

Oh, how the Spring of love resembles
The uncertain glory of an April day;
Which now shows all the beauty of the sun,
And by and by a cloud takes all away!

Reenter PANTHINO.

PAN.   Sir Proteus, your father calls for you;
He's in a hurry, so you'd better go.

PRO.   Well, this is it! My heart consents thereto,
And yet a thousand times it answers, *No.*

Exeunt.

COMMENTS

The answer to how *Proteus* would react to being shipped off to Milan is replaced by the question of how his and *Julia's* love will manage to survive their being torn apart. *Panthino's* otherwise unnecessary exit momentarily relinquishes the stage to *Proteus* for a short but memorable soliloquy on *the uncertain glory of an April day.* And *Panthino's* otherwise unnecessary reentrance provides an echo of the *Lucetta* disruption earlier; once again a lover's heavenly reverie is brought back to earth with a thud, and the act to an end with a smile.

O, how this spring of love resembleth
The uncertain glory of an April day;
Which now shows all the beauty of the sun,
And by and by a cloud takes all away!

Reenter PANTHINO.

PAN.   Sir Proteus, your father calls for you;
He is in haste; therefore, I pray you, go.

PRO.   Why, this it is! my heart accords thereto;
And yet a thousand times it answers, No.

Exeunt.

NOTES

provided — packed (luggage); *stay* — waiting; *look what* — whatever; *hasten on his expedition* — facilitate a quick departure; *vantage* — advantage, i.e., unintended opportunity given him; *excuse* — pretext, i.e., the very excuse I, myself, gave him to keep him from knowing that the letter was from *Julia*; *hath he excepted most against* — has he (in effect) taken greatest possible exception to; *spring of love* — springtime of love; *it is* — is it; *accords thereto* — complies with.

ACT II

SCENE 1 — *Milan. A room in the* DUKE'S *palace.*

Enter VALENTINE *and* SPEED.

SPEED. (*Offers a lady's glove.*)
Sir, your glove.

VAL.   No; mine are being worn.

SPEED. Why, then this may be yours, for this is worn.

VAL.   Hah! Let me see. Yes, give it here; it's mine—

Sweet covering, that graced a thing divine!
Ah, Silvia! Silvia!

SPEED. Madam Silvia! Madam Silvia!

VAL.   Why do you call?

SPEED. She is not within hearing, sir.

VAL.   Who ever told you to call her?

SPEED. You called her yourself, sir; or I misunderstood.

VAL.   You'll always be too brassy.

SPEED. And yet I was last charged with being too dull.

VAL.   Go on! Now tell me, do you know madam Sylvia?

SPEED. She whom your worship loves?

VAL.   Why, how do you know that I'm in love?

COMMENTS

Act II opens with the dangling of a lady's glove. There is a general giggling as even before one word is spoken the audience knows from that glove that *Valentine* has been hopelessly smitten. But lest anyone take his lovesickness seriously—excepting *Valentine*, of course—the diagnosis is revealed not by a lover's soliloquy but by a dialogue with none other than the irreverent *Speed*. The latter

ORIGINAL

ACT II

SCENE 1 — *Milan. A room in the* DUKE'S *palace.*

Enter VALENTINE *and* SPEED.

SPEED. Sir, your glove.
VAL.   Not mine; my gloves are on.
SPEED. Why, then this may be yours, for this is
        but one.
VAL.   Ha! let me see: ay, give it me, it's mine—
Sweet ornament, that decks a thing divine!
Ah Silvia! Silvia!
SPEED. Madam Silvia! madam Silvia!
VAL.   How now, sirrah?
SPEED. She is not within hearing, sir.
VAL.   Why, sir, who bade you call her?
SPEED. Your worship, sir; or else I mistook.
VAL.   Well, you'll still be too forward.
SPEED. And yet I was last chidden for being too
slow.
VAL.   Go to, sir; tell me, do you know madam
Silvia?
SPEED. She that your worship loves?
VAL.   Why, how know you that I am in love?

promptly supports his diagnosis by giving typical symptoms of
young love in medical-chart detail.

———————————

NOTES

Sir, your glove. — the audience sees a lady's glove (*Silvia's*—of
which fact *Speed* is well aware); while *Valentine* thinks he has drop-
ped it, it is more likely that *Speed* impishly filches it onstage.

one — pronounced then like the previous *on* (not "won") and hence a pun; *sirrah* — a form of address to inferiors; *still be too forward* — always be hopelessly impudent, *Valentine* referring to *Speed's* making mockery of the former's cries of *Silvia! Silvia!*; *slow* — *Speed* plays on *forward's* other meaning then of "prompt"; *Go to, sir.* — like the modern "Get out of here!", where the meaning is purely figurative.

MODERN

SPEED. Easy! By these typical signs: First, you have learned, like Sir Proteus, to fold your arms like a study in melancholy, to warble a love-song, like a robin redbreast; to walk alone, like one who has the leprosy; to moan, like a schoolboy who had lost his first school book; to weep, like a young girl who had just lost her grandma; to fast, like someone on a diet; to keep looking around, like someone who fears being robbed; to speak with a whine, like a beggar expecting something extra on a holy day; when you laughed you were inclined to crow like a cock; when you walked, to pace like some kind of lion; when you fasted, it was always right after dinner; whenever you looked sad, it was . . . . . . for lack of money; and now you are metamorphosed by a maiden, that, when I look at you, I can hardly believe you are my master.

VAL.   Are all these things seen in me?

SPEED. They are all seen without you.

VAL.   Without me? They cannot.

SPEED. Without you? No, that's certain, for without you were so simple, nobody else would see them; but you are so these foibles without, that these foibles are within you, and shine through you like the water in a bottle . . . . . . of urine; so that one look at you and who isn't a physician able to diagnose your malady?

ORIGINAL

SPEED. Marry, by these special marks: First you have learned, like sir Proteus, to wreath your arms like a malcontent; to relish a love-song, like a robin red-breast; to walk alone, like one that had the pestilence; to sigh, like a schoolboy that had lost his ABC; to weep, like a young wench that had buried her grandam; to fast, like one that takes diet; to watch, like one that fears robbing; to speak puling, like a beggar at Hallowmas. You were wont, when you laughed, to crow like a cock; when you walked, to walk like one of the lions; when you fasted, it was presently after dinner; when you looked sadly, it was for want of money; and now you are metamorphosed with a mistress, that, when I look on you, I can hardly think you my master.

VAL.   Are all these things perceived in me?

SPEED. They are all perceived without ye.

VAL.   Without me? they cannot.

SPEED. Without you? nay, that's certain, for without you were so simple, none else would; but you are so without these follies, that these follies are within you, and shine through you like the water in an urinal; that not an eye that sees you, but is a physician to comment on your malady.

NOTES

Speed's speech while long in the reading would seem short in the acting; note the opportunities it affords for cavorting, mimicking, and mugging, not to mention noise making.

wreath your arms — fold your arms—in the art and fashion of the day this pose symbolized melancholy; *relish* — sing; *ABC* — primer; *takes diet* — goes on a diet; *watch* — stay awake; *puling* — whiningly; *Hallowmas* — All Saints Day (viz. Halloween) when extra generosity was to be shown to beggars; *lions* — to pace back and forth, referring to lions in captivity, perhaps those in the Tower of London (although some editions would have one believe that

MODERN

VAL.   But tell me, do you know my Lady Silvia?

SPEED.   The one you gaze at so, as she sits at supper?

VAL.   Have you observed that?—she, herself, I mean.

SPEED.   I know not t' what you refer to, but her I know not.

VAL.   You say you know her by my gazing at her, and yet you know her not?

SPEED.   Does she not look hard pressed, sir?

VAL.   Not so much for being hard up, as for taking things hard.

SPEED.   Sir, I know that, heartily.

VAL.   What do you know?

SPEED.   That she is not so hard up as that, with you, she takes things hard.

VAL.   I mean, that she is excellent in bearing, but her charm is infinite.

SPEED.   That's because the one depends on making a proper entrance, and the other on a charming entrance.

VAL.   How proper? And how charming?

SPEED.   Only, sir, that proper as she is no man sees her entrance that entrances.

Speed at this point pointlessly points to the lions in the royal standard presumably displayed in the theater); *presently* — immediately; *sadly* — defined as "seriously" in those editions which footnote it, but Shakespeare here meant "morose, dismal", i.e., "sadly" (cf. Onions); *without ye* — in your outward appearance (the emphasis of *ye* instead of *you* signals the pun to the audience); *for without you* — for unless you; *none else would* — i.e., would perceive them; *for without* — for unless; *so without* — so externally (the personification of); *urinal* — clear glass bottle to submit urine for a physician's examination.

ORIGINAL

VAL.   But tell me, dost thou know my lady Silvia?

SPEED. She that you gaze on so, as she sits at supper?

VAL.   Hast thou observed that? even she, I mean.

SPEED. Why, sir, I know her not.

VAL.   Dost thou know her by my gazing on her, and yet know'st her not?

SPEED. Is she not hard-favored, sir?

VAL.   Not so fair, boy, as well-favored.

SPEED. Sir, I know that well enough.

VAL.   What dost thou know?

SPEED. That she is not so fair as (of you) well favored.

VAL.   I mean, that her beauty is exquisite, but her favor infinite.

SPEED. That's because the one is painted, and the other all out of count.

VAL.   How painted? and how out of count?

SPEED. Marry, sir, so painted, to make her fair, that no man counts of her beauty.

VAL.   How then do you account for me? I see it.

SPEED. You never saw her since she was rigid.

VAL.   Since when has she been rigid!

SPEED. Ever since you loved her.

VAL.   I have loved her ever since I saw her; and still I see her charm.

SPEED. If you love her, you cannot see her.

NOTES

know — also means to know carnally; *even she* — she, herself.

not — also means knot, i.e., virgin knot, maidenhead, with a play on carnality of *know*.

hard-favored — (1) ugly and (2) a play on the female organ (*favor*), with a probable additional stress of the preceding *not*.

Not so fair, boy, as well-favored — several interpretations of this line exist, but it is not troublesome once one is attuned, as is the audience, to the bawdy of *favored; Not so fair* then is "Not so (much) beautiful . . ." as *well-favored* (which in *Valentine's* mind only is "charming").

Sir, I know that well — a play on the previous lines, most probably stressed: Sir, I *know* that well enough.

favor infinite — aside from its obvious bawdy, *favor* in a

MODERN

VAL.   Why?

SPEED. Because love is blind. Oh, if you had my eyes; or your own eyes could see what they once were able to see when you chided Sir Proteus for going ungartered!

VAL.   What would I see then?

SPEED. Your own present folly, and her hard rigidity: for he, being in love, could not see to garter his hose; but you, being in love, cannot even see to put them on.

VAL.   How esteemest thou me? I account of her beauty.

SPEED.   You never saw her since she was deformed.

VAL.   How long hath she been deformed?

SPEED.   Ever since you loved her.

VAL.   I have loved her ever since I saw her; and still I see her beautiful.

SPEED.   If you love her, you cannot see her.

woman denoted both inward and outward charm; hence *Valentine* is saying the modern equivalent of "She's not only pretty; she has personality too."; *painted* — rouged.

   out of all count — an immeasurable, immense *favor*; of course *Valentine's* and *Speed's* reference points differ; (also cf. Partridge at *coun* and *country*).

   counts of her beauty — considers her beauty; *account of her beauty* — take account of . . .

   deformed — also means erection of the sexual organ; from *form* (q.v.); some of the more deformed than informed explanations:—"i.e. transformed." (Pelican), "i.e. distorted by your lover's view." (Signet), "Speed means that when Valentine fell in love, his emotion transfigured his mistress so that he no longer sees her true appearance." (Folger).

ORIGINAL

VAL.   Why?

SPEED.   Because love is blind. O, that you had mine eyes; or your own eyes had the lights they were wont to have when you chid at sir Proteus for going ungartered!

VAL.   What should I see then?

SPEED.   Your own present folly, and her passing deformity: for he, being in love, could not see to garter his hose; and you, being in love, cannot see to put on your hose.

VAL.   It seems, boy, then you are in love; for this morning you could not see to clean my shoes.

SPEED.   True, sir; I was in love with my bed; and, thank you, you whacked me for my love, which makes me all the bolder to chide you for yours.

VAL.   Well, it is true; I am heavily in love with her.

SPEED.   I wish your heavy load were lost; so your desire would cease.

VAL.   Last night she requested me to write a letter to someone she loves.

SPEED.   And did you?

VAL.   I did.

SPEED.   Wasn't it, well, awkward?

VAL.   No, boy, I did my best with it. Quiet! Here she comes.

NOTES

lights — eyes, i.e., sight; *ungartered* — traditional sign of absent-mindedness in a lover; *passing* — surpassing; *swinged* — beaten.

MODERN

Enter SILVIA.

SPEED.   (*Aside*) Oh, what a veritable puppet show! Oh, puppet of puppets! And now will he give her a line.

VAL.   Madam and mistress, a thousand good morrows.

SPEED.   (*Aside*) Oh, God help us tonight—here's a million of mannerisms.

SIL.   Sir Valentine and suitor, to you two thousand.

SPEED.   (*Aside*) He should pay her interest, and she pay him.

VAL.   Belike, boy, then you are in love; for last morning you could not see to wipe my shoes.

SPEED. True, sir; I was in love with my bed: I thank you, you swinged me for my love, which makes me the bolder to chide you for yours.

VAL.   In conclusion, I stand affected to her.

SPEED. I would you were set; so your affection would cease.

VAL.   Last night she enjoined me to write some lines to one she loves.

SPEED. And have you?

VAL.   I have.

SPEED. Are they not lamely writ?

VAL.   No, boy, but as well as I can do them; —Peace! here she comes.

---

stand — also means penis erectus; *affected* — enamored.

set — also bawdy as previously used but, in the context here, with the added sense of orgasm being reached; *lamely* — awkwardly.

ORIGINAL

SPEED. (*Aside*) O excellent motion! O exceeding puppet! Now will he interpret to her.

VAL.   Madam and mistress, a thousand good morrows.

SPEED. (*Aside*) O, give ye good ev'n! here's a million of manners.

SIL.   Sir Valentine and servant, to you two thousand.

SPEED. (*Aside*) He should give her interest, and she gives it him.

VAL.   As you requested me, I wrote your letter
Meant for the secret nameless friend of yours;
But I did do it most reluctantly,
Out of my duty to your ladyship.
SIL.   I thank you gentle suitor—it's very smartly
done.
VAL.   Believe me, madam, it was difficult;
For, being ignorant to whom it goes,
I wrote unsurely, feeling out my way.
SIL.   Perhaps you think I troubled you too much?
VAL.   No, madam; if it helps you, I will write,
If that's your wish, a thousand times as much.
And yet—

NOTES

motion — puppet show (cf. the modern word "movie"); *exceeding* — exceptional; *interpret* — explain the motions of the puppets in terms of the story line (puppets which "speak" are a more recent development).

Various editions go in different directions as to who is the puppet: "Valentine is a puppet being manipulated by Silvia." (Folger); "Speed means that Silvia is a puppet because she has not been able to speak of her love for Valentine, but has had to employ him as an interpreter." (Rowse). It seems unlikely that Shakespeare would have wasted such subtleties on an audience who at this point have no knowledge of any "manipulation" by a Silvia they have not even seen, or, by the same token, do they yet know that "she has not been able to speak of her love".

MODERN

SIL.   A pretty stopping! Well, I can guess the rest;
And yet — no, I will not mention it; *and yet* — I don't
        care;
And yet — take this again; *and yet* — I thank you;
Which means, I'll never trouble you again.

VAL.   As you enjoin'd me, I have writ your letter
Unto the secret nameless friend of yours;
Which I was much unwilling to proceed in,
But for my duty to your ladyship.

SIL.   I thank you, gentle servant: 't is very clerkly
done.

VAL.   Now trust me, madam, it came hardly off;
For, being ignorant to whom it goes,
I writ at random, very doubtfully.

SIL.   Perchance you think too much of so much
pains?

VAL.   No, madam; so it stead you, I will write,
Please you command, a thousand times as much:
And yet—

Almost certainly both are the puppets. *Speed* delivers his *O exceeding puppet!* as *Silvia* enters; and he means by *interpret* that *Valentine* will be going through all sorts of motions to express his love without actually voicing it. *Speed* is merely anticipating a kind of mating dance common to some birds and all young humans.

give (ye) — short for "God give"; *manners* — mannerisms; *servant* — had the additional meaning then of a suitor dedicating himself to "serving" his lady love; *interest* — the humor here, missed by commentators, is "monetary" interest based on the preceding *thousand* and *two thousand*; *clerkly* — scholarly; *hardly off* — with difficulty; *at random* — with no guideline to go by; *doubtfully* — uncertainly; *too much of so much pains* — so much trouble is too much; *so it stead you* — so long as it helps you; *please you* — if it please you to.

ORIGINAL

SIL.   A pretty period! Well, I guess the sequel;
And yet — I will not name it; and yet — I care not;
And yet — take this again; and yet — I thank you;
Meaning henceforth to trouble you no more.

SPEED. (*Aside*) And yet — you will; and yet — another yet.

VAL.   By that what do you mean? You do not like it?

SIL.   Yes, yes; the letter's written skillfully;
But since unwillingly, do take it back;
No—take it.

VAL.   Madam, it is for you.

SIL.   It's true, you wrote it, sir, at my request;
But I'll have none of it; it is for you.
I only wish it were more passionate.

VAL.   Please, let me write your ladyship another.

SIL.   And when it's done, for my sake read it over;
And should it please you, good; if not, good too.

VAL.   If it pleases me, madam! What then?

SIL.   Well, should it please you, keep it for your effort.
And so good morrow, suitor.

Exit SILVIA.

NOTES

period — stopping, halting (of the sentence); *take this again* — she is returning the letter; *quaintly writ* — well written.

In having unwittingly written himself a letter, how *Valentine* has changed. And in having portrayed him as a sensible young man in Act I, how Shakespeare shows the change that love has wrought. Yet scholars rebuke him for his *Valentine*, as does Charlton:

"In classical comedy the hero is simply the protagonist, the central figure who is the biggest butt of the comic satire. But here the protagonist is the upholder of the faith on which the play is built, the man with whom the audience is called upon to rejoice admiringly, and not the fellow at whom it is derisively to laugh. He is to play the hero in every sense of the word. Yet in the event, the prevailing spirit of romance endows him with sentiments and provides him with occupations which inevi-

SPEED. (*Aside*) And yet — you will; and yet — another yet.

VAL.   What means your ladyship? do you not like it?

SIL.   Yes, yes; the lines are very quaintly writ:
But since unwillingly, take them again;
Nay take them.

VAL.   Madam, they are for you.

SIL.   Ay, ay, you writ them, sir, at my request;
But I will none of them; they are for you:
I would have had them writ more movingly.

VAL.   Please you, I'll write your ladyship another.

SIL.   And when it's writ, for my sake read it over:
And if it please you, so; if not, why, so.

VAL.   If it please me, madam! what then?

SIL.   Why, if it please you, take it for your labor.
And so good morrow, servant.

Exit SILVIA.

tably frustrate the heroic intention. The story renders him a
fool.''

. . . and not him alone, Mr. Charlton, if you honestly believe that
Shakespeare would have had *Valentine* sit right down and write
himself a letter if the audience were intended to look upon him ''admiringly''.

MODERN

SPEED. Oh, joke unseen, inscrutable, invisible,
As a nose on a man's face, or a weathervane on a steeple!
First he makes suit for her; and now she's taught her
                suitor,
He being her pupil, to become her tutor.
Oh, what a clever scheme! Has there ever been one
                better,
Where he, unwittingly, has written himself a letter?
        VAL.   Well now, sir? What—are you talking to
yourself?
        SPEED. Just making rhyme; it's you who has the
reason.
        VAL.   To do what?
        SPEED. To be a spokesman for Madam Silvia.
        VAL.   To whom?
        SPEED. To yourself—she woos you with her piece.
        VAL.   What piece?
        SPEED. Her epistle—the letter, I should say.
        VAL.   Why, she has not written me.
        SPEED. She need not, when she has made you write
to yourself. Why, can't you see the joke?
        VAL.   No, believe me.
        SPEED. Unbelieveable, indeed, sir—but did you
notice her earnest intention?
        VAL.   I noticed no tension, except an angry word.

————————

NOTES

    her tutor — i.e., in the art of courting; *reasoning with* — talk-
ing to (leading to a play on *rhyme-reason*); *spokesman from* — i.e.,
on behalf of.
    **figure* — also means the male or female organ; editors vari-
ously define this as "device, rhetorical device, figure of speech, in-
direct means", etc., all facets of the same definition, and all wrong
here—Shakespeare never used *figure* as synonymous with a *letter*

ORIGINAL

SPEED. O jest unseen, inscrutable, invisible,
As a nose on a man's face, or a weathercock on a steeple!
My master sues to her; and she hath taught her suitor,
He being her pupil, to become her tutor.
O excellent device! was there ever heard a better,
That my master, being scribe, to himself should write
the letter?

VAL.   How now, sir? what are you reasoning with
yourself?

SPEED. Nay, I was rhyming; 't is you that have the
reason.

VAL.   To do what?

SPEED. To be a spokesman from madam Silvia.

VAL.   To whom?

SPEED. To yourself: why, she woos you by a figure.

VAL.   What figure?

SPEED. By a letter, I should say.

VAL.   Why? She hath not writ to me.

SPEED. What needs she, when she hath made you
write to yourself? Why, do you not perceive the jest?

VAL.   No, believe me.

SPEED. No believing you, indeed, sir; but did you
perceive her earnest?

VAL.   She gave me none, except an angry word.

(i.e., a piece of correspondence), or for that matter has anyone else,
ever.

letter — also means sexual organ but of the female only (also
cf. Partridge at "O"); there is of course a non-bawdy play here on
figure and *letter* (i.e., character of the alphabet).

earnest — sincerity (misinterpreted by *Valentine* as meaning
earnest in its figurative sense of "promise").

MODERN

SPEED. Why, she has given you a letter.

VAL.   That's the letter I wrote to her friend.

SPEED. That same letter she's now delivered, and that's the end.

VAL.   I hope it gets no worse.

SPEED. Indeed, it's going well,

For often have you written her, and she, in modesty,
Or else for lack of idle time, just could not make reply,
Or else not trusting anyone her secret to discover,
Herself has taught her love himself, to write unto her
                    lover.—

All that I say is letter perfect, for I found it all in a letter. Sir, why do you mope? It's dinnertime.

VAL.   I have dined.

SPEED. I'll say this, sir—though lovers and lizards can live on air, I for one am nourished by my stomach and need to have my meat. Oh, don't be like your lady; be bold, be bold.

Exeunt.

NOTES

her mind discover — reveal her secret.

speak in print — several conjectures—"speak by rote" (Pelican), "utter authoritatively" (Folger), etc.—but most likely "precisely, exactly, to the letter" (Staunton); *in print I found it* — since the verse is obviously beyond *Speed's* ad libbing ability he confesses to an amazed audience, perhaps by plucking a paper from his pocket, that he plagiarized it.

I have dined — by feasting his eyes on *Silvia*, of course; *chameleon love* — chameleons were mistakenly thought to be able to live on air just as lovers, then and now, were and are seemingly able to do so.

fain — rather; *be moved* — become enamored, i.e., be aggressive.

ORIGINAL

SPEED. Why she hath given you a letter.

VAL. That's the letter I writ to her friend.

SPEED. And that letter hath she delivered, and there an end.

VAL. I would it were no worse.

SPEED. I'll warrant you 't is as well.

For often have you writ to her, and she, in modesty,
Or else for want of idle time, could not again reply,
Or fearing else some messenger, that might her mind
discover,
Herself hath taught her love himself, to write unto her
lover.—

All this I speak in print, for in print I found it—Why muse you, sir? 't is dinnertime.

VAL. I have dined.

SPEED. Ay, but hearken, sir; though the chameleon Love can feed on the air, I am one that am nourished by my victuals, and would fain have meat. O, be not like your mistress; be moved, be moved.

Exeunt.

MODERN

ACT II

SCENE 2 — *Verona. A room in JULIA'S house.*

Enter PROTEUS *and* JULIA.

PRO.   Have patience, gentle Julia.

JUL.   I must, there is no other way.

PRO.   As soon as possible, I will return.

JUL.   Sooner yet, if you stay true to me.
Here—for my sake now keep your Julia's ring.

PRO.   And I will give you mine; here now take
this.

They exchange.

JUL.   And seal the bargain with a holy kiss.

PRO.   Here, take my hand, I pledge my faithful-
ness;
And should there ever be an hour go by
Where I forget to sigh in love of you,
Before a second hour has passed may fate
Torment me for my love's forgetfulness!
My father waits—You need not answer me.
The tide is high—Now, now . . . no tide of tears;
They'll only keep me longer than I should—

Exit JULIA.

Julia, farewell—What! Gone without a word?
Yes, so true love should do—it cannot speak,
For truth is better served by deeds than words.

Enter PANTHINO.

PAN.   Sir Proteus, you are waited for.

PRO.   Go; I come, I come—
Oh, how this parting strikes poor lovers dumb.

Exeunt.

ORIGINAL

ACT II

SCENE 2 — *Verona. A room in* JULIA'S *house.*

Enter PROTEUS *and* JULIA.

PRO.   Have patience, gentle Julia.

JUL.   I must, where is no remedy.

PRO.   When possibly I can, I will return.

JUL.   (*Giving a ring.*) If you turn not, you will
return the sooner:

Keep this remembrance for thy Julia's sake.

PRO.   Why, then we'll make exchange; here take
you this.

JUL.   And seal the bargain with a holy kiss.

PRO.   Here is my hand for my true constancy;

And when that hour o'erslips me in the day,

Wherein I sigh not, Julia, for thy sake,

The next ensuing hour some foul mischance

Torment me for my love's forgetfulness!

My father stays my coming; answer not;

The tide is now: nay, not thy tide of tears;

That tide will stay me longer than I should:

Exit JULIA.

Julia, farewell—What! gone without a word?

Ay, so true love should do: it cannot speak;

For truth hath better deeds than words to grace it.

Enter PANTHINO.

PAN.   Sir Proteus, you are stay'd for.

PRO.   Go; I come, I come—

Alas! this parting strikes poor lovers dumb.

Exeunt.

COMMENTS

As the lovers *Valentine* and *Silvia* court in Milan, the lovers *Proteus* and *Julia* betroth in Verona. The scene has been criticized as too short on action and too short period; but these critics read the betrothal as something tender and touching whereas the Elizabethans saw it as hilarious irony.

But in addition to the laughter it provides, this scene is an important foundation stone for action later in the play; indeed, in being recalled by the audience then it will add poignancy and intensity to that later action; this "ring" scene then—what it is and where it is placed—is one more example of masterly dramaturgy.

NOTES

turn — i.e., to another lover; a conjecture has been made (Signet) of a possible bawdy meaning here—but that is so unlikely as to be not so.

MODERN

ACT II

SCENE 3 — *Verona. A street.*

Enter LAUNCE *and* DOG.

LAUN.   I still cannot keep from weeping; indeed, the whole clan of the Launces have this family weakness. Now I've received an awful lot, like the prodigious son, and I'm going with Sir Proteus to the high-muck-a-muck's court. I think Crab, my dog, be the sourest-natured dog that lives—my mother weeping, my father wailing, my sister crying, our maid howling, our cat wringing her hands, and all our house in a great perplexity, yet did not this cruel-hearted cur shed one tear; he is like stone, the hardest kind of stone, and has no more pity in him than a dog; the very devil would have wept to see my leaving; why, my granny, having no eyes, you see, wept herself blind at my leaving. Here, *tide is now* — Verona is no more a seaport here than in Act I, but the audience came to see a comedy, not a travelogue, so veracity was not theatrically important; indeed, had Shakespeare made a gentlemen's bet with his associates that no one would spot the discrepancy, he probably would have won.

father stays — father waits; *tide will stay me* — i.e., keep me.

Some scholars suggest that this extremely short scene was abridged from a longer original and concomitantly suggest that the abridgement was made by a non-Shakespearean hand. One trouble with this kind of speculation is that who is to say that any abridgement did not improve the play—ipso facto it probably did. The other trouble is in the conjecture here of a non-Shakespearean abridger based on the fact that the first two lines are in prose and that even the remainder—all verse—is jarred by *Proteus'* second *I come*; such speculation presumes to know what mixture of verse and prose the bard would have considered proper; indeed, to please the critics by "improving" *Proteus'* speech to read, *Go: I come.*, would make it sound like a line out of *Tarzan.*

ORIGINAL

ACT II

SCENE 3 — *The same. A street.*

Enter LAUNCE, *leading a Dog.*

LAUN. Nay, 't will be this hour ere I have done weeping; all the kind of the Launces have this very fault: I have received my proportion, like the prodigious son, and am going with sir Proteus to the imperial's court. I think Crab my dog be the sourest-natured dog that lives: my mother weeping, my father wailing, my sister crying, our maid howling, our cat wringing her hands, and all our house in a great perplexity, yet did not this cruel-hearted cur shed one tear; he is a stone, a very pebble-stone, and has no more pity in him than a dog; a Jew would have wept to have seen our parting; why, my grandam, having no eyes, look you, wept herself blind at my parting. Nay, I'll show you the manner of it: This

let me show you how it went. Say this shoe is my father;
—no, this left shoe is my father; no, no, this left shoe is
my mother; no—that can't be so either; yes, it is so, it is
so, because it has the worst sole. Yes, this shoe with the
hole in it, is my mother, and this my father. A curse
upon it! So there. Well, sir, now, this stick is my sister;
because, see, she is as white as a lily, and as small as a
wand. This hat is Nan, our maid;

NOTES

This is the only scene which Shakespeare animates with a dog.
It is generally believed that the scene was created with the great
comedian of the time, William Kempe (or Kemp) in mind; it is in
fact believed that Kempe, along with his trained dog, portrayed
Launce in the original performances of the play.

Will Kempe was probably the most popular comedian of that
day and something of a zany. Long before the Guinness Book of
Records was a comma in a publisher's eye, Kempe—in 1600—did a
nine day marathon dance stint from London to Norwich. He probably performed the role of *Launce* very extempore, which leads the
Folger edition to observe:

"Launce and his dog Crab doubtless occupied a much larger
place in the play than the printed text suggests, for Launce was
played by the most famous clown of the Elizabethan stage,
Will Kemp, and Kemp's dog was a trained beast capable of all
sorts of vaudeville tricks."

MODERN

I am the dog:—no, the dog is himself, and I am the
dog—Oh, the dog is me, and I am myself; Yes, so, so.
Now I come to my father; *Father, your blessing*; now
the shoe is weeping so much nothing comes from it;
now I will kiss my father; well, he weeps on:—now I
come to my mother. Oh, if she could spout off now like
a woman would—well, I kiss her: there, like so; here's

shoe is my father;—no, this left shoe is my father; no, no, this left shoe is my mother;—nay, that cannot be so neither:—yes, it is so, it is so; it hath the worser sole. This shoe, with the hole in it, is my mother, and this my father. A vengeance on 't! there 't is: now, sir, this staff is my sister; for, look you, she is as white as a lily, and as small as a wand: this hat is Nan, our maid;

If it is logical to assume that Shakespeare consulted Kempe on this scene, even coauthored it with him, it may be equally assumed that the bard would have made sure that the final script was not dependent on Kempe playing the part; this would have been the case not only because such would be essential to the whole idea of repertory, but also as provision against the sudden incapacity of Kempe, or his dog, to perform. Indeed, if this edition's speculation is correct (cf. *Induction*) this scene was performed many times after Kempe left Shakespeare's acting group in 1599. At the very least, Shakespeare would have rewritten the scene when Kempe left if such had been necessary.

All of this is to say that the existing script plays perfectly well with any good comedian and with any old untrained curbstone setter.

kind — kin, kinfolk; *fault* — weakness (of the family); *proportion* — portion (a malapropism); *prodigious* — prodigal (a semi-malapropism with sexual connotation); *sole* — with a possible, but unlikely, play on "soul".

*hole — also means the female organ.

ORIGINAL

I am the dog:—no, the dog is himself, and I am the dog— O, the dog is me, and I am myself; ay, so, so. Now come I to my father; *Father, your blessing*; now should not the shoe speak a word for weeping; now should I kiss my father; well, he weeps on:—now come I to my mother; O, that she could speak now, like a would-woman; —well, I kiss her; —why, there 't is; here's my my mother's breathing up and down; now I come to my sister—hark the moan she makes: now the dog all this while sheds not a tear, nor speaks a word; but see how I settle the dust with my tears.

Enter PANTHINO.

PAN.   Launce, away, away, get aboard; your master is already on board, and now you'll need to use a rowboat. What's the matter? Why do you weep, man? Get going, ass; you'll miss the tide if you linger any longer.

LAUN.   That is one tied that would not be missed, for it is the unkindest tied that ever man tied.

PAN.   What's the unkindest tide?

LAUN.   Why, he that's tied there—Crab, my dog.

COMMENTS

The bawdy of this "dog" scene is rather gross, but it is so imaginatively so that it somehow sublimates the bawdy. In all the commentary on this scene, and it has been considerable, not once has there been the slightest suggestion that the dog of this scene does anything other than stand or sit stage center. Neither is there anything in the dialogue to suggest, as does Folger, that the dog does "tricks".

Nothing would be more un-Shakespearean, or uninteresting, than such an un-dog. Of course the dog's stage business, if not his business on stage, can only be conjectured; this is more appropriately a subject for the *Notes* and can be found there.

NOTES

should — this edition does not agree with those who find a play here on *shoe*.

*speak — also means sexually emit.

*word — also means sexual emission.

he weeps on — i.e., he **whips* on.

that she could — misguidedly "corrected" in some editions to *that SHOE could.*

mother's breath up and down; now come I to my sister; mark the moan she makes: now the dog all this while sheds not a tear, nor speaks a word; but see how I lay the dust with my tears.

Enter PANTHINO.

PAN.   Launce, away, away, aboard; thy master is shipped, and thou art to post after with oars. What's the matter? why weep'st thou, man? Away, ass; you'll lose the tide if you tarry any longer.

LAUN.   It is no matter if the tied were lost; for it is the unkindest tied that ever man tied.

PAN.   What's the unkindest tide?

LAUN.   Why, he that's tied here; Crab, my dog.

---

would-woman — so in the original, but various scholars variously "corrected" this to read "wood" woman (mad or wild woman), "wold" (country) woman, or "ould" (old) woman, with some so desperate for meaning that they suggested *Launce* was wearing wooden shoes; *would* was then beginning to lose the 'l' sound, but its disyllabic pronunciation was not lost until later (cf. Kökeritz et al); thus *would* would have permitted a play on "wooed" woman; an equally tenable case, which no one has noticed, could be made for "wood-woman" as a play on "woodman", a sexually promiscuous male; the "wooed" woman, however, seems more appropriate because "to woo" then did not imply some distance but rather a bodily contact "wooing" (cf. Partridge).

mother's breath up and down — mother's heavy breathing.

A scenario based on the above requires conjecture. This is because there are no other Shakespeare dog scenes to compare it with or to support a given interpretation. Equally nonce, for Shakespeare, is the play on "weep-whip" only indirectly supported by the "weed-wick" homonymic in Comedy of Errors III-2 (also cf. Kökeritz), the author's use of "sheep-ship" in the previous act and elsewhere, and his bawdy use of *whip (cf. *Glossary*). Nevertheless, the scenario below should render the meaning reasonably near, if not on, the mark:

SCENARIO

Enter LAUNCE *with* DOG.

LAUN. (*With mock weeping and whipping his staff up and down.*) Nay, 't will be this hour ere I have done weeping; all the Launces have this very fault. I have . . . etc. (*Sits down. Taking one shoe off.*) this cruel-hearted cur . . . has no more pity in him than a dog. A Jew would have wept . . . (*Removes other shoe.*) . . . Nay, I'll show you the manner of it. This shoe is my father; . . . (*Unobtrusively extracts bit of meat from pocket and smears it on toes of shoes*) . . . This shoe with the hole in it, is my mother, and this my father. A vengeance on 't! (*Whacks it with the staff.*) . . . this staff (*Cradling it.*) is my sister . . . this hat (*Lifting it, displaying its well, then twirling it on the staff.*) is Nan, our maid; I am the dog: . . . ay, so, so. (*Kneels down on all fours next to dog, blending with dog, indicating that he is a dog, that he is "the" dog.*) Now come I to my father; (*Kissing one shoe as he might a bishop's ring.*)

MODERN

PAN.   Come on!—I mean you'll miss high tide; and in missing high tide you'll miss the boat; and in missing the boat miss your master; and in missing your master lose your job; and in losing your job—Why do you cover my mouth?

LAUN.   For fear you would lose your tongue.

PAN.   Where could I lose my tongue?

LAUN.   In your tale.

PAN.   In your tail?

Father, your blessing; (*The shoe instantly whips.*) now should not the shoe speak a word for weeping; (*Putting shoe near dog's nose.*) now should I kiss my father; (*The dog interjects himself and licks the shoe.*) well, he weeps on:—now (*Picking up other shoe.*) come I to my mother —O, that she could speak now, like a would woman: —well, (*The dog again interposes.*) I kiss her;—why, (*Manipulating shoe as dog licks toe.*) there 't is; here's my mother's breath (*Breathes heavily.*) up and down; now come I to my sister (*Thrusting staff which dog instinctively grabs with teeth.*) mark the moan she makes: (*Sullenly.*) now the dog all this while sheds not a tear, nor speaks a word; but see how I (*Still on all fours, suddenly raising one leg dog-fashion.*) lay the dust with my tears. (*Interrupted by* PANTHINO, *resumes mock weeping.*)

Enter PANTHINO, ETC.

is shipped — has shipped out; *post* — hasten, hurry; *oars* — rowboat.

ORIGINAL

PAN.　　Tut, man, I mean thou'lt lose the flood; and, in losing the flood, lose thy voyage; and, in losing thy voyage, lose thy master; and, in losing thy master, lose thy service; and, in losing thy service—Why dost thou stop my mouth?

LAUN.　　For fear thou shouldst lose thy tongue.

PAN.　　Where should I lose my tongue?

LAUN.　　In thy tale.

PAN.　　In thy tail?

LAUN.   Miss the tide, and the boat, and the master, and so the job, and the tied! Why man, if the river went dry I could fill it again, for I'm a man of much . . . tears; and if the wind went down I could drive the boat with . . . well, I come from a family of most powerful wails, howls, moans, and sighs.

PAN.   Come, come away, man; I was sent to call you.

LAUN.   Sir, call me whatever you . . . dare to.

PAN.   Will you go?

LAUN.   Very well, I'll go.

Exeunt.

COMMENTS

Just as the playwright has bridged into this interlude of bawdy with *Launce* moseying to his departure, so the scene is bridged out with his being booted to his departure by *Panthino.*

NOTES

flood — high tide.
tongue — also means male organ.
tail — also means podex.

LAUN.   Lose the tide, and the voyage, and the master, and the service, and the tied! Why man, if the river were dry, I am able to fill it with my tears; if the wind were down, I could drive the boat with my sighs.

PAN.   Come, come away, man; I was sent to call thee.

LAUN.   Sir, call me what thou darest.

PAN.   Wilt thou go?

LAUN.   Well, I will go.

Exeunt.

thou, thee, thy — the familiar form of address is used here in sarcasm, not friendliness.

if the river were dry, etc. — some commentators, perplexed by this sudden flowery burst have ascribed it to a reviser other than Shakespeare; others suggest it is a "parody" of *Valentine's* earlier speech which, if it were, would certainly have been lost on the Elizabethan audience; more likely, *Launce* is alluding back to his monologue, which is to say that he delivers his *tears* and *sighs* to the audience with a figurative wink.

MODERN

ACT II

SCENE 4 — *Milan. A room in the DUKE'S Palace.*

Enter VALENTINE, SILVIA, THURIO *and* SPEED.

SIL.   Suitor!
VAL.   Mistress.
SPEED.   Master, Sir Thurio frowns on you.
VAL.   Yes, boy, it's for love.
SPEED.   Not of you.
VAL.   Of my mistress then.
SPEED.   You ought to knock him flat.

Exit SPEED.

SIL.   Suitor, you are sad.
VAL.   Indeed, madam, I seem so.
THU.   Do you seem to be what you are not?
VAL.   Happily maybe.
THU.   So you're two-faced.
VAL.   So are you.
THU.   What do I seem to be that I am not?
VAL.   Wise.
THU.   What do you observe to the contrary?
VAL.   You have two heads.
THU.   How do you see that?
VAL.   I see one over your coat—and one under it.
THU.   That means I'm doubly wise.
VAL.   That means each head is a half-wit.
THU.   How dare—

———————

COMMENTS

Enter *Thurio*, the rich and snobbish rival for *Silvia's* hand. He adds no dramatic conflict to the play since everyone knows that he has no more chance of winning the heroine than had the spoiled playboy in all those early American films. And like the playboy he

ORIGINAL

ACT II

SCENE 4 — *Milan. A room in the* DUKE'S *Palace.*

Enter VALENTINE, SILVIA, THURIO *and* SPEED.

SIL.   Servant!
VAL.   Mistress.
SPEED.   Master, sir Thurio frowns on you.
VAL.   Ay, boy, it's for love.
SPEED.   Not of you.
VAL.   Of my mistress then.
SPEED.   'T were good you knocked him.

Exit SPEED.

SIL.   Servant, you are sad.
VAL.   Indeed, madam, I seem so.
THU.   Seem you that you are not?
VAL.   Haply I do.
THU.   So do counterfeits.
VAL.   So do you.
THU.   What seem I that I am not?
VAL.   Wise.
THU.   What instance of the contrary?
VAL.   Your folly.
THU.   And how quote you my folly?
VAL.   I quote it in your jerkin.
THU.   My jerkin is a doublet.
VAL.   Well, then, I'll double your folly.
THU.   How?

will, to the delight of the audience, be cut down to size by the hero.
Beyond that he will afford additional delight by virtue of his being,
if this edition suspects correctly, what was then called a fantastic or
fantastico—an outlandish, in costume as well as action, personality;
such a role, distinct from that of the clown (*Speed* and *Launce*),
often turned out to be an out-and-out scene stealer.

NOTES

Mistress. — so in the original, but most editions have "corrected" the period to a question mark; the exclamation mark of the previous line suggests that *Silvia* is calling to *Valentine* from a distance, probably entering at the opposite end of the stage, and his reply of *Mistress* is almost inaudibly faint from lovesickness.

knocked him — would hit him.

Exit SPEED. — the original script does not oblige with a designated exit for *Speed*, so the commentators do and usually at this point; but more, they have criticized the author for the unnecessariness of *Speed's* presence for a mere three lines and the lack of motivation for his exit, some inevitably laying it all to that nameless "reviser"; this edition stands alone in feeling that *Speed* was really conveniently exiting (i.e., leaving *Valentine*) at the scene's opening and, further, that it was by design; again, by "using" *Speed* in similar fashion at the opening of a later scene, and "using" *Thurio* likewise—not to mention instances in other plays—Shakespeare is providing attention-getting diversity of scene openings at those

MODERN

SIL.   What? Angry, Sir Thurio? Turning colors?

VAL.   Leave him be, madam, he's some kind of chameleon.

THU.   That would rather drink your blood than breathe in your hot air.

VAL.   You don't say!

THU.   Said and done too, for now anyway.

VAL.   For you, sir, it's *done* and *said*; for your're at your wit's end before you begin.

SIL.   A fine volley of words, gentlemen; I can see you're both quick to shoot off.

VAL.   Yes, indeed, madam, and we have you to thank.

SIL.   How is that?

times when the audience has been distracted by an intermission or interruption between scenes.

The same absence of proper exits in the original applies to entrances as well, which is why most editions—including this—delete the *Duke's* entrance from this scene's opening stage direction and insert it later on. While the editorial need to supply entrances and exits in this play is unusual, two other plays also have this "massed-entry" problem (cf. *Induction*; also Greg and McKerrow).

haply — a play on its two meanings (1) not sad and (2) perhaps; he is deliberately twisting *Thurio's, Seem you that* (Pretend you are someone) *you are not* to mean *Seem you that you are not* (sad).

counterfeits — fakers, phonies.

*folly — also means male or female organ.

how quote — how regard, observe, with a play on verb form of "coat" since such was then the pronunciation of *quote; I quote it* — (1) observe it (2) coat it.

jerkin — a long outer jacket worn over or in place of a doublet; *doublet* — a close-fitting or inner jacket, leading to a play on *double*.

ORIGINAL

SIL.   What, angry, sir Thurio? do you change color?

VAL.   Give him leave, madam, he is a kind of chameleon.

THU.   That hath more mind to feed on your blood, than live in your air.

VAL.   You have said, sir.

THU.   Ay, sir, and done too, for this time.

VAL.   I know it well, sir; you always end ere you begin.

SIL.   A fine volley of words, gentlemen, and quickly shot off.

VAL.   'T is indeed, madam; we thank the giver.

SIL.   Who is that, servant?

VAL.   It was your radiance, sweet lady, that fired off the volley. Indeed, Sir Thurio's wit exists only in the reflection of your radiance, and is therefore both borrowed and spent in your company.

THU.   Sir, if you spend word for word with me, I shall make your wit bankrupt.

VAL.   I know that well, sir: you have a treasure chest of words, and, I think, no other treasure to give your hangers-on; for it appears by the poverty of their clothes that they live by the poverty of your vocabulary.

SIL.   No more, gentlemen, no more; here comes my father.

NOTES

give him leave — leave him be; *chameleon* — as before, a lizard believed to live on air; *in your air* — allusion to chameleon and to the obnoxiousness of *Valentine's* proximity; *you have said* — you don't say!; *ere you begin* — i.e., to say something meaningful; *gave the fire* — fueled the fire, sparked it; *kindly* — in kind, i.e., accordingly; *exchequer* — treasury.

MODERN

Enter DUKE.

DUKE.   My daughter, I can see your hands are full.
Sir Valentine, your father's in good health;
How would you like a letter from your friends
Of much good news?

VAL.   My lord, I would be thankful
For any such good news that comes from home.

DUKE.   Know you don Antonio, your countryman?

VAL.   Yes, my good lord, I know the gentleman.
He's both of worth and worthy reputation,
And well deserves to be so well respected.

VAL.   Yourself, sweet lady; for you gave the fire: Sir Thurio borrows his wit from your ladyship's looks, and spends what he borrows, kindly, in your company.

THU.   Sir, if you spend word for word with me, I shall make your wit bankrupt.

VAL.   I know it well, sir; you have an exchequer of words, and, I think, no other treasure to give your followers; for it appears, by their bare liveries, that they live by your bare words.

SIL.   No more, gentlemen, no more; here comes my father.

---

bare liveries — threadbare uniforms, clothes; *live* — play on *liveries*; *bare words* — barren, i.e., stupid words.

Some commentators see a conflict here in *Valentine's* reference to threadbare clothes since there are several other references in the play to *Thurio's* wealth; but *Valentine* refers here not to *Thurio's* own clothes but to those of his followers—pointing up, if anything, the probable sumptuousness of *Thurio's* garments.

ORIGINAL

Enter DUKE.

DUKE.   Now. daughter Silvia, you are hard beset.
Sir Valentine, your father's in good health:
What say you to a letter from your friends,
Of much good news?

VAL.   My lord, I will be thankful
To any happy messenger from thence.

DUKE.   Know you don Antonio, your countryman?

VAL.   Ay, my good lord, I know the gentleman
To be of worth, and worthy estimation,
And not without desert so well reputed.

DUKE.   Has he not a son?

VAL.   Yes, my good lord, a son who well deserves
The honor and regard of such a father.

DUKE.   You know him well?

VAL.   As well as I do know myself; from infancy
We have been close, and spent our hours together,
And though myself I've been an idle truant,
Not making best advantage of my time
To shape my own old age to sheer perfection,
Yet has Sir Proteus, for that's his name,
Made use and good advantage of his days;
His years still young, but his experience old;
A youth unmellowed, and yet in judgment ripe,
And in a word (for nowhere near his worth
Are all the praises that I here bestow)
He does not lack for looks or splendid mind,
With all good grace to grace a gentleman.

NOTES

hard beset — i.e., fighting off two ardent suitors; *happy mes-senger* — good-news messenger; *desert* — deserving; *convers'd* — associated; *omitting* — neglecting; *mine age* — my old age; *unmel-low'd* — still young; *complete in feature* — not lacking in hand-someness.

MODERN

DUKE.   Oh, hogwash, sir! If he is all that good
He'd be as worthy of any empress' love
As he'd be fit to counsel emperors.
At any rate, this gentleman has come
Well recommended by great potentates;
And he intends to stay here for awhile,
Which I would think is welcome news to you.

VAL.   If I had wished at all, I'd wish for him.

DUKE. Hath he not a son?

VAL.   Ay, my good lord; a son that well deserves
The honor and regard of such a father.

DUKE. You know him well?

VAL.   I know him, as myself; for from our infancy
We have convers'd and spent our hours together:
And though myself have been an idle truant,
Omitting the sweet benefit of time
To clothe mine age with angel-like perfection,
Yet hath sir Proteus, for that's his name,
Made use and fair advantage of his days,
His years but young, but his experience old;
His head unmellow'd, but for his judgment ripe;
And in a word (for far behind his worth
Come all the praises that I now bestow)
He is complete in feature and in mind,
With all good grace to grace a gentleman.

ORIGINAL

DUKE. Beshrew me, sir, but if he make this good
He is as worthy for an empress' love,
As meet to be an emperor's counselor.
Well, sir; this gentleman is come to me
With commendation from great potentates,
And here he means to spend his time awhile:
I think 't is no unwelcome news to you.

VAL.   Should I have wish'd a thing, it had been he.

DUKE.   Then welcome him in keeping with his
             worth.
Silvia, I'm talking to both you and Thurio,
For Valentine needs no reminding from me.
And Proteus, I will send him in right now.

Exit DUKE.

VAL.   That is the gentleman I told you of.
He would have come with me except his mistress
Had hypnotized him with alluring looks.
SIL.   It seems she must have freed him from her
             spell;
No doubt she's found new lovers' eyes to hold.
VAL.   No, I am sure she holds his pris'ner still.
SIL.   No, then he would be blind, and being
             blind,
How could he see his way to seek you out?
VAL.   Why, lady, love has twenty pairs of eyes.
THU.   They say that love has not an eye at all.
VAL.   Not for such lovers, Thurio, as yourself;
To certain homely objects love is blind.

NOTES

beshrew — mild oath; *make this good* — is this good; *meet* —
fit; *cite* — alert, remind; *presently* — right now; *had come* — would
have come; *lock'd in her crystal looks* — there was a belief that a

MODERN

Enter PROTEUS.

SIL.   Now let's be done!—Here comes the
             gentleman.
VAL.   Welcome, dear Proteus! Mistress, I do beg
             you,
Show him he's welcome in some special way.

DUKE.   Welcome him then according to his worth;
Silvia, I speak to you; and you, sir Thurio:
For Valentine, I need not cite him to it.
I will send him hither to you presently.

Exit DUKE.

VAL.   This is the gentleman I told your ladyship,
Had come along with me, but that his mistress
Did hold his eyes lock'd in her crystal looks.

SIL.   Belike that now she hath enfranchis'd them
Upon some other pawn for fealty.

VAL.   Nay, sure I think she holds them prisoners
          still.

SIL.   Nay, then he should be blind; and, being
          blind,
How could he see his way to seek out you?

VAL.   Why, lady, love hath twenty pairs of eyes.

THU.   They say that love hath not an eye at all.

VAL.   To see such lovers, Thurio, as yourself;
Upon a homely object love can wink.

person whose image was "caught" in a crystal ball was under the
control of the ball's owner; *belike* — likely; *enfranchis'd* — set free;
some other pawn for fealty — some other (lover's) pledge of loyalty; *not an eye at all* — i.e., love is blind; *Love can wink* — Love
can make itself blind.

ORIGINAL

Enter PROTEUS.

SIL.   Have done, have done; here comes the
          gentleman.

VAL.   Welcome, dear Proteus! Mistress, I beseech
          you,
Confirm his welcome with some special favor.

SIL.   His character assures his welcome here,
If this is he you often highly spoke of.
VAL.   It is; sweet lady please encourage him
To be my fellow suitor of your ladyship.
SIL.   Oh, I'm too lowly for so high a suitor.
PRO.   Not so, sweet lady; I'm too poor a suitor
For any notice by so fine a mistress.
VAL.   Let's stop this contest in humility;
Sweet lady, let him be another suitor.
PRO.   I promise you the greatest loyalty.
SIL.   And loyalty has never lacked reward;
I, undeserving as I am, accept you.
PRO.   I'll slay the man who says so, but yourself.
SIL.   That I accept you?
PRO.   That you are undeserving.
THU.   Madam, my lord your father would speak
          with you.
SIL.   I wait upon his pleasure. Come, sir Thurio.
Go with me. Once more, new suitor, welcome.
I'll leave you to relate your news from home;
When you are done we look to hear from you.
PRO.   We'll both be with your ladyship anon.

Exeunt SILVIA *and* THURIO.

COMMENTS

In here establishing *Valentine's* naivete and other-world nobleness Shakespeare is laying the groundwork for *Valentine's* even
more incredulous action yet to come. Lest it be misunderstood,
Valentine was every bit as valid a caricature of the "noble" in-
dividual to the Elizabethans as was *Don Quixote* to the Spanish
(both Cervantes and Shakespeare died in the same year)—or *Li'l
Abner* to the modern American.

It is this very innocents-abroad vulnerability of the truly pure
mind, the clean-living honest soul, the proverbial "nice guy" that is
the essence of the satire here. It is certainly not the literary emphasis
of "friendship" which was common then and which most scholars
have enlisted as an explanation of, if not the very raison d'etre of,

SIL.   His worth is warrant for his welcome hither,
If this be he you oft have wish'd to hear from.
VAL.   Mistress, it is. Sweet lady, entertain him
To be my fellow servant to your ladyship.
SIL.   Too low a mistress for so high a servant.
PRO.   Not so, sweet lady; but too mean a servant
To have a look of such worthy mistress.
VAL.   Leave off discourse of disability—
Sweet lady, entertain him for your servant.
PRO.   My duty will I boast of, nothing else.
SIL.   And duty never yet did want his meed;
Servant, you are welcome to a worthless mistress.
PRO.   I'll die on him that says so, but yourself.
SIL.   That you are welcome?
PRO.   That you are worthless.
THU.   Madam, my lord your father would speak
        with you.
SIL.   I wait upon his pleasure. Come, sir Thurio.
Go with me. Once more, new servant, welcome:
I'll leave you to confer of home affairs;
When you have done, we look to hear from you.
PRO.   We'll both attend upon your ladyship.

Exeunt SILVIA *and* THURIO.

the play. To say that the story is about "friendship" is only to state the obvious and offers no more insight than to add that it is also a boy-meets-girl plot.

A drama of friendship is no drama at all because it lacks dramatic conflict. Friendship is however, a vehicle for motivation in conflict when, as here for example, two friends love the same woman, a common enough "triangle" plot line with many playwrights then (and now). That "friendship" in fiction was more idealized then is true, but it is hardly incomprehensible or even in need of explanation to a culture raised on Huckleberry Finn and Tom Sawyer and still living with Ronald Reagan and Bob Cummings of "Kings Row" memory . . . not to mention the multitude of other "friendship" plots in films, American, British and otherwise.

As to innumerable scholars of yore and today who have spumed oceans of words anent this play being an example of the so-called "friendship literature", this edition agrees that it is so—and so?

NOTES

warrant — assurance; *entertain* — engage, employ; *fellow-servant* — fellow suitor; *low* — lowly; *but too mean a servant* — I'm too lowly a suitor; *to have a look of* — to be looked at by; *leave off discourse of disability* — stop these expressions of humility; *my duty* — i.e., to *Silvia*; *boast of* — be proud of; *want his meed* — lack its reward; *die on him* — i.e., on his dead body.

It is noteworthy, as a precursor of later events, that not once, but twice *Valentine* here entreats *Silvia* to accept *Proteus* as another suitor, although *Valentine* is naively thinking on a Platonic level.

THU.   Madam, my lord your father would speak with you — this line raises the question of how could *Thurio* know this unless

MODERN

VAL.   Now tell me, how is everyone at home?
PRO.   Your friends are well; they send their best
        regards.
VAL.   Your family?
PRO.   They're all in best of health.
VAL.   How is your lady? And how goes your love?
PRO.   My tales of love are apt to weary you;
I know you're bored with any talk of love.
        VAL.   Yes, Proteus, but my life is all changed now.
I've paid a price for my contempt of love.
My high imperious thoughts have punished me
With abstinence, with groans of self-denial,
With nightly tears, and daily heartsore sighs;
For, in revenge of my contempt of love,
Love has chased sleep out of my spellbound eyes,
And made them witness of my own heart's sorrow.
Oh, gentle Proteus, Love's a mighty lord,

he has gone offstage earlier to return later, but the original gives him no such exit and reentrance. The authorities have over the years done the usual handsprings over this point, some taking the liberty of writing in an exit and a reentrance for *Thurio* while others elect to leave him onstage and "create" an *Enter SERVANT* to deliver this line.

This edition leaves the original script intact here, although it thus becomes the only modern edition to do so. Firstly, it would be unnatural for *Thurio* to leave amid the excitement of a newcomer's arrival in the court and equally natural for him to be silent as all attention goes to that newcomer. Secondly, why send *Thurio*—or a servant—dashing on and off stage when the line can make sense using simpler means?—for instance, *Thurio* notices the *Duke* gesturing in the wings and after his own pointing toward "Who? Me?", "Who? Her?", both he and the audience are prepared for the line; and that is only one way of handling the "problem".

ORIGINAL

VAL.   Now tell me: how do all from whence you came?

PRO.   Your friends are well, and have them much commended.

VAL.   And how do yours?

PRO.   I left them all in health.

VAL.   How does your lady? and how thrives your love?

PRO.   My tales of love were wont to weary you;
I know you joy not in a love-discourse.

VAL.   Ay, Proteus, but that life is alter'd now:
I have done penance for contemning love;
Whose high imperious thoughts have punish'd me
With bitter fasts, with penitential groans,
With nightly tears, and daily heart-sore sighs;
For, in revenge of my contempt of love,
Love hath chas'd sleep from my enthrall'd eyes,

And has so humbled me as, I confess,
No woe compares to his harsh punishment,
Nor to his blessing no such joy on earth!
Now, no more talk, unless it be of love;
Now I can breakfast, lunch and dine, and sleep,
All in the name of love, and love alone.

     PRO.   Enough; yes, I can see love in your eye;
Was this the goddess that you worship so?

     VAL.   No one else; and is she not a heavenly saint?

     PRO.   No—but she is an earthly specimen.

NOTES

commended — sent regards; *whose high* . . . — probably means "which high . . ."; some editions read "those high . . ." (after Johnson); *enthrall'd* — captivated, spellbound; *no woe to* — no woe like, i.e., compared to; *correction* — punishment; *to his service* — like serving him; *very naked* — mere; *fortune* — condition, state.

MODERN

     VAL.   Call her divine.

     PRO.   I will not flatter her.

     VAL.   Then flatter me, for love delights in praises.

     PRO.   For lovesickness you gave me bitter pills;
Now I must give the selfsame dose to you.

     VAL.   Then speak the truth—if she is not divine,
Then surely she's a kingdom here on earth,
Sovereign to all the creatures living here.

     PRO.   Except my mistress.

     VAL.   Boy, except not any;
Unless you take exception to my love.

     PRO.   Don't I have reason to prefer my own?

And made them watchers of mine own heart's sorrow.
O, gentle Proteus, Love's a mighty lord;
And hath so humbled me as, I confess,
There is no woe to his correction,
Nor to his service no such joy on earth!
Now, no discourse, except it be of love;
Now can I break my fast, dine, sup, and sleep,
Upon the very naked name of love.

    PRO.   Enough; I read your fortune in your eye;
Was this the idol that you worship so?

    VAL.   Even she; and is she not a heavenly saint?

    PRO.   No; but she is an earthly paragon.

ORIGINAL

    VAL.   Call her divine.

    PRO.   I will not flatter her.

    VAL.   O, flatter me, for love delights in praises.

    PRO.   When I was sick, you gave me bitter pills;
And I must minister the like to you.

    VAL.   Then speak the truth by her; if not divine,
Yet let her be a principality,
Sovereign to all the creatures on the earth.

    PRO.   Except my mistress.

    VAL.   Sweet, except not any;
Except thou wilt except against my love.

    PRO.   Have I not reason to prefer mine own?

VAL.   And I will help you give her preference;
For she alone will have the highest honor
To hold my lady's train, lest lowly earth
Should manage from her dress to steal a kiss,
And growing then to be so smug and proud,
Refuse to raise the summer-swelling flower,
Creating winter everlastingly.
      PRO.   Why, Valentine, what braggartism is this?
      VAL.   Well, Proteus, all that I can say is nothing
Compared to her, whose worth makes all worth nothing;
She stands alone.
      PRO.   Then let her alone.

COMMENTS

The uncivility of *Valentine's* braggartism, almost to the point of a personality change, establishes that Love has "smit" him even more deeply than *Proteus*.

NOTES

truth by her — truth about her; *principality* — some commentators cite an abstruse (even to the educated Elizabethan) passage

MODERN

VAL.   Not for the world! Why, man she is my
               own;
And I'm as rich in having such a jewel
As twenty seas, if all their sand were pearl,
The water nectar, and the rocks pure gold.
Forgive me if I am neglecting you;
As you can see, I dote upon my love.
My foolish rival, whom her father likes
Only because he has such huge possessions,
Has left along with her; and I must follow,
For love, you know, is full of jealousy.

VAL.   And I will help thee to prefer her too:
She shall be dignified with this high honor;
To bear my lady's train; lest the base earth
Should from her vesture chance to steal a kiss,
And, of so great a favor growing proud,
Disdain to root the summer-swelling flower,
And make rough winter everlastingly.
PRO.   Why, Valentine, what braggartism is this?
VAL.   Pardon me, Proteus: all I can say is nothing
To her, whose worth makes other worthies nothing;
She is alone.
PRO.   Then let her alone.

referring to "principality" as part of a hierarchy of angels, while
more likely the bard simply meant a kind of kingdom of all the earth
as distinguished from the "divine"; *sweet* — used sarcastically here;
except thou wilt except against — except that (unless) you will take
exception to; *prefer* — (1) rather have (2) acclaim, recommend;
vesture — dress, skirt; *all I can is* — all I can say is; *worth makes
other worthies nothing* — praiseworthiness makes other praise-
worthy persons as nothing; *alone* — first usage—in her beauty, second usage—be alone, i.e., do not involve her.

ORIGINAL

VAL.   Not for the world: why, man, she is mine
         own;
And I as rich in having such a jewel
As twenty seas, if all their sand were pearl,
The water nectar, and the rocks pure gold.
Forgive me, that I do not dream on thee,
Because thou seest me dote upon my love.
My foolish rival, that her father likes,
Only for his possessions are so huge,
Is gone with her along; and I must after,
For love, thou know'st, is full of jealousy.

PRO.   But does she love you?

VAL.   Indeed—we are betrothed;
And more—our marriage hour,
With all our clever planning to elope
Decided on—How I must climb her window;
The ladder made of cords; and ev'rything
Plotted, agreed on, for my happiness.
Good Proteus, go with me to my lodging,
To aid and counsel me in these affairs.

PRO.   Go on ahead; I'll find you on my own.
I must go to the roadstead to unpack
Some necessary items that I need;
And then I'll promptly come to join you.

VAL.   Will you make haste?

NOTES

dream on — consider, think about; *determin'd of* — decided.

and I must after / For love, thou know'st, is full of jealousy — more than one commentator find a contradiction here between *Valentine* saying he must follow *Thurio* and then almost immediately afterward asking *Proteus* to go with him and give him counsel; of course that mysterious "reviser" once again comes in for the blame, when in truth it is once again a case of Shakespeare's subtlety being inexcusably unappreciated.

Harking back to *Proteus'* excessiveness upon meeting *Silvia*, any actor who could not transmit to the audience that *Proteus* falls in love with *Silvia* at first sight is simply not an actor; knowing of this infatuation, the audience is excited and *Proteus* stunned when

PRO.   But she loves you?

VAL.   Ay, and we are betroth'd:
Nay, more, our marriage hour,
With all the cunning manner of our flight,
Determin'd of: How I must climb her window;
The ladder made of cords; and all the means
Plotted and 'greed on, for my happiness.
Good Proteus, go with me to my chamber,
In these affairs to aid me with thy counsel.

PRO.   Go on before; I shall inquire you forth:
I must go unto the road, to disembark
Some necessaries that I needs must use;
And then I'll presently attend you.

VAL.   Will you make haste?

Valentine, after hesitating (note *Proteus'* meter-broken line), an-
nounces the betrothal and, after another hesitation (again note the
meter), blurts out the whole elopement scheme; the audience, fasci-
nated, completely forgets the reference to following *Thurio*.

If, however, a Shakespearean scholar were in the audience and
insisted on a retrospective analysis on the spot, he could only (or
should only) conclude that *Valentine*, not having yet taken *Proteus*
into his confidence, was using *Thurio* as an excuse to leave so he
could attend to the business of his elopement; and once that he had
decided to take *Proteus* into his confidence the "white lie" excuse
did not need excuse.

inquire you forth — seek you out; *road* — roadstead (nautical
term for marina or place for mooring boats); *presently* — promptly.

MODERN

PRO.   I will—

Exit VALENTINE.

Even as one wind another wind expels,
Or as one wave will wash another out,
So the remembrance of my former love
Is by a newer object quite forgotten.
Is it just my, or Valentine's, perception,
Her true perfection—or my own false lust,
That makes me reasonless to reason thus?
She is fair; but so is Julia, whom I love—
That I did love, for now my love is thawed,
Which, like a doll of wax thrown in a fire,
Bears no resemblance to the thing it was.
I think my warmth for Valentine is cold,
And that I love him not, as once I did—
Oh! but I love his lady too-too much,
And that's the reason I love him so little.
How much I'll dote on her with time to think,
When with no thought at all I'm deep in love!
Yet I have only seen her formally,
And even that has dazzled reason's light;
But if I should behold her beauty close,
There's reason to believe I will be blind.
If I can check my erring love, I will;
If not, to conquer her I'll use my every skill.

Exit.

———————

COMMENTS

With *Proteus'* avowal to use every skill to conquer *Silvia* the
play has acquired a villain which, by a process of elimination,
makes *Valentine* a hero.

ORIGINAL

PRO.   I will—

Exit VALENTINE.

Even as one heat another heat expels,
Or as one nail by strength drives out another,
So the remembrance of my former love
Is by a newer object quite forgotten.
Is it mine, or Valentine's praise,
Her true perfection, or my false transgression,
That makes me reasonless to reason thus?
She is fair; and so is Julia, that I love—
That I did love, for now my love is thaw'd;
Which, like a waxen image 'gainst a fire,
Bears no impression of the thing it was.
Methinks, my zeal to Valentine is cold;
And that I love him not, as I was wont:
O! but I love his lady too-too much;
And that's the reason I love him so little.
How shall I dote on her with more advice,
That thus without advice begin to love her!
'T is but her picture I have yet beheld,
And that hath dazzled my reason's light;
But when I look on her perfections,
There is no reason but I shall be blind.
If I can check my erring love, I will;
If not, to compass her I'll use my skill.

Exit.

NOTES

heat expels — a popular truism of the day based on the fact that a burn receives symptomatic relief when kept warm (increasing blood flow), albeit a relief as temporary as it was relative; *nail* — the "nail" analogy was also popular at the time.

Is it mine . . . — so begins the most problematical, or at least the most conjectured, three lines of the play. Just some of the versions—the most generally accepted—are:

Is it mine, or Valentine's praise (Cambridge)
Is it mine then, or Valentinean's praise (Second Folio)
Is it mine eye or Valentinus' praise (Dyce)
Is it mine eyne, or Valentino's praise (Capell)
Is it mine unstaid mind, or Valentine's praise (Bond)
Is it my mind, or Valentinus' praise (Alexander)
Is it her mien, or Valentinus' praise (Malone, from Blakeway)
It is mine eye, or Valentine's praise (Steevens)

Other equally distinguished authorities cannot repress the urge to, as it were, get in the act. Rowe removes the comma from the Second Folio line and opts for "Valentin*o*"; Theobald and Warburton go along with that, but only if *then* is changed to *eye* and the comma is put back in; Craig and Chambers go along with that, but only if "Valentino" is changed to "Valentin*us*"; and Young goes along with that, but only if . . . . . .

Or is this pontificating carried on with anything less than such dead seriousness as to be in its own way hilarious. Indeed it constitutes a comedy in its own right—a kind of spin-off from the original comedy that Shakespeare wrote.

Even disregarding that pushed around comma and the variations on *Valentine* (to "improve" on the bard's meter) a considerable number of nuances are expressed above. The point of beginning of course is the original 1623 Folio which reads—

It is mine, or Valentines praise?
Her true perfection, or my false transgression?
That makes me reasonless, to reason thus?

Clearly, either the *It is* must be changed to "Is it" or the question marks must go. The latter choice was taken by Munro and Steevens, and that for the most tenuous of reasons, but most authorities opt for the former. This edition does also since—meaning of the passage aside—an error of transposition is more likely to have slipped the eye than an unwanted question mark, especially when all three lines (none of which is asseverative) end with a question mark in the original. The same rationale of likelihood suggests that no other errors in the passage occurred simultaneously with the first error; which is another way of saying that all of the words are those of and intended by Shakespeare—no more, no less. Or again, the bard made perfectly good sense without the scholarly contributions of "then", "eye", "eyne", "mind", "unstaid mind", "mien", etc. This edition then accords with the 1863 (Old) Cambridge edition noted above, and for meaning offers:

praise — modern usage implies "expressed", but usage then included unexpressed praise, i.e., appraisal, admiration, so *Proteus* is questioning whether *Silvia's* beauty is merely in the eye of the beholder (his or *Valentine's*) or "true" beauty; *my false transgression* — i.e., my sinning falsely or perfidiously (against her); *reasonless* — mad, insane.

waxen image — witches were supposed to fashion and then burn a wax likeness of a person they wished to harm; *more advice* — advisement, thinking about.

'T is but her picture . . . — so begins four lines for which Shakespeare (or his "reviser") has been severely criticized for what appears to be a glaring conflict with the fact that *Proteus* has just met *Silvia* "in the flesh"; the criticism is entirely unjustified since here, and elsewhere, the author's meaning is *Silvia's* outward clothed "appearance"; This is confirmed by *Proteus'* adding *when I* (shall) *look on her perfections*—i.e., her "endowments"— *. . . I shall be blind.*

no reason — no doubt; *compass her* — encompass, i.e., conquer her.

Shakespeare's *Proteus* was in all probability the namesake of the mythological Proteus who had and used the power to change himself into different forms. This of course befits his sudden switch of affection from *Julia* to *Silvia*. Interestingly, in a later play (Totenham-Court, by Thomas Nabbes) acted in 1633 the phrase "*Proteus* love" is used synonymously with fickle, changeable love; and since a character in the same play says he would rather attend performances of plays of Shakespeare and Jonson than study and read books, it is possible that a revival of *The Two Gentlemen of Verona* was then extant and the audience accordingly expected to grasp the allusion to "*Proteus* love". (Also cf. 3rd Henry VI at III-2-192.)

MODERN

ACT II

SCENE 5 — *A Street in Milan.*

Enter SPEED *and* LAUNCE.

SPEED. Launce! Well I swear! Welcome to Milan.

LAUN.   You better not swear, my friend—for I am not welcome. I always figure this—that a man is never all spent until he's completely shot; and never welcome to a tavern until he's had his shot and the waitress says, *Welcome!*

SPEED. Come on, you madcap, I'll go to the tavern with you right now where for one shot in a pint of ale you'll have five thousand welcomes. But, my friend, how did your master part with madam Julia?

LAUN.   Well now!—after they got together seriously, they parted jokingly.

SPEED. But will she marry him?

LAUN.   No.

SPEED. Well, then—will he marry her?

LAUN.   No—neither.

SPEED. Did they break off?

LAUN.   No, they are both as whole as a fish in a fish.

SPEED. Well then, how does the matter stand with them?

LAUN.   It's like this—when it stands well with him, it stands well with her.

SPEED. What an ass you are! You don't make sense.

LAUN.   What a blockhead you are if you can't! My rod understands me.

———————————

NOTES

Milan — ''Padua'' in the original, but this geographical ''error'' made by *Speed* (the original scene heading has no place designated) may be an as yet undeciphered pun or perhaps simply a ''geographic malapropism''; predictably, some critics are less kind.

ORIGINAL

ACT II

SCENE 5 — *The same. A Street.*

Enter SPEED *and* Launce.

SPEED. Launce! by mine honesty, welcome to Milan.

LAUN. Forswear not thyself, sweet youth; for I am not welcome. I reckon this always—that a man is never undone till he be hanged; nor never welcome to a place till some certain shot be paid, and the hostess say, Welcome.

SPEED. Come on, you madcap, I'll to the alehouse with you presently; where, for one shot of fivepence, thou shalt have five thousand welcomes. But, sirrah, how did thy master part with madam Julia?

LAUN. Marry, after they closed in earnest, they parted very fairly in jest.

SPEED. But shall she marry him?

LAUN. No.

SPEED. How then? shall he marry her?

LAUN. No, neither.

SPEED. What, are they broken?

LAUN. No, they are both as whole as a fish.

SPEED. Why then, how stands the matter with them?

LAUN. Marry, thus; when it stands well with him, it stands well with her.

SPEED. What an ass art thou! I understand thee not.

LAUN. What a block art thou, that thou canst not! My staff understands me.

---

forswear not thyself — do not swear to something that may not be.

undone — also means sexually spent.

hanged — also means made sexually limp.

shot — here (1) tavern bill or tab (2) ejaculation.

Welcome — Well *come.

closed — embraced; *whole as a fish* — a play on an old expression ''as whole (sound, healthy) as a fish''; *stands — as earlier, erection.

*matter — also means flesh of genitalia.

block — blockhead.

MODERN

SPEED. What are you saying?

LAUN. Yes, and what I'm doing, too. Look, I'll just lean, and my rod understands me.

SPEED. It stands under you, all right.

LAUN. Well, stand under and understand is all one.

SPEED. But tell me the truth, will they make a match?

LAUN. Ask my dog. If he says *yea*, they will. If he says *nay*, they will. And if he shake his tail, and says nothing, they will.

SPEED. The conclusion then is that they will.

LAUN. You'll never get such a secret from me except by a parable.

SPEED. I prefer it that way. But, Launce, what do you say, that my high and mighty master has become a notable lover?

LAUN. I never knew your high and mighty to be otherwise.

SPEED. Than how?

LAUN. A notable lubber, as you report him to be.

SPEED. Why, you son of a whore, you took me wrong.

LAUN. Why, fool, I did not mean you, I meant your high and mighty.

SPEED. Let me tell you, my master has become a hot lover.

ORIGINAL

SPEED. What thou say'st?

LAUN. Ay, and what I do, too: look thee, I'll but lean, and my staff understands me.

SPEED. It stands under thee, indeed.

LAUN. Why, stand under and understand is all one.

SPEED. But tell me true, will 't be a match?

LAUN. Ask my dog: if he say ay, it will; if he say no, it will; if he shake his tail, and say nothing, it will.

SPEED. The conclusion is then, that it will.

LAUN. Thou shalt never get such a secret from me but by a parable.

SPEED. 'T is well that I get it so. But, Launce, how say'st thou, that my master has become a notable lover?

LAUN. I never knew him otherwise.

SPEED. Than how?

LAUN. A notable lubber, as thou reportest him to be.

SPEED. Why, thou whoreson ass, thou mistakest me.

LAUN. Why, fool, I meant not thee, I meant thy master.

SPEED. I tell thee, my master is become a hot lover.

LAUN.   And let me tell you, I don't care if he ends up sorely burning. Now, if you want, go with me to the tavern; if not, then you can stew in your juice, while I brew in mine. Will you go?

SPEED.   Lead on. I'm at your service.

Exeunt.

_____

COMMENTS

This scene is so slight that it seems to have the sole purpose of breaking up an otherwise too lengthy speech of *Proteus*; indeed the next scene picks *Proteus* up exactly where he had left off.

Interestingly *Speed*-the-comic of Act I becomes straight man to *Launce*-the-comic here and elsewhere, leaving no question as to which was the leading comic role.

LAUN.   Why, I tell thee, I care not though he burn himself in love, If thou wilt, go with me to the alehouse; if not, thou art an Hebrew, a Jew, and not worth the name of a Christian.

SPEED.   Why?

LAUN.   Because thou hast not so much charity in thee as to go to the ale with a Christian: Wilt thou go?

SPEED.   At thy service.

Exeunt.

NOTES

lean — lean his weight on.

my *master — a bawdy play on *Speed's* "master".

*burn himself — contract a venereal disease.

Hebrew — "he-brew", a reference to a gross common joke of that day having nothing to do with "Hebrew"; for the intended humor see ACT III for *she brews* and *you brew*, as well as Merry Wives of Windsor III-5; the idea remains in modern jokes but is omitted in the *Modern* text here.

Having reached for "Hebrew" all words following are merely by way of extricating the playwright from his pun and closing the scene.

worth — worthy of; *ale* — a church ale party given for charity, punning here on *charity*, but of course he means an alehouse.

MODERN

ACT II

SCENE 6 — *A Room in the Palace.*

Enter PROTEUS.

PRO.   To leave my Julia, I'll be a betrayer;
To love fair Silvia, I'll be a betrayer;
To wrong my friend, I'm all the more betrayer.
The very force which made me swear my love
Incites me to this triple perjury.
Love made me vow, love makes me disavow.
Oh, sweet, suggestive Love, if you once sinned,
Show me, your servant, how to make excuse.
At first I did adore a twinkling star,
But now I worship a celestial sun.
Oh, thoughtless vows may thoughtfully be broken,
And he lacks sense who lacks determined will.
To use good sense to barter bad for better—
For shame, irreverent tongue!—to call her bad,
Whose excellence so often you've extolled
With twenty thousand reverential oaths.
I cannot stop my loving, yet I do;
I cease to love just there where I should love.
Julia I lose, and Valentine I lose:
If I keep them, then I must lose myself;
If I lose them—for losing Valentine
I find myself; for losing Julia—Silvia.

COMMENTS

All the world loves an antithesis whether it be comic (I love garlic, but garlic doesn't love me), tragic (You always hurt the one you love), or something in between (The more things change the more they are the same). Therein lies the magic of a sudden reversal, a stimulating "punch line" effect. The Elizabethans especially

ORIGINAL

ACT II

SCENE 6 — *The same. A Room in the Palace.*

Enter PROTEUS.

PRO.　　To leave my Julia, shall I be forsworn;
To love fair Silvia, shall I be forsworn;
To wrong my friend, I shall be much forsworn,
And even that power which gave me first my oath,
Provokes me to this threefold perjury.
Love bade me swear, and love bids me forswear.
O sweet-suggesting Love, if thou hast sinned,
Teach me, thy tempted subject, to excuse it.
At first I did adore a twinkling star,
But now I worship a celestial sun.
Unheedful vows may heedfully be broken;
And he wants wit that wants resolved will
To learn his wit to exchange the bad for better.
Fie, fie, unreverend tongue! to call her bad,
Whose sovereignty so oft thou hast preferr'd
With twenty thousand soul-confirming oaths.
I cannot leave to love, and yet I do;
But there I leave to love, where I should love.
Julia I lose, and Valentine I lose:
If I keep them, I needs must lose myself;
If I lose them, thus find I, by their loss,
For Valentine, myself; for Julia, Silvia.

delighted in, and Shakespeare especially excelled in, the antithesis.

This scene, this monologue scintillates with, is sustained by, these sudden inversions of ideas. Unfortunately, the reading of such lines has nothing like the impact of hearing them in performance. Consider merely the first three lines of this scene—the movement from a feeling of shame to painful ecstasy, then back to shame again; consider the actor's shift of inflection, volume, posture, feeling that would emanate from the stage; and consider finally the "anti" of antithesis, the conflict of ideas that reinforces dramatic conflict, here the inner struggle of *Proteus.*

But the play must go on, and so the inner struggle, having given motivation to, now gives way to the outer struggle as the scene closes on the suspenseful details of *Proteus'* scheming.

MODERN

I'm dearer to myself than any friend,
For always love's more precious in one's self:
And Silvia—thanks to Heaven, that made her fair!—
Shows Julia up as no more than exotic.
I will forget that Julia is alive,
Rememb'ring that my love to her is dead;
And Valentine I'll call my enemy,
Regarding Silvia as a sweeter friend.
I cannot now be loyal to myself
Without disloyalty to Valentine—
Tonight he means to use a rope-made ladder
To reach celestial Silvia's chamber window;
Myself his trusted co-conspirator,
Without delay I'll tell her father all:
Of their deception and intended flight;
And in his rage he'll banish Valentine,
For Thurio's whom he wants to wed his daughter.
With Valentine once gone, I'll double cross,
By some sly trick, dumb Thurio's stupid courtship.
Love, wing me to my goal with speed extreme
Now that you gave me wit to plot this scheme!

Exit.

NOTES

still — always; *shows Julia* — shows up *Julia* (by comparison); *aiming at* — in favor of; *constant* — true; *used to* — used toward, against; *in counsel, his competitor* — in his confidence, his accom-

NOTES

suggesting — suggestive, tempting; *excuse it* — excuse it away, rationalize it; *unheedful* — thoughtless; *wants* — lacks; *learn his wit* — teach himself; *unreverend* — irreverent; *preferr'd* — extolled; *soul-confirming* — devout; *leave* — cease.

ORIGINAL

I to myself am dearer than a friend,
For love is still more precious in itself:
And Silvia, witness Heaven, that made her fair!
Shows Julia but a swarthy Ethiope.
I will forget that Julia is alive,
Rememb'ring that my love to her is dead,
And Valentine I'll hold an enemy,
Aiming at Silvia as a sweeter friend.
I cannot now prove constant to myself,
Without some treachery us'd to Valentine—
This night, he meaneth with a corded ladder
To climb celestial Silvia's chamber-window;
Myself in counsel, his competitor:
Now presently I'll give her father notice
Of their disguising, and pretended flight;
Who, all enrag'd, will banish Valentine;
For Thurio, he intends, shall wed his daughter:
But, Valentine being gone, I'll quickly cross,
By some sly trick, blunt Thurio's dull proceeding.
Love, lend me wings to make my purpose swift,
As thou hast lent me wit to plot this drift!

Exit.

plice; *disguising* — deceiving; *pretended* — intended; *cross* — double-cross; *blunt Thurio* — not very sharp *Thurio*; *proceeding* — progress (in courting *Silvia*); *my purpose* — achieving my purpose; *drift* — scheme.

MODERN

ACT II

SCENE 7 — *Verona. A Room in JULIA'S House.*

Enter JULIA *and* LUCETTA.

JUL.   Come talk, Lucetta! dear, sweet girl, please help me!
Out of our very love I do implore you—
Since you are like a book where all my thoughts
Are openly engraved and written down—
Give me advice, and show me some good way,
And yet with honor, I may undertake
A journey to my loving Proteus.

LUC.   Oh, dear!—The way is wearisome and long.

JUL.   A true, devoted pilgrim does not weary
Though crossing kingdoms with his feeble steps;
Much less will she who has love's wings to fly!
And when the flight is made to one so dear,
Of such divine perfection as Sir Proteus.

LUC.   You better wait till Proteus has returned.

JUL.   Oh, don't you know, his gaze is my soul's food?
Then pity how I'm starved from all my pining,
My longing for that food so long a time.
If you could know the inner feel of love,
You would as soon go start a fire with snow,
As try to quench the fire of love with words.

LUC.   I do not try to quench your love's hot fire;
Just to reduce the fire's excessive rage,
Lest it should burn beyond the bounds of reason.

———————————

NOTES
even in kind love — precisely because it is in the nature of love;
conjure — adjure, implore; *table* — tablet; *character'd* — written;
lesson — teach; *mean* — means; *with my honor* — with honor

ORIGINAL

ACT II

SCENE 7 — *Verona. A Room in* JULIA'S *House.*

Enter JULIA *and* LUCETTA.

JUL.   Counsel, Lucetta! gentle girl, assist me!
And, even in kind love, I do conjure thee—
Who art the table wherein all my thoughts
Are visibly character'd and engrav'd—
To lesson me; and tell me some good mean,
How, with my honor, I may undertake
A journey to my loving Proteus.

LUC.   Alas! the way is wearisome and long.

JUL.   A true devoted pilgrim is not weary
To measure kingdoms with his feeble steps;
Much less shall she that hath love's wings to fly!
And when the flight is made to one so dear,
Of such divine perfection, as sir Proteus.

LUC.   Better forbear, till Proteus make return.

JUL.   O, know'st thou not, his looks are my
                soul's food?
Pity the dearth that I have pined in,
By longing for that food so long a time.
Didst thou but know the inly touch of love,
Thou wouldst as soon go kindle fire with snow,
As seek to quench the fire of love with words.

LUC.   I do not seek to quench your love's hot
                fire;
But qualify the fire's extreme rage,
Lest it should burn above the bounds of reason.

(without losing it); *measure* — walk across; *looks* — gazes; *dearth* — famine (of food for the soul); *inly* — inner; *qualify* — mollify, reduce.

MODERN

JUL.   The more you damper it, the more it burns.
The stream that moves so smoothly murmuring,
If stopped, you know, impatiently will rage;
But when his free flow is not hindered,
He makes sweet music with the polished stones,
And gently kissing all the marshy grass
He passes over in his pilgrimage;
And so by many winding nooks he strays,
With playful will, to the wild ocean's span.
Then let me go, and stand not in my way—
I'll be as patient as a gentle stream,
And make a game out of each tiring step,
Till the last step has brought me to my love;
And there I'll rest, like, after much turmoil,
Good souls, in peace, rest in Elysium.
        LUC.   Now how will you be dressed for traveling?
        JUL.   No woman's dress, because I must ward off
The propositions of lascivious men.
Dear, sweet Lucetta, fit me with such clothes
As might be worn by some respected page.
        LUC.   Why, then your ladyship must cut your
                 hair.
        JUL.   No, girl; I'll braid it up in silken strings,
With twenty odd, peculiar lover's knots—
To look too clever may suggest a youth
Who's older than I else would seem to be.

NOTES

    enamel'd — smooth and shiny; *sedge* — a kind of plant common to wet places; *sport* — sportfulness.
    wild — disagreement exists between scholars—Collier (or less precisely, his "annotator") changed the word to "wide" arguing that it otherwise conflicts with *Julia's* coming to *rest* five lines farther, and the New Cambridge edition, for one, seconds this argument; Sisson defends *wild* as meaning "open or unenclosed"; this

ORIGINAL

JUL.   The more thou damn'st it up, the more it
            burns;
The current that, with gentle murmur glides,
Thou know'st, being stopp'd, impatiently doth rage;
But, when his fair course is not hindered,
He makes sweet music with the enamel'd stones,
Giving a gentle kiss to every sedge
He overtaketh in his pilgrimage;
And so by many winding nooks he strays,
With willing sport, to the wild ocean.
Then let me go, and hinder not my course:
I'll be as patient as a gentle stream,
And make a pastime of each weary step,
Till the last step have brought me to my love;
And there I'll rest, as, after much turmoil,
A blessed soul doth in Elysium.
        LUC.   But in what habit will you go along?
        JUL.   Not like a woman; for I would prevent
The loose encounters of lascivious men:
Gentle Lucetta, fit me with such weeds
As may beseem some well-reputed page.
        LUC.   Why, then, your ladyship must cut your
            hair.
        JUL.   No, girl; I'll knit it up in silken strings,
With twenty odd-conceited true-love knots:
To be fantastic, may become a youth
Of greater time than I shall show to be.

edition agrees with the defense, but for a different reason. *Wild* appears to be used here as Shakespeare has used it elsewhere—viz.,
wild forests, wild hills, wild field—to mean unchanged by man,
pristine; Collier seems wrong because if the metaphor here were as
unmixed as he suggests it would follow that *Julia* comes to "rest"
in an "ocean".

    pastime — game; *Elysium* — mythological final resting place of
blessed souls; *habit* — clothing; *prevent* — in its "avert" sense

here; *loose* — sexually loose; *weeds* — clothing; *odd-conceited* — cleverly contrived; *true-love knots* — complicated knots so named from their being "interwoven"; *fantastic* — imaginative, creative; *of greater time* — older.

MODERN

LUC.   What style of breeches, madam, shall I make you?

JUL.   That sounds as rich as—*Tell me now, good sir,*
What fullness would you like your skirt to have?
Whatever fashion you think best, Lucetta.

LUC.   Then you must have them with a codpiece, madam.

JUL.   Oh no, Lucetta! That would be outrageous.

LUC.   Men's garments, madam, now aren't worth a pin,
Unless you have a codpiece stuck with stickpins.

JUL.   Lucetta, as you love me, let me have
What you think best, so I look mannerly.
But tell me, imp, how will the world regard me,
For undertaking such a naughty journey?
I fear that they will think me scandalous.

LUC.   If you think so, then stay at home; don't go.

JUL.   No, that I will not.

LUC.   Then do not worry about scandal—Go.
If Proteus would be glad to see you come,
Then it's no matter who's not pleased you've gone—
But I'm afraid he'll not be pleased with it.

JUL.   That is the least, Lucetta, of my fears—
A thousand vows, an ocean of his tears,
And times of an infinity of love,
Prove I'll be welcome to my Proteus.

LUC.   All these are tools used by deceitful men.

ORIGINAL

LUC.   What fashion, madam, shall I make your breeches?

JUL.   That fits as well as—*Tell me, good my lord,*
What compass will you wear your farthingale?
Why, ev'n what fashion thou best likes, Lucetta.

LUC.   You must needs have them with a cod-piece, madam.

JUL.   Out, out, Lucetta! that will be ill favor'd.

LUC.   A round hose, madam, now's not worth a pin,
Unless you have a codpiece to stick pins on.

JUL.   Lucetta, as thou lov'st me, let me have
What thou think'st meet, and is most mannerly.
But tell me, wench, how will the world repute me,
For undertaking so unstaid a journey?
I fear me, it will make me scandaliz'd.

LUC.   If you think so, then stay at home, and go not.

JUL.   Nay, that I will not.

LUC.   Then never dream on infamy, but go.
If Proteus like your journey, when you come,
No matter who's displeas'd, when you are gone:
I fear me, he will scarce be pleased withal.

JUL.   That is the least, Lucetta, of my fear:
A thousand oaths, an ocean of his tears,
And instances of infinite of love,
Warrant me welcome to my Proteus.

LUC.   All these are servants to deceitful men.

NOTES

breeches — any garment covering part or all of the upper leg; *fits as well as* — i.e., is as ridiculous as; *what compass* — how wide (full); *farthingale* — hoop skirt; *ev'n what* — exactly that; *likes* — vernacular for "likest"; *round hose* — puffed short breeches; *pins* — decorative pins, a fashion of the nobility. (For excellent illustrations of Elizabethan fashions in dress see Harrison's edition.)

meet — suitable; *mannerly* — conservative, with a pun on "man"; *unstaid* — improper, naughty; *never dream on infamy* — don't dwell on (worry about) scandal; *withal* — with it.

And instances of infinite of love — so in the original and another poser for the scholars:

MODERN

JUL.   Vile men, who put them to so vile a use!
But Proteus' birth was under truer stars:
His words are bonds, his vows are made in heaven;
His love sincere, his thoughts immaculate;
His tears, pure messengers sent from his heart;
His heart as far from fraud as heaven from earth.

LUC.   Pray Heaven he proves so, when you come
          to him!

JUL.   Now, as you love me, don't do him that
          wrong—
To have a doubt, or question that he's true:
Please, just return my love by loving him;
And now if you'll go with me to my chamber,
To make a note of what I stand in need of,
To take with me upon my long . . . ing journey.
All that I own I leave in your good hands,
My goods, my lands . . . my reputation;
And all I ask is—Speed me on my way!
Don't answer. Come. Just do it right away—
I'm losing patience with my own delay.

Exeunt.

And instances <u>as</u> infinite of love (Second Folio)
And instances of <u>the</u> infinite of love (Malone)
And instances of <u>infinity</u> of love (Bond)

Most editors simply leave the line as is and define *infinite* as "an infinity"; this is essentially correct since wherever *infinite* is used as a noun prefixed by "of" (cf. Staunton, also O.E.D.) it is in this sense; further, a rapturous onstage delivery would easily convey the idea of "trysts of unlimited lovemaking."

warrant — assure; *servants to* — tools (guiles) of.

ORIGINAL

JUL.   Base men, that use them to so base effect!
But truer stars did govern Proteus' birth:
His words are bonds, his oaths are oracles;
His love sincere, his thoughts immaculate;
His tears, pure messengers sent from his heart;
His heart as far from fraud as heaven from earth.
LUC.   Pray Heaven he prove so, when you come
        to him!
JUL.   Now, as thou lov'st me, do him not that
        wrong,
To bear a hard opinion of his truth:
Only deserve my love, by loving him;
And presently go with me to my chamber,
To take a note of what I stand in need of,
To furnish me upon my longing journey.
All that is mine I leave at thy dispose,
My goods, my lands, my reputation;
Only, in lieu thereof, dispatch me hence;
Come, answer not, but to it presently:
I am impatient of my tarriance.

Exeunt.

COMMENTS

If Scene 6 was a plot thickener, what with *Proteus'* scheme to steal *Silvia*, Scene 7 is a plot boiler as—unknown to unsuspecting *Proteus*—unsuspecting *Julia* plans to pay him a visit . . . and in disguise.

NOTES

oracles — divine promises; *deserve my love* — repay my love; *presently* — now; *take a note of* — make a note of; *longing* — filled with longing (as a longing look); *dispatch me* — speed me; *presently!* — immediately!; *tarriance* — delay.

The Arden and New Cambridge editions, among others, are distressed by what they see as a glaring inconsistency here: *Julia*, who has a father earlier in the play, is now—like an orphan—bequeathing all of her goods, lands, and reputation to her maid. The bequest of her "reputation" should have tipped them to what the playwright intended—and surely what the audience understood. It is all part of the grand hyperbole of young love; but more than that, one can almost see *Lucetta's* broad smile on *my goods*, her even broader smile on *my lands*, and her sudden grimace on *my reputation*.

ACT III

SCENE 1 — *An Anteroom in the* DUKE'S *Palace.*

Enter DUKE, THURIO *and* PROTEUS.

DUKE.   Sir Thurio, let us be alone awhile;
A confidential matter has come up.

Exit THURIO.

Now tell me, Proteus, what you wish with me.
      PRO.   My gracious lord, that which I would
            reveal,
The bonds of friendship say I should conceal.
But, when I call to mind the gracious favors
You did me, undeserving as I am,
My duty spurs me on to tell you what
I otherwise for all the world would not.
Hear this, my prince—SIr Valentine, my friend,
Tonight intends to steal away your daughter;
He even made me privy to the plot.
I know you have decided to betroth her
To Thurio, whom your gentle daughter hates;
And if she should be seized away from you,
It would, in your late years, be burdensome.
So, from my sense of duty, I have chosen
To now expose my friend in what he plots,
For, by concealing it, I'd load you with
A pack of sorrows, which would send you down,
If not prevented, to an early grave.
      DUKE.   Proteus, I thank you for your great
            concern;
For which I'll give you anything you ask.

ORIGINAL

ACT III

SCENE 1 — *An Anteroom in the* DUKE'S *Palace.*

Enter DUKE, THURIO *and* PROTEUS.

DUKE.   Sir Thurio, give us leave, I pray, awhile;
We have some secrets to confer about.

Exit THURIO.

Now tell me, Proteus, what's your will with me?
    PRO.   My gracious lord, that which I would
           discover,
The law of friendship bids me to conceal:
But, when I call to mind your gracious favors
Done to me, undeserving as I am,
My duty pricks me on to utter that
Which else no worldy good should draw from me.
Know, worthy prince, sir Valentine, my friend,
This night intends to steal away your daughter;
Myself am one made privy to the plot.
I know you have determin'd to bestow her
On Thurio, whom your gentle daughter hates;
And should she thus be stol'n away from you,
It would be much vexation to your age.
Thus, for my duty's sake, I rather chose
To cross my friend in his intended drift,
Than, by concealing it, heap on your head
A pack of sorrows, which would press you down,
Being unprevented, to your timeless grave.
    DUKE.   Proteus, I thank thee for thine honest care;
Which to requite, command me while I live.

NOTES

give us leave, I pray — please leave us be alone; *discover* — reveal; *law* — i.e., obligation; *worldly good(s)* — i.e., wealth, money; *cross* — cross up (double-cross); *drift* — scheme; *being unprevented* — (the scheme) being not prevented; *timeless* — untimely; *care* — concern; *to requite, command me* — to repay (you), ask anything of me.

Act III opens with a problem—at least for students of Shakespeare: What in the world is *Thurio* doing on that stage only to immediately exit without saying so much as a word?

The New Cambridge editors, and a few others, regard this as one more flaw due to a ghost writer's hand. Whether right or wrong these commentators are at least to be commended for offering some explanation; most editors just look the other way despite the glaringness of *Thurio's* "curtain-going-up" exit.

It could be explained away by assuming that *Thurio* was really never there but rather an illusion easily created by the *Duke's* speaking back over his shoulder as he entered; but this would merely raise a larger question of "Why bother?" Indeed, the opening seems to be

MODERN

This love of theirs I've often seen myself,
By chance, when they have thought me fast asleep;
And often I've intended to deny
Sir Valentine her company, and my court.
But fearing my suspicions may be wrong,
And so, unjustly, bring disgrace on him—
A rash accusing, something I've not done—
I always smiled at him, so I might find
That which you now have told me all about.
As proof of how I've lived in fear of this—
Knowing how youth is tempted easily—
I nightly keep her in an upper tower,
The key to which alone is kept by me;
So that from there she can't be carried off.

so utterly pointless as to preclude attributing it to a hack rewriter; even the rankest amateur playwright—not to mention every actor in the cast—would catch the flaw in rehearsal.

A transposer's error then, working from various actors' parts? One so obvious as this would probably have been detected by the distinguished associates of Shakespeare from whom the Folio comes.

What then? Perhaps no one will ever know, but this edition offers a possibility. It will be recalled that in an earlier scene *Valentine* was so vicious in his ridicule of *Thurio* as to almost be out of character. This derision would be more understandable to the audience, however, if *Thurio* were made out to be particularly repugnant. An extremely foppish costume and peacock strut would do it for the Elizabethans. *Valentine's* earlier remarks about the poor clothing of *Thurio's* followers did not include *Thurio's* clothes, which probably were by way of contrast, garishly bejeweled and plumed. Add to this *Valentine's* pointed reference to *Thurio's folly* plus other reference to his *huge possessions*, and *Thurio* could have been a minor scene stealer just by his appearance—a kind of running sight-gag. And a sight-gag could have been an effective act opener.

ORIGINAL

This love of theirs myself have often seen,
Haply, when they have judg'd me fast asleep;
And oftentimes have purpos'd to forbid
Sir Valentine her company, and my court.
But, fearing lest my jealous aim might err,
And so, unworthily, disgrace the man,
(A rashness that I ever yet have shunn'd)
I gave him gentle looks; thereby to find
That which thyself hast now disclos'd to me.
And, that thou mayest perceive my fear of this,
Knowing that tender youth is so soon suggested,
I nightly lodge her in an upper tower,
The key whereof myself have ever kept;
And thence she cannot be convey'd away.

PRO.   Then know, my lord, that they've devised
         a means
Whereby her chamber window can be reached,
And with a rope-made ladder take her down;
To get the ladder now is where he's gone,
And he'll be coming this way with it soon;
Where, if you wish to, you may intercept him.
But, please my lord, do it so cleverly
That he might not suspect my role in this;
For it's my love of you, not hate of him,
That made me tell you all about this plot.
    DUKE.   Upon my honor, he will never know
That I had any word of this from you.
    PRO.   Adieu, my lord—Sir Valentine is coming.

                    Exit PROTEUS.

NOTES

haply — by chance; *purpos'd* — intended; *jealous aim* —
suspicious guess; *shunn'd* — avoided; *tender* — immature; *soon
suggested* — easily tempted; *corded* — rope; *presently* — very soon;
my discovery be not aimed at — my disclosure be not guessed at;
publisher — revealer; *pretense* — intention, plot; *light* — enlighten-
ment, information.

MODERN

Enter VALENTINE.

    DUKE.   Sir Valentine, where are you rushing so?
    VAL.   Excuse me, sir, but there's a messenger
Who waits to bear my letters to my friends,
And I am going to deliver them.
    DUKE.   Are they of much importance?
    VAL.   The tenor of them merely indicates
My health and happiness here in your court.

PRO. Know, noble lord, they have devis'd a mean
How he her chamber window will ascend,
And with a corded ladder fetch her down;
For which the youthful lover now is gone,
And this way comes he with it presently;
Where, if it please you, you may intercept him.
But, good my lord, do it so cunningly,
That my discovery be not aimed at;
For love of you, not hate unto my friend,
Hath made me publisher of this pretense.
    DUKE. Upon mine honor, he shall never know
That I had any light from thee of this.
    PRO. Adieu, my lord; sir Valentine is coming.

Exit PROTEUS.

ORIGINAL

Enter VALENTINE.

DUKE. Sir Valentine, whither away so fast?
    VAL. Please it your grace, there is a messenger
That stays to bear my letters to my friends,
And I am going to deliver them.
    DUKE. Be they of much import?
    VAL. The tenor of them doth but signify
My health, and happy being at your court.

DUKE.   Well then, no matter; stay with me awhile;
I'd like to speak with you of some affairs,
Quite close to me, and which you must keep secret.
I'm sure you are aware that I have sought
To wed my friend, Sir Thurio, to my daughter.
      VAL.   Indeed, I know, my lord; and think the
                  match
Both rich and honorable. Besides, the gentleman
Is full of virtue, bounty, worth, and qualities
All suiting such a wife as your fair daughter:
Can't you convince her, sir, that she should like him?
      DUKE.   Believe me, no; she's peevish, sullen, willful
Proud, disobedient, stubborn, disrespectful;
Neither remembering that she's my child,
Nor willing to obey me as her father.
And may I say to you, this pride of hers,
I must conclude, has killed my love for her;
Where once I thought that my declining years
Would have been cared for by her sense of duty,
I've now resolved to take myself a wife,
And turn her out—to who will take her in:
Then let her beauty be her wedding dowry,
For she cares not for me or for my wealth.
      VAL.   What does your grace want me to do in this?

NOTES

break with thee of — broach; *trust me* — believe me; *regarding that she is* — regarding herself as being; *fearing* — obeying; *advice* — deliberation; *drawn my love from her* — turned me against her; *remnant of mine age* — rest of my years; *cherish'd* — comforted; *childlike* — daughter-like.

DUKE.   Nay then, no matter; stay with me awhile;
I am to break with thee of some affairs,
That touch me near, wherein thou must be secret.
'T is not unknown to thee, that I have sought
To match my friend, sir Thurio, to my daughter.
    VAL.   I know it well, my lord; and, sure, the match
Were rich and honorable; besides, the gentleman
Is full of virtue, bounty, worth, and qualities
Beseeming such a wife as your fair daughter:
Cannot your grace win her to fancy him?
    DUKE.   No, trust me; she is peevish, sullen, froward,
Proud, disobedient, stubborn, lacking duty;
Neither regarding that she is my child,
Nor fearing me as if I were her father:
And, may I say to thee, this pride of hers,
Upon advice, hath drawn my love from her;
And, where I thought the remnant of mine age
Should have been cherish'd by her childlike duty,
I now am full resolv'd to take a wife,
And turn her out to who will take her in:
Then let her beauty be her wedding dower;
For me and my possessions she esteems not.
    VAL.   What would your grace have me to do in
            this?

MODERN

DUKE.   There is a lady from Verona here,
Whom I adore; but she is cool and shy,
And is not moved by my old eloquence.
Now, therefore, would I like to have you coach me—
For I have long forgotten how to court;
Besides, the customs and the times have changed—
How, and which way, I should conduct myself
To be respected in her lovely eye.
            VAL.   Win her with gifts, if you cannot with
                        words;
Mute jewels often, in their silent way,
More than bright words, a woman's mind will sway.
            DUKE.   But she refused a present that I sent her.
            VAL.   A woman sometimes scorns what most
                        contents her.
Send her another; never let her go,
For early scorn is food that makes love grow.
If she should frown, it's not in hate of you,
But rather to excite more love in you.
If she should scold, it's not to have you gone;
Indeed—the fools go mad if left alone.
Take no offense, whatever she might say:
For *Go*, she does not mean to go *away*.
Flatter, and praise, commend, extol their graces;
Though they look bleak, say they have angels' faces.
That man who has a tongue, I say, is no man,
If with his tongue he cannot win a woman.
            DUKE.   But what I mean is that she has been
                        promised
To some quite youthful gentleman of wealth;
And kept most strictly from the reach of men,
So no man has a way of seeing her.
            VAL.   Well then I would go visit her at night.
            DUKE.   Yes, but the doors are locked, and keys
                        kept safe,
So no man can get in to her at night.

ORIGINAL

DUKE.   There is a lady in Verona here
Whom I affect; but she is nice, and coy,
And nought esteems my aged eloquence:
Now, therefore, would I have thee to my tutor,
—For long agone I have forgot to court;
Besides, the fashion of the time is chang'd—
How, and which way, I may bestow myself
To be regarded in her sun-bright eye.
     VAL.   Win her with gifts, if she respects not
                words;
Dumb jewels often, in their silent kind,
More than quick words, do move a woman's mind.
     DUKE.   But she did scorn a present that I sent her.
     VAL.   A woman sometimes scorns what best
                contents her:
Send her another; never give her o'er;
For scorn at first makes after-love the more.
If she do frown, 't is not in hate of you,
But rather to beget more love in you:
If she do chide, 't is not to have you gone;
Forwhy, the fools are mad, if left alone.
Take no repulse, whatever she doth say:
For *get you gone*, she doth not mean *away*:
Flatter, and praise, commend, extol their graces;
Though ne'er so black, say they have angels' faces.
That man that hath a tongue, I say, is no man,
If with his tongue he cannot win a woman.
     DUKE.   But she I mean is promis'd by her friends
Unto a youthful gentleman of worth;
And kept severely from resort of men,
That no man hath access by day to her.
     VAL.   Why then I would resort to her by night.
     DUKE.   Ay, but the doors be lock'd, and keys kept
                safe,
That no man hath recourse to her by night.

NOTES

in Verona here — since the action here takes place in Milan, these words have been altered to read "of Verona" (Halliwell), "in Milan" (many editors), or—to preserve meter—"in Milano", "sir, in Milan", etc. by others. The question should be asked—Why does the *Duke* mention any city in the first place? Since this is the very opening line of his gambit he may well associate the *lady* with Verona to throw *Valentine* off the track; also, what could be more natural than to seek information about courting a lady from Verona from a gentleman of Verona? Finally, the line as it stands in the Folio could be correct as to *in* Verona since the word *here* can be construed as "who is here".

affect — have affection for; *nice* — shy; *coy* — reserved, distant; *nought* — not at all (the Archaic adverbial usage); *agone* — ago); *bestow myself* — conduct myself; *respect not words* — is not moved by words.

dumb jewels — begins a sudden burst of rhyme. Some authorities feel that the roughness of the rhyming and its (in their judgment) inappropriateness considering what comes before and after point to a non-Shakespearean pen. There does seem to be a sense

MODERN

VAL. What hinders you from entering her
      window?

DUKE. Her chamber's very high, far from the
      ground;
And jutting out so much that one can't climb it
Without an obvious hazard to his life.

VAL. Why then, a ladder, woven well with ropes,
To cast up with a pair of anchoring hooks,
Would serve to scale another Hero's tower,
If bold Leander dared to venture it.

DUKE. Now, as you are a gentleman well bred,
Advise me where I may find such a ladder.

VAL. When would you use it? Can you tell me
      that?

here of reading a poem which has been plucked from a playwright's sketchbook and plumped into the play almost as a filler; certainly this "poem" could be removed from the play with neither the actors nor the audience missing a beat; indeed, it could almost stand on its own as a witty ditty on the inanity of courtship.

And yet there is very much Shakespearean in these lines: the holding up to everyman—and everywoman—his own folly, the plethora of ideas in a dearth of lines, and the dramatist's building of the lines to a kind of moral-of-the-story climax.

Pettet for one sees *Valentine* as somewhat "Machiavellian" here. Far from scheming, *Valentine* is demonstrating a naive overconfidence to the point of cockiness, an irrepressible character trait which he manifests again in the next act. Moreover, this "hot air" was undoubtedly calculated on the part of Shakespeare because the audience knows what *Valentine* does not—that the *Duke* knows . . . and will at any moment prick *Valentine's* balloon.

silent kind — silent way; *quick* — lively; *forwhy* — since, because; *ne'er so black* — ever so dark ("angels" then had fair, light skin); *friends* — family, relatives; *resort to her by night* — have resort to her at night.

ORIGINAL

VAL.   What lets but one may enter at her window?
DUKE.   Her chamber is aloft, far from the ground;
And built so shelving that one cannot climb it
Without apparent hazard of his life.
VAL.   Why, then, a ladder, quaintly made of
        cords,
To cast up with a pair of anchoring hooks,
Would serve to scale another Hero's tower,
So bold Leander would adventure it.
DUKE.   Now, as thou art a gentleman of blood,
Advise me where I may have such a ladder.
VAL.   When would you use it? pray, sir, tell me
        that.

DUKE. Why now, tonight—for love is like a child
Who longs for everything that he can come by.

VAL.   By seven o'clock I'll get you such a ladder.

DUKE. But listen—I'll be going there alone;
What way's the best to get the ladder there?

VAL.   It will be light, my lord, so you can take it
Under a cloak with any length at all.

DUKE. A cloak as long as yours would turn the
          trick?

VAL.   Yes, my good lord.

DUKE.   Then let me see your cloak:
I'll get myself a cloak of equal length.

VAL.   Why, any cloak will turn the trick, my lord.

DUKE. But can I get accustomed to a cloak?—
Allow me sir—let me try on your cloak—
What letter is this here? What's this?—*To Silvia!*
And here's a ladder fit for what I planned!
I'll be so bold for once to break the seal.

NOTES

lets — hinders; *so shelving* — so shelf-like, i.e., projecting; *apparent* — obvious; *quaintly* — cleverly; *so bold* — if bold; *blood* — noble blood; *is of any length* — has any length at all; *serve the turn* — turn the trick; *such another length* — another of the same length; *fashion me to wear* — fancy me to wear, get used to wearing; *feel* — try on; *engine* — contrivance, ingenious device.

E. M. W. Tillyard is so critical of this play as to be condemnatory. He comments on this scene—

"It [Scene 1 of Act III] begins with Proteus betraying to the Duke that Valentine is about to elope with his daughter and

DUKE.   This very night; for love is like a child,
That longs for everything that he can come by.
　　VAL.　　By seven o'clock I'll get you such a ladder.
　　DUKE.   But, hark thee; I will go to her alone;
How shall I best convey the ladder thither?
　　VAL.　　It will be light, my lord, that you may bear
　　　　　　it
Under a cloak that is of any length.
　　DUKE.   A cloak as long as thine will serve the turn?
　　VAL.　　Ay, my good lord.
　　DUKE.　　　　　　　　Then let me see thy cloak:
I'll get me one of such another length.
　　VAL.　　Why, any cloak will serve the turn, my
　　　　　　lord.
　　DUKE.   How shall I fashion me to wear a cloak?—
I pray thee, let me feel thy cloak upon me—
What letter is this same? What's here?—*To Silvia!*
And here an engine fit for my proceeding!
I'll be so bold to break the seal for once.

　　　　will be passing shortly, carrying the rope ladder necessary for
　　　　the deed. All that the plot required here was that the Duke
　　　　should confront Valentine, unmask him, and send him into ex-
　　　　ile. But Shakespeare decided that here was an opportunity for
　　　　a big scene and proceeded to elaborate . . . The scene, though
　　　　unnecessarily drawn out for the purposes of the play, is
　　　　superbly dramatic, a perfect gift to actors with any command
　　　　of facial expression with Valentine of schoolboy aspect giving
　　　　himself away and the Duke glowering ferociously behind a
　　　　superficial mask of good humor.''
With enemies the likes of Mr. Tillyard, Mr. Shakespeare needs no
friends.

MODERN

(*Reads*) *My thoughts seek haven with my Silvia nightly;*
  Like slaves obeying me, I send them flying:
Oh, could their master come and go as lightly,
  Then I would live where lifeless they are lying.
In your pure bosom rest my wing sent thoughts;
  While I their king, who sent them on their mission,
Do curse this king, his Grace, who has so graced them,
  Because I'm not myself in their position.
I curse myself, for they were sent by me,
And now have haven where their lord should be.
What's here?—
  Silvia, tonight's the night I'll make you free.
It's so; and here's the ladder for the purpose.
You would-be sun-god's son (You mortal son—)!
Would you, like Phaeton, dare to enter heaven,
And then burn up the world with sun's own chariot,
Then drive it to the stars . . . because they're there?
Go, you intruder! You pretentious rogue!
Fawn smilingly on those of your own class;
And thank my patience, not what you deserve,
For letting you depart from here alive:
Thank me for this more than for all the favors
Which, all too much, I have bestowed on you.
But if you linger in my territories
One minute longer than the shortest time
You need to speed you from this royal court,
By Heav'n, my wrath will far exceed the love
I ever bore my daughter or yourself.
Get out! I will not hear your lame excuse,
And, if you love your life, make speed from here.

                    Exit DUKE.

ORIGINAL

(*Reads*) *My thoughts do harbor with my Silvia nightly;*
   And slaves they are to me, that send them flying:
O, could their master come and go as lightly,
   Himself would lodge, where senseless they are lying.
My herald thoughts in thy pure bosom rest them;
   While I, their king, that thither them importune,
Do curse the grace that with such grace hath bless'd them,
   Because myself do want my servants' fortune:
I curse myself, for they are sent by me,
That they should harbor where their lord should be.
What's here?—
   Silvia, this night I will enfranchise thee.
'T is so; and here's the ladder for the purpose.
Why, Phaeton (for thou art Merops' son),
Wilt thou aspire to guide the heavenly car,
And with thy daring folly burn the world?
Wilt thou reach stars, because they shine on thee?
Go, base intruder! overweening slave!
Bestow thy fawning smiles on equal mates;
And think, my patience, more than thy desert,
Is privilege for thy departure hence:
Thank me for this, more than for all the favors,
Which, all too much, I have bestow'd on thee.
But if thou linger in my territories,
Longer than swiftest expedition
Will give thee time to leave our royal court,
By Heaven, my wrath shall far exceed the love
I ever bore my daughter, or thyself.
Be gone; I will not hear thy vain excuse,
But, as thou lov'st thy life, make speed from hence.

Exit DUKE.

Notes

One scholar (Bond) notes that *Valentine's* letter to *Silvia* is in the form of a sonnet without the first quatrain, and he also suggests an inconsistency of unwritten thoughts (*flying*) and written thoughts (*lying*); if *lying* is taken figuratively, which it probably should be, there is no inconsistency. What is a little troublesome, however, is that all of the thoughts seem figurative, the kind of verse a poet would write to himself, not in a love letter, and above all not in a letter he intends to personally deliver—and beyond that, why bring a letter at all when he can tell her whatever he wishes when he sees her later that night? Could it be that stagecraft required that an incriminating letter be found by the *Duke*, and that Shakespeare accommodated by dusting off an old sketch of a sonnet? In any case, it did an excellent job of incriminating.

lightly — easily; *senseless* — insensate; *herald* — heralding; *rest them* — rest themselves; *importune* — impel; *curse the grace that* — curse the king (himself) who, *grace* being used appelatively

MODERN

VAL.   And why not death rather than living
        torment?
To die is to be banished from myself;
And Silvia is myself: banished from her
Is self from self—a deadly banishment!
What light is light, if Silvia is not seen?
What joy is joy, if Silvia's not near by?
Unless it is to think that she's near by,
And dream about her image of perfection.
And if I'm not near Silvia in the night,
There is no music in the nightingale;
Unless I look on Silvia in the day,
There is no day for me to look upon.
She is my essence; and I cease to be,
If I be not within her radiance—
Nourished, illumined, cherished, kept alive.
I don't flee death to flee his deadly doom:
Yet if I linger here I ask for death;
But if I fly, I fly away from life.

here; *want* — lack; *servants' fortune* — servant-thoughts' good fortune (being with *Sylvia*); *enfranchise* — liberate.

Phaeton — the archetypal overreacher of classical myth. His stepfather, Merops, was a mere mortal, but then he learned his true father was no less than god of the sun. He promptly asked to borrow the family car—the sun chariot—and equally promptly hot-rodded it all over earth until the Chief of Gods, Zeus, made a fatality out of Phaeton. It has been said that Shakespeare had his mythology wrong since Phaeton was the sun-god's son, not Merops'. Shakespeare did not; his *for thou art Merops' son* should be read *in truth you, Valentine, are but a common mortal's son.* The New Cambridge editors suggest a pun on *Merops* and the ladder's "ropes"; not only—as so many commentators—do they side-step explaining what the pun is supposed to be, but they overlook one detail—nowhere in the play is there a "rope"; it is always a ladder of *cord*.

reach — reach for; *equal mates* — persons of your own class; *think* — realize; *is privilege for* — gives you the privilege of.

ORIGINAL

VAL.   And why not death, rather than living torment?
To die is to be banish'd from myself;
And Silvia is myself: banish'd from her,
Is self from self: a deadly banishment!
What light is light, if Silvia be not seen?
What joy is joy, if Silvia be not by?
Unless it be to think that she is by,
And feed upon the shadow of perfection.
Except I be by Silvia in the night,
There is no music in the nightingale;
Unless I look on Silvia in the day,
There is no day for me to look upon:
She is my essence; and I leave to be,
If I be not by her fair influence
Foster'd, illumin'd, cherish'd, kept alive.
I fly not death, to fly his deadly doom:
Tarry I here, I but attend on death;
But, fly I hence, I fly away from life.

Enter PROTEUS *and* LAUNCE.

PRO.   Run, boy, run, run, and seek him out.

LAUN.   So-ho! So-ho! We hunt the hare!

PRO.   What do you see?

LAUN.   Him we want to find. There's not a hair on's head but it's a valentine.

PRO.   Valentine?

VAL.   No.

PRO.   Who then? His spirit?

VAL.   Neither.

PRO.   What then?

VAL.   Nothing.

NOTES

Is self from self: a deadly banishment! — the New Cambridge editors changed this line's ending to read *Ah! Deadly banishment!* Not only did they fail to "improve" Shakespeare, they failed to get the point; this line, however, surely did not fail to get a laugh as *Valentine* contemplates the removal of himself from himself and concludes that such would be a *dead*ly banishment.

the shadow — her image; *leave to be* — leave off being, cease to exist; *influence* — there was a belief then that not only stars affected the destinies of men, but that men also had interlocking destinies which "influenced" one another.

I fly not death, to fly his deadly doom — there are many conjectured constructions of this line:

I fly not death_to fly his deadly doom (Fourth Folio)

I fly not death; to fly is deadly doom (Singer)

I fly not death, to fly this deadly doom (Dyce)

. . . and those who stay with the original quibble over whether *his* means "Death's" or the "*Duke's*" deadly doom. Similarly, the following two lines have received differing interpretations.

Once again too many commentators seem to be looking at a comedy through tragedians' eyes. They miss the humorous bravado. *Valentine* is saying that he does not fly from death because he fears it—he is not afraid of death at all, not him! . . . . . . but . . . . . . on the other hand, when one stops to think about it, is there any point, really, in hanging around there and, well, asking for it, so to

Enter PROTEUS *and* LAUNCE.

PRO.   Run, boy, run, run, and seek him out.

LAUN.   So-ho! so-ho!

PRO.   What seest thou?

LAUN.   Him we go to find: There's not a hair on's head, but 't is a Valentine.

PRO.   Valentine?

VAL.   No.

PRO.   Who then? his spirit?

VAL.   Neither.

PRO.   What then?

VAL.   Nothing.

speak . . . . . . and yet, alas, and woe, to leave town is to leave *Silvia*, and that, alas and woe, is to *fly away from life.* Of course, just minutes later he is wasting no time on his way to the town's *North gate*, having apparently decided that it is far, far better to *fly away from life* than to *attend on death.*

attend on — wait for; *so-ho* — a hunting call, here by *Speed* as he pretends to be a dog hunting a hare (his sarcastic response to *Proteus' run, boy, run*).

hair — Malone first suggested a pun here on "hare" in keeping with the preceding *so-ho* call; it seems to fit. This edition speculates that *Proteus* enters in quest of *Valentine* who, on hearing someone approach, hides somewhere with his hat (or worse) still exposed. It would certainly explain *Speed's* detecting the hat with *There's not a hair* (hare) *on's head, but 't is a Valentine.* Interestingly, a heart-shaped hat or a heart patch somewhere else would not have been unlikely costuming, depending on how broadly the comedy was played (cf. the dramatis personae of Microcosmus, by Thomas Nabbes, 1637—"*Love. A Cupid* in a flame colour'd habite; Bow and quiver, a crowne of flaming hearts, &c.").

MODERN

LAUN.   Can *nothing* speak? Master, shall I strike?
PRO.   Whom would you strike?
LAUN.   *Nothing.*
PRO.   You devil!—Stop!
LAUN.   Why, sir, I'll strike nothing. Please let me—
PRO.   Rascal, I say, stop it—Friend Valentine, a
word—
VAL.   My ears are stuffed and cannot hear good
news,
So much of bad news has now filled them up.
PRO.   Then I will keep my news in speechless
silence
For it is harsh, unfortunate, and bad.
VAL.   Is Silvia dead?
PRO.   No, Valentine.
VAL.   No Valentine, indeed, for sacred Silvia!—
Has she disowned me?
PRO.   No, Valentine.
VAL.   No valentine, if Silvia has disowned me!—
What is your news?
LAUN.   Sir, there is a proclamation that you are
vanished.
PRO.   That you are *banished*. Oh, that's the
news—
From here, from Silvia, and from me, your friend.
VAL.   Oh, I've already heard this news too much,
So much of it that I am sick of it.
Does Silvia know that I am banished yet?
PRO.   Oh, yes, she's tried to stop your banish-
ment—
Which if not stopped, stands in effective force—
With seas of melting pearl, which some call tears,
That she wept at her surly father's feet,
And humbly threw herself upon her knees,
Wringing her hands, whose whiteness was so fitting,
As if just then they had waxed pale for woe:

ORIGINAL

LAUN. Can nothing speak? Master, shall I strike?
PRO. Who wouldst thou strike?
LAUN. Nothing.
PRO. Villain, forbear.
LAUN. Why, sir, I'll strike nothing: I pray you—
PRO. Sirrah, I say, forbear: Friend Valentine, a word.
VAL. My ears are stopp'd, and cannot hear good news,
So much of bad already hath possess'd them.
PRO. Then in dumb silence will I bury mine,
For they are harsh, untunable, and bad.
VAL. Is Silvia dead?
PRO. No, Valentine.
VAL. No Valentine, indeed, for sacred Silvia!—
Hath she forsworn me?
PRO. No, Valentine.
VAL. No Valentine, if Silvia have forsworn me!—
What is your news?
LAUN. Sir, there is a proclamation that you are vanished.
PRO. That thou art banished. Oh, that's the news;
From hence, from Silvia, and from me, thy friend.
VAL. O, I have fed upon this woe already,
And now excess of it will make me surfeit.
Doth Silvia know that I am banished?
PRO. Ay, ay; and she hath offer'd to the doom
(Which, unrevers'd, stands in effectual force)
A sea of melting pearl, which some call tears:
Those at her father's churlish feet she tender'd;
With them, upon her knees, her humble self;
Wringing her hands, whose whiteness so became them,
As if but now they waxed pale for woe:

NOTES

stopp'd — stopped up; *possess'd* — filled; *bury mine* — keep my news; *for they are harsh, untunable* — for the news is harsh, disagreeable (*news* was singular or plural then); *no Valentine, if Silvia* — no *Valentine* (himself) exists; *O, that's the news* — wrongly conjectured by the (Old) Cambridge edition to be spoken by *Val-*

MODERN

But neither bended knees, pure hands held up,
Sad sighs, deep groans, or silver-shedding tears,
Could penetrate her uncompassionate sire;
He said, if taken, Valentine must die.
What's more, her intercession chafed him so,
That when she sought repeal on your behalf,
He ordered her confined—to stay at home—
And threatened her with long restriction there.
      VAL.   No more, unless the next word that you
             speak
Has some malignancy to end my life;
If so, I beg you, breathe it in my ear
As ending death-song to my endless grief.
      PRO.   Oh, cry not over that which you can't help,
But seek what help there is before you cry.
Time is the nurse and healer of all wounds.
If you stay here, you cannot see your love;
Besides, your staying here would mean your life.
Hope is a lover's crutch; go walk with that,
And level it against despairing thoughts.
Be here, through letters, even though you're there—
Whatever you write me will be delivered
Right to the milk-white bosom of your love.
It's no time now for conversation here—
Come, I'll conduct you through the city gate;
Before we part our ways we'll talk at length
Of ev'rything about your love affairs.

entine—Proteus, after correcting *Launce's "vanished"*, merely confirms the *news* now that *Launce* has blurted it out; *surfeit —* sick of it all; *offer'd to the doom —* offered up (in response) to the banishment; *unreversed, stands in effectual force —* if unreversed (by *Silvia's* pleading) stands in full force; *father's churlish feet —* surly father's feet; *but now —* right now, right then and there.

ORIGINAL

But neither bended knees, pure hands held up,
Sad sighs, deep groans, nor silver-shedding tears,
Could penetrate her uncompassionate sire;
But Valentine, if he be ta'en, must die.
Besides, her intercession, chaf'd him so,
When she for thy repeal was suppliant,
That to close prison he commanded her,
With many bitter threats of 'biding there.
    VAL.   No more; unless the next word that thou
                speak'st
Have some malignant power upon my life;
If so, I pray thee, breathe it in mine ear,
As ending anthem of my endless dolor.
    PRO.   Cease to lament for that thou canst not
                help,
And study help for that which thou lament'st.
Time is the nurse and breeder of all good.
Here if thou stay, thou canst not see thy love;
Besides, thy staying will abridge thy life.
Hope is a lover's staff; walk hence with that,
And manage it against despairing thoughts.
Thy letters may be here, though thou art hence:
Which, being writ to me, shall be deliver'd
Even in the milk-white bosom of thy love.
The time now serves not to expostulate:
Come, I'll convey thee through the city gate;
And, ere I part with thee, confer at large
Of all that may concern thy love-affairs:

For Silvia's sake, then, if not for your own,
Beware, take care, now come along with me.
    VAL.   I'll ask you, Launce, that if you see my boy,
Tell him make haste to meet me at the North gate.
    PRO.   Go, rascal, seek him out. Come, Valentine.
    VAL.   Oh my dear Silvia! Luckless Valentine!

    Exeunt VALENTINE *and* PROTEUS.

NOTES

thy repeal — your banishment's repeal; *close prison* — confinement; *'biding* — abiding, remaining; *ending anthem* — funeral song; *study help for* — seek solutions to; *manage it* — use it; *even in the milk-white bosom* — right into the milk-white bosom, i.e., secretly; *expostulate* — talk; *convey* — conduct; *at large* — at length.

Critics note that *Proteus* enters and relates the (off-stage) confrontation of *Silvia* and the *Duke*, and *Launce* mentions a *procla-*

MODERN

    LAUN.   You don't have to be a bat to own one, or a gamecock to have one, so even though my higher-up is not an elephant he has a trunk—but that's all one and the same thing, if it all comes out of the same trunk. No one in the world knows that I am in love, yet I am in love; but a team of horse will not drag it from me, or who it is I love. And yet it's a woman, but which woman — that's some tale, and I'll never tell. And yet it's a milk-maid—yet it's not a maid, for gossipers call her made, yet it's a maid, for she is her master's maid and serves for wages. She has better qualities than a water-spaniel—which is saying a lot for an ailing Christian. Here is the sweet roll of what she has to offer: (*Produces a paper.*) party of the Second Part . . . can carry everything on her back. Why a horse can do no more; nayyy, a horse cannot carry *on* on its back; therefore she is better than a nag. Item—*She can milk*; well now, that's a sweet virtue in a maid with clean hands.

As thou lov'st Silvia, though not for thyself,
Regard thy danger, and along with me.
    VAL.   I pray thee, Launce, an if thou seest my boy,
Bid him make haste, and meet me at the North gate.
    PRO.   Go, sirrah, find him out. Come, Valentine.
    VAL.   O my dear Silvia! hapless Valentine!
    Exeunt VALENTINE *and* PROTEUS.

mation has been issued, yet the *Duke* has just made his exit. Such a "time squeeze" was as accepted by the audience then as "light dimming" between scenes is to the audience of today. If common sense does not confirm a lapse of time, then *Valentine* does when he states that he is sick and tired of hearing about the banishment.

    Such criticism would have been better addressed to the question of why *Valentine* has been hanging around Verona so long—under pain of death. It could simply be a trade off between stagecraft and realism. To date at least it appears that only the playwright knows the answer.

ORIGINAL

    LAUN.   I am but a fool, look you; and yet I have the wit to think my master is a kind of a knave: but thats all one, if he be but one knave. He lives not now that knows me to be in love; yet I am in love; but a team of horse shall not pluck that from me; nor who 't is I love, and yet 't is a woman: but what woman, I will not tell myself; and yet 't is a milkmaid; yet 't is not a maid, for she hath had gossips: yet 't is a maid, for she is her master's maid, and serves for wages. She hath more qualities than a water-spaniel—which is much in a bare Christian. Here is the cate-log of her condition. (*Produces a paper.*) *Imprimis*, She can fetch and carry. Why, a horse can do no more: nay, a horse cannot fetch, but only carry; therefore is she better than a jade. *Item*, She can milk: look you, a sweet virtue in a maid with clean hands.

Enter SPEED.

SPEED.   Say now, signor Launce? I see your leader-
ship is part of the readership—what's the news?

LAUN.   With my leader's ship? Why, it's at sea.

SPEED.   Well, still up to your old tricks—mistaking
the word. Then, what's the news in your paper?

LAUN.   The blackest news that you ever heard of.

SPEED.   How is that?

LAUN.   Because the ink is black.

SPEED.   Let me read it.

LAUN.   Get out of here, dolt-head! You can't read.

SPEED.   You lie—I can.

NOTES

(*kind of*) **knave* — also means male organ, as do **fool, *wit*
and **master* here; other editions, agonizing for meaning here, "correct" this to *kind of kind* or *kind of in love*, or say this alludes to
Proteus' "double treachery", or the knave here is a "moderate
knave", or it derives from the "proverb of the two knaves", or
refers to the "four knaves in a deck of cards", etc.; this is not even
to touch on the "problem" most editors find with *Launce's* referring to his master's knavery when he is not supposed to know what
knavery his master may have been up to.

(*but one*) *knave* — additional meaning here of "nave" (the
word then for navel) thereby completing the jest.

*horse — also means and pronounced then like "whores" (cf
Kökeritz); of course most modern editors have by now painstaking-
ly "corrected" the original to read "*horses*".

*tell — bawdy as before; *maid* — three usages here are (1)
milkmaid (2) virgin (3) servant; *gossips* — godparents (for her child),
i.e., she is no maid (virgin), with play on "taleteller" gossips.

bare— pronounced then (and rurally yet) as "beer"; hence
"beer (drinking) Christian" as a play against "water (drinking)
spaniel"; *cate-log* — a play on catalog and "cates" (food delicacies,
sweets).

*condition — also means male or female organ.

fetch and carry — although not used elsewhere in Shakespeare,
the joke about animals being able to carry but not fetch, whereas

Enter SPEED.

SPEED. How now, signior Launce? What news with your mastership?

LAUN. With my master's ship? Why, it is at sea.

SPEED. Well, your old vice still; mistake the word: What news then in your paper?

LAUN. The blackest news that ever thou heard'st.

SPEED. Why, man, how black?

LAUN. Why, as black as ink.

SPEED. Let me read them.

LAUN. Fie on thee, jolt-head! Thou canst not read.

SPEED. Thou liest, I can.

---

women could do both, was common; *carry* had the same meaning as *bear, while to *fetch* meant to physically arouse the male organ; even today *fetch* is used in the sense of to draw a breath, "fetching" refers only to the charm of a female, and the whole phrase "fetch and carry", devoid of its bawdy, is still occasionally used to describe the menial tasks of a female domestic: (cf II-2 of Every Woman in Her Humour, Anon.—not the Ben Jonson one—1609; I-2 of Every Man in His Humour, the Ben Jonson one—1598; and III-3 of Ralph Roister Doister by Nicholas Udall circa—1540, et al).

jade — (1) nag (2) dissolute woman; *she can milk . . . with clean hands* — likely a bawdy suggestion; *mastership* — a vernacular, slangy greeting; *old vice* — Mahood sees a play here on "Old Vice"—the buffoon character of the old morality dramas—but such a wordplay here would be so feeble as to be more Victorian than Elizabethan (or modern day) humor.

MODERN

LAUN. I'll test you. Tell me this—Who begot you?

SPEED. Well now, the son of my grandfather.

LAUN. Oh ill-littered loiterer! It was the sin of your grand . . . mother; this proves you can't read.

SPEED. Come On, fool—try your paper on me.

LAUN. There it is, and may the saints speed you.

SPEED. Party of the Second Part . . . *can milk.*

LAUN. What and whomever she can.

SPEED. Item, *She brews good ale.*

LAUN. And from that comes the proverb—Bless your hard heart, you brew good ale.

SPEED. Item, *She can sow.*

LAUN. That's as much as to say, can she so?

SPEED. Item, *She can knit.*

LAUN. Well, a man need not worry then if he has a sock with a hole—she can knit him a new sock.

SPEED. Item, *She can wash and rub.*

LAUN. Especially good, for then she need not be washed an-d-rubbed.

SPEED. Item, *She can spin.*

LAUN. Then can I retire and make the rounds, when she can spin for her living.

SPEED. Item, *She has many unnamed virtues.*

LAUN. That's as much as to say, bastard virtues which indeed don't know their fathers, and therefore have no names.

SPEED. *Here follow her vices.*

LAUN. Close on the heels of her virtues.

SPEED. Item, *She should not be fasting, because of her breath.*

LAUN. Well, I'll cure her of that with a fast break . . . fast with her.

ORIGINAL

LAUN. I will try thee: tell me this: Who begot thee?

SPEED. Marry, the son of my grandfather.

LAUN. O illiterate loiterer! it was the son of thy grandmother: this proves that thou canst not read.

SPEED. Come, fool, come: try me in thy paper.

LAUN. There; and St. Nicholas be thy speed!

SPEED. Imprimis, She can milk.

LAUN. Ay, that she can.

SPEED. Item, She brews good ale.

LAUN. And thereof comes the proverb—*Blessing of your heart, you brew good ale.*

SPEED. Item, She can sew.

LAUN. That's as much as to say, *Can she so?*

SPEED. Item, She can knit.

LAUN. What need a man care for a stock with a wench, when she can knit him a stock.

SPEED. Item, She can wash and scour.

LAUN. A special virtue; for then she need not be washed and scoured.

SPEED. Item, She can spin.

LAUN. Then may I set the world on wheels, when she can spin for her living.

SPEED. Item, She hath many nameless virtues.

LAUN. That's as much as to say, *Bastard virtues*; that, indeed, know not their fathers, and therefore have no names.

SPEED. Here follow her vices.

LAUN. Close at the heels of her virtues.

SPEED. Item, She is not to be fasting, in respect of her breath.

LAUN. Well, that fault may be mended with a breakfast: Read on.

NOTES

I will try thee — Launce, probably butchering the Latin and only slightly less the English, cleverly inveigles *Speed* into reading for him with this jest.

*son — (i.e., "sun") the female organ; occasionally the male organ (i.e., "son", both words being pronounced alike then as now); with a play on *illiterate* and *grandmother*; hence the line reads, *Oh* ILL-LITTERED *loiterer! it was the* SUN *of thy (grand) mother.*

St. Nicholas — patron saint of scholars; *speed* — obvious pun; *ay, that she can* — yes, whomever that she can; *she brews . . . you brew* — variation of the "He-brew" joke previously mentioned as unmentionable.

can sow — so in the original (sowe) but changed to *sew* in most modern editions; a milkmaid, being a farm girl, is as likely to know how to sow as sew, which latter at any rate is somewhat redundant with the immediately following *knit.*

a stock with a wench — a stocking with a hole; this edition admits to no support for this rendering basing it solely, if not wholly,

MODERN

SPEED.   Item, *She has a sweet mouth.*

LAUN.   That makes up for her foul breath.

SPEED.   Item, *She walks in her sleep.*

LAUN.   There's nothing the matter with that, just so she runs before she walks.

SPEED.   Item, *She is slow in words.*

LAUN.   Oh, villain who wrote this down as one of her vices! To be slow in words is a woman's special virtue. By all means, out with it and make it instead her chief virtue.

SPEED.   Item, *She is passionate.*

LAUN.   Out with that too. It's to be expected from one who is related to Eve, and comes from a bone.

SPEED.   Item, *She has no teeth.*

on intuition; most editions offer the standard meaning then for the first *stock* of "dowry", but how that would even titillate the audience goes unexplained.

scour — first usage (1) clean (2) skewer, probably with sexual implication; second usage (3) beat.

spin — possibly bawdy meaning (cf. Partridge) but this edition is satisfied with a play here on *spin*ning wheel and *world on wheels*, i.e., carefree; *nameless* — (1) sundry (cf. Hulme), but twisted by *Launce* into its other meaning of (2) unnamed.

not to be fasting — i.e., not to be "fast in" sexually; most editions have erroneously "corrected" this (Rowe) to read *kissed fasting* based on the popular belief then that fasting caused bad breath (which, albeit true, is nevertheless no license for doctoring the line —and killing the meaning).

breath — breadth, i.e., in respect of her vulva.

fault — also means male or female organ.

break — i.e., break the hymen . . . hence—

breakfast — "break fast"; i.e., mended or corrected fast with a "break".

ORIGINAL

SPEED. Item, She hath a sweet mouth.

LAUN. That makes amends for her sour breath.

SPEED. Item, She doth talk in her sleep.

LAUN. It's no matter for that, so she sleep not in her talk.

SPEED. Item, She is slow in words.

LAUN. O villain that set this down among her vices! To be slow in words is a woman's only virtue: I pray thee, out with't; and place it for her chief virtue.

SPEED. Item, She is proud.

LAUN. Out with that too; it was Eve's legacy, and cannot be ta'en from her.

SPEED. Item, She hath no teeth.

LAUN.   That doesn't bother me either, because I love crusts.

SPEED.   Item, *She is crusty, and growls.*

LAUN.   That's all right, since she has no teeth to bite.

SPEED.   *She will often praise her liquor.*

LAUN.   If her liquor be good, she will; if she shall not, I shall—for good things should be praised.

SPEED.   Item, *She is too liberal.*

LAUN.   With her tongue she cannot, for it's written down there that she's slow in that; with her purse she will not, for that I'll keep shut; now with another thing she may . . . and that I cannot help. Well, proceed.

SPEED.   Item, *She has more hair than brains, and she has more airs than hairs . . . and lets more* air than she has airs . . . but she has a rich uncle . . . and she's the only heir.

NOTES

sweet mouth — usually connoted as "lovely mouth" or "sweet tooth", either of which will do since the line is merely a setup to get another laugh out of *sour breath* (see below). The 1921 New Cambridge offers "wantonness" for the meaning, and it would be interesting to know in what glossary or dictionary they found that—not to overlook that *Speed* is the straight man and any bawdy would normally be in the response that follows; of course it was unquestionable that the unquestioning new editors of the later 1942 "New Cambridge" blithely continued the "wanton" footnote.

sour breath — also harks back to her "breadth", hence a play on a play on words.

*sleep not in her talk — the *sleep* is usually found incorrectly corrected to *slip*; this one-liner was a fairly common joke and

LAUN. I care not for that neither, because I love crusts.

SPEED. Item, She is curst.

LAUN. Well, the best is, she hath no teeth to bite.

SPEED. Item, She will often praise her liquor.

LAUN. If her liquor be good, she shall; if she will not, I will; for good things should be praised.

SPEED. Item, She is too liberal.

LAUN. Of her tongue she cannot; for that's writ down she is slow of; of her purse she shall not; for that I'll keep shut: now of another thing she may; and that cannot I help. Well, proceed.

SPEED. Item, She hath more hair than wit, and more faults than hairs, and more wealth than faults.

alludes to unintended premature sexual excitation before one even gets to bed (while tantalized, thinking about or "talking" about sex). A clarifying example occurs in a later play (The City-Night-Cap, II-1, by Robert Davenport, performed 1624) where the Clown is guiding the lover, Francisco, to Dorothea's bed for a tryst; in the total darkness of the bed chamber Francisco apparently accidentally gropes the Clown who promptly whispers—"would you would groap out the bed; for I sleep in my talke, I am sure of that."

slow in words — play on "slow inwards", orgasmically; *only* — with a play on another connotation then of "one-ly" or unique; *proud* — in heat, passionate; *curst* — nagging, ill-tempered, followed by a possibly bawdy response; *liquor* — licker (viz. Launce); *liberal* — (1) frank (2) extravagant (3) wanton.

MODERN

LAUN.   Stop there—I'll take her! I took her on and put her off two or three times in that last article—*re-hairs* that once more.

SPEED.   Item, *She has more hair than brains*—

LAUN.   More hair than brains—harebrained? It may be that I will remedy that. For if the lass knows less, it's because her lover knows more; so if the lass has less, and if I have more, I cannot help but to make her smart.

SPEED.   *And more airs than hairs*—

LAUN.   Oh, that's high society! She must have a society disease!

SPEED.   *And more wealth than airs.*

LAUN.   Why, that makes all the difference in the world. There's nothing like fresh airs for one's wealth. Well, I'll have her; and if it becomes a match—

SPEED.   What then?

LAUN.   Well, I'll tell you what then—that your master is waiting for you at the North gate.

SPEED.   For me?

LAUN.   For you? And who are you? He has waited for a better man than you.

SPEED.   And must I go to him?

LAUN.   You better run to him, for you have stayed so long that just going will hardly do.

SPEED.   Why didn't you tell me sooner?—Well, you know what you can do with your love letters!

Exit SPEED.

LAUN.   Now he'll be switched for reading my let-ter—an ill-mannered knave who will stick his nose into other people's business! I'll follow him, to rejoice in the boy's comeuppance.

Exit.

ORIGINAL

LAUN.   Stop there; I'll have her: she was mine, and not mine, twice or thrice in that article: rehearse that once more.

SPEED.   Item, She hath more hair than wit—

LAUN.   More hair than wit: it may be I'll prove it: the cover of the salt hides the salt, and therefore it is more than the salt; the hair that covers the wit is more than the wit; for the greater hides the less. What's next?

SPEED.   And more faults than hairs—

LAUN.   That's monstrous: O, that that were out!

SPEED.   And more wealth than faults.

LAUN.   Why, that word makes the faults gracious: well, I'll have her: and if it be a match, as nothing is impossible—

SPEED.   What then?

LAUN.   Why, then will I tell thee—that thy master stays for thee at the *North gate.*

SPEED.   For me?

LAUN.   For thee? Ay—who art thou? He hath stayed for a better man than thee.

SPEED.   And must I go to him?

LAUN.   Thou must run to him, for thou hast stayed so long that going will scarce serve the turn.

SPEED.   Why didst not tell me sooner?—'pox of you love letters!

Exit SPEED.

LAUN.   Now will he be swinged for reading my letter—an unmannerly slave that will thrust himself into secrets! I'll after, to rejoice in the boy's correction.

Exit.

NOTES

A redundancy has been noted in *Launce's stop there; I'll have her* and his *well, I'll have her* a dozen lines later; and as usual a "reviser" has been blamed for injecting those twelve supposedly superfluous lines; further, Arden sees in *I'll have her* what is almost a non sequitur since she is already *Launce's woman.*

Taking the last criticism first, Arden is reading a serious romance into what is no more than a prop for bawdy. As to the "reviser", it must be remembered that this play closed while Shakespeare was still active in the performing company, so any revision would in all probability have had to have had his approval; or should it ever be forgotten that the play was published by—in a way certified by—the bard's own lifelong associates and respectful friends.

Finally, there is no redundancy here and no reason to believe the lines are anything other than true Shakespeare. The first *I'll have her* is a response to the straight uses of *hair, wit* and *faults,* all of which is a setup for the subsequent bawdy uses. The final *I'll have her,* far from being redundant, is a reinforcement of what kind of woman *Launce* will marry if the price is right.

LAUN. More hair than *wit — delivered suggestively; while the line is bawdy here, it is a play on a common expression then of someone stupid, i.e., someone with "more hair than wit" (also cf. Steevens).

it may be I'll prove it — so the original (now usually "corrected" to *It may be, I'll prove it:*); *prove* then had more the meaning of "probe, experience", hence "maybe I'll find out".

*cover — (1) salt cellar cover (2) also means to mount sexually; *salt* — also means lewd (woman) . . . which imagery leads to—

hair that covers the wit — i.e., hare (lewd woman) who covers the (male) **wit* . . . leading to—

greater hides the less — i.e., the greater hide (piece of flesh) is the "lass"; for the same play on *less* cf. *Measure for Measure,* I-4-17 and II-2-128.

And more faults than hairs — a ludicrous line were it not that this was a readily recognized reference to syphilis—"the pox"; this derived from the symptomatic skin pocks which, being likened to a multitude of miniature pudenda, became embedded in Elizabethan humor.

gracious — cf. **grace,* i.e., pudend.

stays — waits; *go* — often meant "walk" as distinct from run or ride; *scarce serve the turn* — hardly do; *'pox* — as noted before, here a mild expletive; *swinged* — whipped; *after* — follow; *correction* — punishment.

The New Cambridge editors, in furtherance of their theory that "Speed's part in this scene was added by the adapter", hold that, "All the wit in this scene lies in Launce's comments upon the 'catalogue', comments which he could have made without Speed's help." One may as well argue that Costello did not need Abbott—or did Gracie need George.

MODERN

ACT III

SCENE 2 — *The same. A Room in the* DUKE'S *Palace.*

Enter DUKE *and* THURIO *with* PROTEUS *behind.*

DUKE.   Sir Thurio, have no fear that she will love
                    you,
Now Valentine is banished from her sight.

THU.   His exile made her but despise me more,
Reject my company, and rail at me,
So that I now despair of winning her.

DUKE.   This superficial love is like a figure
That's traced in ice, which with an hour of heat
Dissolves to water, and has lost its form.
A little time will melt her frozen thoughts,
And worthless Valentine will be forgot—
Tell me, Sir Proteus! Is your countryman,
In keeping with our proclamation, gone?

PRO.   Gone, my good lord.

DUKE.   My daughter takes his going grievously.

PRO.   A little time, my lord, will end her grief.

DUKE.   I think so too, but Thurio disagrees—
Proteus, the high regard I hold you in—
For you have earned a measure of respect—
Makes me the more disposed to talk with you.

PRO.   Longer than I prove loyal to your grace
Let me not live to look upon your grace.

DUKE.   You know how much I want to bring about
A match between Sir Thurio and my daughter.

PRO.   I do, my lord.

DUKE.   And also, I'm sure you're not unaware
How very much she goes against my will.

PRO.   I know she did when Valentine was here.

DUKE.   Yes, and perversely she still perserveres.
What might we do to make the girl forget
Her love of Valentine . . . and love Sir Thurio?

ORIGINAL

ACT III

SCENE 2 — *The Same. A Room in the* DUKE'S *Palace.*

Enter DUKE *and* THURIO; PROTEUS *behind.*

DUKE.   Sir Thurio, fear not but that she will love
        you,
Now Valentine is banish'd from her sight.

THU.   Since his exile she hath despis'd me most,
Forsworn my company, and rail'd at me,
That I am desperate of obtaining her.

DUKE.   This weak impress of love is as a figure
Trenched in ice; which with an hour's heat
Dissolves to water, and doth lose his form.
A little time will melt her frozen thoughts,
And worthless Valentine shall be forgot—
How now, sir Proteus! Is your countryman,
According to our proclamation, gone?

PRO.   Gone, my good lord.

DUKE.   My daughter takes his going grievously.

PRO.   A little time, my lord, will kill that grief.

DUKE.   So I believe; but Thurio thinks not so—
Proteus, the good conceit I hold of thee,
(For thou hast shown some sign of good desert)
Makes me the better to confer with thee.

PRO.   Longer than I prove loyal to your grace,
Let me not live to look upon your grace.

DUKE.   Thou know'st how willingly I would effect
The match between sir Thurio and my daughter.

PRO.   I do, my lord.

DUKE.   And also, I think, thou art not ignorant
How she opposes her against my will.

PRO.   She did, my lord, when Valentine was here.

DUKE.   Ay, and perversely she perseveres so.
What might we do, to make the girl forget
The love of Valentine, and love sir Thurio?

NOTES

THURIO . . . she hath despis'd me most — the Arden edition once again notes a "time lapse" problem here where there would not have been enough time between *Valentine's* banishment and this scene for *Silvia's* harsh treatment of Thurio to have occurred. Actually, Shakespeare has more than adequately provided for a

MODERN

PRO.   The best way is to slander Valentine
As coward, false, and of the lower class—
Three things that women totally detest.
    DUKE.   True, but she'll think it's being said in hate.
    PRO.   True—if it's said by enemies of his.
Therefore it must most credibly be spoken
By one whom she believes to be his friend.
    DUKE.   Then you must be the one to slander him.
    PRO.   And that, my lord, I will be loathe to do.
It's shameful business for a gentleman;
Especially against his own true friend.
    DUKE.   Since here your praise can no more do him
        good,
So neither can your slander do him bad;
Thus since on him your act has no effect,
Think of it as a favor done for me.
    PRO.   You have convinced me, sir. If I can do it—
In any way I can discredit him—
She'll not for long be still in love with him.
But even if this takes her love from him,
It does not follow that she'll love Sir Thurio.
    THU.   Therefore, as you unwind her love from
        him,
Lest it unravel, favoring no one,
You must make sure to wind it on to me;
Which should be done by praising me as much
As you disparage this Sir Valentine.

"lapse" with the interposing of the previous "milkmaid" scene.

forsworn — rejected; *desperate* — despairing; *impress* — impression; *trenched* — etched, cut into; *his form* — its form; *conceit* — conception, opinion; *good desert* — deserving good; *better* — better disposed; *opposes her* — opposes herself, i.e., goes against.

ORIGINAL

    PRO.   The best way is to slander Valentine
With falsehood, cowardice, and poor descent;
Three things that women highly hold in hate.
    DUKE. Ay, but she'll think that it is spoke in hate.
    PRO.   Ay, if his enemy deliver it:
Therefore it must, with circumstance, be spoken
By one whom she esteemeth as his friend.
    DUKE. Then you must undertake to slander him.
    PRO.   And that, my lord, I shall be loth to do:
'T is an ill office for a gentleman;
Especially, against his very friend.
    DUKE. Where your good word cannot advantage
           him,
Your slander never can endamage him;
Therefore the office is indifferent,
Being entreated to it by your friend.
    PRO.   You have prevail'd, my lord: if I can do it,
By aught that I can speak in his dispraise,
She shall not long continue love to him.
But, say this weed her love from Valentine,
It follows not that she will love sir Thurio.
    THU.   Therefore, as you unwind her love from
           him,
Lest it should ravel, and be good to none,
You must provide to bottom it on me;
Which must be done by praising me as much
As you in worth dispraise sir Valentine.

NOTES

poor descent — lower class lineage; *circumstance* — substance, i.e., circumstantial evidence; *very friend* — very own friend; *the office is indifferent* — your mission does not affect (*Valentine* one way or another); *by your friend* — by (me) your friend.

PROTEUS. You have prevail'd — the New Cambridge editors, looking to support their rewrite theory, suggest that this is too sudden a consent on *Proteus'* part and further speculate that the *Duke's* argument was possibly longer in the original version. They misread *Proteus'* motivation and character; although he was deviously playing hard-to-get, he was ready to slander *Valentine* at the drop of the *Duke's* hat; indeed, he must have delivered *You have prevail'd* in the tone of, "I thought you would never ask!"

MODERN

DUKE.   And, Proteus, we dare trust you in this way
Because we know, as Valentine has said,
You are a staunch supporter of all love,
And are not apt to quickly change your mind.
With this in mind I'll see you're free to act,
So you and Silvia may converse at length—
For she is sluggish, moody, melancholy,
And for your friend's sake glad to talk with you.
Then you may soften her by your persuasion
To hate young Valentine, and love my choice.
PRO.   As much as I can do, I will effect—
But you, Sir Thurio, are not sharp enough;
You must lay lures to capture her desires,
By wailful sonnets whose well crafted rhymes
Should swell with promises to cherish her.
DUKE.   Yes, great is the force of Heaven-sent
              poetry.
PRO.   Say that upon the altar of her beauty
You sacrifice your tears, your sighs, your heart.
Write till your ink is dry; and with your tears

weed - so in the original, but the New Cambridge suggests this is a printing error of what was originally "wend" or "wind". Indeed, if the original had had *wend* or *wind* (to go, proceed) this edition would have suggested a printing error for what must have been "weed"; what is more, Shakespeare has only used "wend" three times in his entire oeuvre, and two of those were for the sake of rhyme. (Rowe suggested "wean", but why would take "away" be a better connotation than take "out"?) Farmers then commonly spoke of weeding the fields or weeding certain plants *from* the fields; Shakespeare is merely using the latter sense of "pluck from" figuratively.

provide — arrange, make sure; *bottom it on me* — bottom is a core or clew on which thread is wound, so *Thurio* is imaginatively picturing *Silvia's* "thread of love" being wound around himself.

ORIGINAL

DUKE.   And, Proteus, we dare trust you in this kind;
Because we know, on Valentine's report,
You are already love's firm votary,
And cannot soon revolt and change your mind.
Upon this warrant shall you have access
Where you with Silvia may confer at large;
For she is lumpish, heavy, melancholy,
And, for your friend's sake, will be glad of you;
Where you may temper her, by your persuasion,
To hate young Valentine, and love my friend.
PRO.   As much as I can do, I will effect—
But you, sir Thurio, are not eager enough;
You must lay lime, to tangle her desires,
By wailful sonnets, whose composed rhymes
Should be full fraught with serviceable vows.
DUKE.   Ay, much is the force of heaven-bred
          poesy.
PRO.   Say that upon the altar of her beauty
You sacrifice your tears, your sighs, your heart.
Write till your ink be dry; and with your tears

Wet it again, and form some soulful line
As evidence of such sincerity:
For Orpheus' lute was strung with poets' sinews;
Where golden touch could soften steel and stones,
Make tigers tame, and huge sea-going whales
Forsake unsounded depths to dance on sands.
After your dire, lamenting elegies,
Visit by night your lady's chamber window
With some musicians. Have them play a song
Of very mournful tone. The night's dead stillness
Will well enhance such bittersweet-like sadness—
This, or else nothing, will inherit her.

COMMENTS

This scene heightens the action with a scheming plot to trans-
fer *Silvia's* affections from *Valentine* to *Thurio*, with a subscheme
of *Proteus'* to undermine the main scheme. Apart from being ex-
pository, the scene also adds baseness to the already base character
of *Proteus*.

NOTES

kind — way, manner; *votary* — devotee, supporter; *revolt* —
i.e., do a complete about-face; *warrant* — assurance; *at large* — at
length; *lumpish* — lethargic, sluggish of body and/or spirit; *glad of
you* — glad to see you; *where* — whereupon; *temper* — bend.

love my friend — the Arden edition sees an "absurdity" for the
Duke to use *my friend* here (for *Thurio*); not so—(1) it is a play
against *your friend* two lines earlier (2) it preserves meter, where
"Thurio" would not (3) onstage the *Duke* would eliminate any am-
biguity with a nod or shoulder clap.

sharp — keen, eager; *lime to tangle* — a sticky substance
spread on tree branches to trap birds; *composed* — i.e., ad hoc,
composed as befitting the occasion; *full fraught* — jam-packed; *serviceable vows* — vows to serve her.

heaven-bred poesy — this hyperbole releases the gush of hypo-
critical lines which follow (and is not to show the *Duke's* ridiculous-

Moist it again; and frame some feeling line,
That may discover such integrity:
For Orpheus' lute was strung with poets' sinews;
Whose golden touch could soften steel and stones,
Make tigers tame, and huge leviathans
Forsake unsounded deeps to dance on sands.
After your dire-lamenting elegies,
Visit by night your lady's chamber window,
With some sweet consort: to their instruments
Tune a deploring dump: the night's dead silence
Will well become such sweet complaining grievance:
This, or else nothing, will inherit her.

---

ness as the Arden editors suggest); *feeling line* — line full of feeling;
discover — uncover, i.e., exhibit or show.

   such integrity — such "heartfelt sincerity" . . . so in the Folger
edition, which could not be more right, and so seemingly nowhere
else: *such true emotion* (Pelican); *such devotion* (Signet); *soot,
sweet, or sooth integrity* (per Kellner depending on which section
of his book one is reading); the Arden, terming the phrase
"laboured", then offers the unlabored reading—*such single heart-
edness as your weeping shows you have.* Such remarkable disagree-
ment shows what can happen where the glossarist Onions decided
to omit a word—here *integrity*—altogether.

   Admittedly, even prior to Onions, Mr. Staunton suspected
"some corruption in the words *such integrity*", and the eminent
scholar Malone thought a whole line to be missing here. Then again,
this controversy may be the very reason "integrity" never made it
to Onions' glossary in the first place.

   Integrity at that time, in addition to its meaning of an intrinsic
quality, was used in a specific sense—a mother's integrity to her
daughter (Coriolanus), one's integrity to heaven (Henry VIII),
prayers of integrity (Richard II), oaths vowed with integrity (Love's
Labor), et al—where the meaning is "loyalty" and/or "sincerity".
Hence here where *Proteus*, having just urged a most willing *Thurio*
to be excessively dramatic with *Silvia*, need only gaze at the gal-
leries as he sarcastically answers the equivalent of—"and feed her a
line full of feeling that will show . . . *such integrity.*" Far from be-

ing "laboured", or "corrupt", or "missing" something, the line is very simple and very effective.

    Orpheus' lute . . . dance on sands — these four lines have been criticized as either too "elaborate" (Arden) or "irrelevant" (New Cambridge); while they do read like something salvaged from a sketch for a sonnet, they serve to intensify *Proteus'* mockery by

MODERN

    DUKE.   This shows you are experienced in love.

    THU.   And your advice tonight I'll put in practice.
Therefore, friend Proteus, my instruction-giver,
Let's go into the city right away
To pick some good, professional musicians.
I have a sonnet that will serve the need
And put to use your excellent advice.

    DUKE.   Then to it, gentlemen!

    PRO.   We'll keep your company till after supper,
And afterward decide on our proceedings.

    DUKE.   Go to it now!—And so you are excused.

Exeunt.

NOTES

    discipline — instruction; *presently* — right now; *sort* — sort out, select; *serve the turn* — serve the need; *give the onset to* — start things off with; *wait* — attend; *determine* — finally determine, decide upon; *pardon you* — i.e., from staying for supper.

comparing *Thurio* to the fabled musician who could even enchant stones.

    sinews — tendons (of animals were used to string musical instruments); *consort* — musical ensemble; *deploring* — mournful; *dump* — a sad, down-in-the-dumps tune; *sweet-complaining grievance* — bitter-sweet grieving; *inherit* — win.

ORIGINAL

DUKE.   This discipline shows thou hast been in love.
THU.   And thy advice this night I'll put in practice.
Therefore, sweet Proteus, my direction-giver,
Let us into the city presently
To sort some gentlemen well skill'd in music:
I have a sonnet that will serve the turn,
To give the onset to thy good advice.
   DUKE.   About it, gentlemen.
   PRO.   We'll wait upon your grace till after supper;
And afterward determine our proceedings.
   DUKE.   Even now about it: I will pardon you.

Exeunt.

ACT IV

SCENE 1 — *A Forest near Mantua.*

Enter several OUTLAWS.

1st OUT.   Fellows, stand fast. I see a traveler.

2nd OUT. If there are ten, shrink not, but down
with 'em.

Enter VALENTINE *and* SPEED.

3rd OUT. Stand, sir, and hand us that which you
are wearing.

If not, we'll make you sit, and strip you clean.

SPEED.   Sir, we are undone. These are the
villains

That all the travelers do fear so much.

VAL.   My friends—

1st OUT.   That's not so, sir; we are your enemies.

2nd OUT. Peace! We'll hear him.

3rd OUT. Aye, by my beard will we, for he's a
handsome man.

VAL.   You'll find that I have little wealth to
lose;

I am a man who's met adversity.

My riches are these poor old clothes on me,

Of which if you should hereby steal from me,

You take the sum and substance that I have.

2nd OUT. Whither travel you?

VAL.   To Verona.

1st OUT.   From where?

VAL.   From Milan.

3rd OUT. Have you long sojourned there?

VAL.   Some sixteen months. I might have
stayed there longer

If warped misfortune had not thwarted me.

ORIGINAL

ACT IV

SCENE 1 — *A Forest, near Mantua.*

Enter certain OUTLAWS.

1st OUT.   Fellows, stand fast; I see a passenger.
2nd OUT. If there be ten, shrink not, but down
     with 'em

Enter VALENTINE *and* SPEED.

3rd OUT.   Stand, sir, and throw us that you have
     about you,
If not, we'll make you sit, and rifle you.
SPEED.   Sir, we are undone! these are the villains
That all the travelers do fear so much.
VAL.   My friends—
1st OUT.   That's not so, sir; we are your enemies.
2nd OUT. Peace! we'll hear him.
3nd OUT. Ay, by my beard, will we; for he is a
     proper man!
VAL.   Then know that I have little wealth to
     lose;
A man I am cross'd with adversity.
My riches are these poor habiliments,
Of which if you should here disfurnish me,
You take the sum and substance that I have.
2nd OUT. Whither travel you?
VAL.   To Verona.
1st OUT.   Whence?
VAL.   From Milan.
3rd OUT. Have you long sojourn'd there?
VAL.   Some sixteen months; and longer might
     have stay'd
If crooked fortune had not thwarted me.

COMMENTS

This scene is a good example of Elizabethan bawdy in the humor of sex per se. This humor has nothing to do with what would today be called homosexuality . . . or bisexuality . . . or perverted, inverted or converted heterosexuality. It is simply sex without preoccupation, without hang-ups. For understanding here see the scenario offered later in *Notes*.

NOTES

New Cambridge faults this scene for its "irrational mingling of verse and prose" as well as the "poor quality of much of the 'verse'"; as usual they suggest an "adapter". Their observation is unobserving; this scene has a good deal of action which could easily explain the text; consider the choreography of just the scene's opening—outlaws leaping from wings, perhaps from a tree (balcony), possibly even from the audience; to have orchestrated

MODERN

1st OUT.   What? Were you banished from there?
VAL.   I was.
2nd OUT. For what offense?
VAL.   For that which now torments me to
            relate.
I stabbed a man—an upshot I regret,
But yet I slew him in a manly struggle,
With no mean edge, and not a thing concealed.
    1st OUT.   Then don't regret it if you did it so.
But were you banished for so small a thing?
    VAL.   I was—and rather glad for such release.
    1st OUT. Know you many tongues?
    VAL.   Why that's the story of my happy life—
How I made friends . . . else I'd gone off alone.

this scene with a singsong cadence throughout the text would have been absurd. The action here determined the speech, not vice versa.

    passenger — traveler.

    Stand . . . throw . . . sit — at least one commentator (Charlton) sees a timidity here on the part of the *Outlaws* because of these three words; however *throw* in respect to garments then (and now —"throw something warm on") did not mean hurl or fling, but rather put on or take off; and since *stand* meant "halt" here, *sit* is a bit of wordplay on the more usual meaning of *stand*. Incredibly— and yet, alas, not so incredibly—a few scholars to this day gullibly "buy" the very blarney of these *Outlaws* and interpret them as merely poor little Whiffenpoof lambs: e.g., (Wright and LaMar, The Folger Guide to Shakespeare) "All have been outlawed for minor offenses and are gentlemen rather than ruffians".

    rifle — strip; *proper* — good looking (rather respecting the body than the face, hence, well-built); *am cross'd with* — came across, met with; *disfurnish me* — rob me of everything; *whence?* — from where?; *sixteen months* — a fabrication, obvious to the audience.

ORIGINAL

1st OUT.   What, were you banish'd thence?
VAL.   I was.
2nd OUT.   For what offense?
VAL.   For that which now torments me to
             rehearse.
I killed a man, whose death I much repent,
But yet I slew him manfully in fight,
Without false vantage or base treachery.
1st OUT.   Why, ne'er repent it, if it were done
             so.
But were you banish'd for so small a fault?
VAL.   I was, and held me glad of such a
             doom.
1st OUT.   Have you the tongues?
VAL.   My youthful travail therein made me
             happy,
Or else I often had been often miserable.

3rd OUT. By the bare scalp of Robin Hood's fat
                    friar,
This fellow is a king for our wild faction!
1st OUT.   We'll have him. Sirs—a word.

OUTLAWS *withdraw.*

SPEED.   Master, be one of them.
It is an honorable kind of thievery.
VAL.   Quiet, knave!

OUTLAWS *return.*

2nd OUT. Tell us this—have you anything to fall
back on?
VAL.   Nothing but my drawn lot.
3rd OUT. You'll see that some of us are gentlemen
Such that the wildness of our reckless youth
Did wrench us from the lives of lawful men.
And I, myself, was exiled from Verona
For plotting the abduction of a lady,
And heiress . . . niece related to the Duke.

NOTES

I *killed a man* — *kill* also means the male role in copulation (cf. keel); this bawdy term has never been detected despite its rifeness then, which explains why the literati wrote reams of conjecture on why Shakespeare would allow *Valentine* to tell a "lie" and without any explanation to the audience—which latter of course never, at any point, needed one.

repent — also means weep (sexually, "tears" of orgasm).

fight — also means contend sexually; *false* — (1) unfair (2) *faults; doom* — sentence, punishment.

tongues — (1) foreign languages (2) here allusive to fellatio.

travail . . . happy — the Oxford English Dictionary cites this particular line from Shakespeare, but assigning the "labor" rather than the "travel" meaning to *travail* (which then had both meanings, depending on context) arrives at the meaning of "apt, dexterous," for *happy*; even allowing that lexicographers are not ex-

3rd OUT. By the bare scalp of Robin Hood's fat
                  friar,
This fellow were a king for our wild faction!
          1st OUT. We'll have him. Sirs—a word.

                  OUTLAWS *withdraw.*

          SPEED.   Master, be one of them;
It is an honorable kind of thievery.
          VAL.   Peace, Villain!

                  OUTLAWS *return.*

          2nd OUT. Tell us this—have you anything to
take to?
          VAL.   Nothing but my fortune.
          3rd OUT. Know then that some of us are
                  gentlemen
Such as the fury of ungovern'd youth
Thrust from the company of awful men.
Myself was from Verona banished
For practicing to steal away a lady,
And heir and niece, allied unto the Duke.

pected to recognize bawdy when they see it, surely "travel" is
more readily associated with *the tongues* than "labor", not to mention that *happy* is in obvious counterpoint to the following line's
miserable; so *happy* here simply means "happy", and the O.E.D. is
clearly wrong.

   often . . . miserable — virtually all editions have "corrected"
the original by deleting the second *often*, which should remain
since it here has the bawdy meaning of "off-ing" sexually; the
meter of the line is maintained with a monosyllabic treatment of
miserable, which is not unknown in Shakespeare (e.g., Cymbaline
I-6-6).

   fat friar — is of course Friar Tuck, counterpart of today's "dirty
old man"; all those authorities who for centuries criticized Shakespeare for his deficiencies in authenticity of Italian ambience seem
to blithely ignore this reference and the evidence it constitutes as to
just how much the Elizabethan audience cared about such authenticity—after all, an Italian Robin Hood?

anything to take to — any resources.

*fortune — also means male or female organ.

Know, then . . . unto the Duke — the Arden edition notes that this six-line speech by "The 3rd Outlaw tells, substantially, Valentine's own story . . . The dramatist was doubtless saving the trouble of further invention . . ." There is no "doubtless" about it. The lines are of both invention and intention; and they are a bit of Shakespearean theatricality. *Valentine* does a take on the outlaw's banishment—so like his own—in the opening lines. He does a stronger take learning that the outlaw was banished from, of all places,

MODERN

2nd OUT. And I from Mantua, for a gentleman
Whom, in my heat, I stabbed straight to the heart.

1st OUT.   And I for suchlike petty crimes as these.
But to the point—we raise our shortcomings
To help explain why we lead lawless lives,
And partly due to your fine handsomeness,
With well-built shape (and by your own report
A linguist); and a man of such perfection
As we do in our specialty much need.

2nd OUT. Indeed, because you're banished, just
                    like us,
You're all the more desirable to us.
Are you content to be our general?
To make a virtue of necessity,
And live—as we do—in this wilderness?

3rd OUT. What do you say? Will you come with
                    our group?
Say, *Aye*, and be the captain of us all.
We will respect you, and be ruled by you.
Love you as our commander and our king.

1st OUT.   But if you scorn our offer, then you die.

2nd OUT. You will not live to brag about this offer.

Verona. He is holding his breath at the self-same offense of plotting
to abduct a lady. His heart stops with *an heir* and then gasps in
relief when the word *niece*, instead of "daughter" of the *Duke*,
restores him to normal.

Modern readers are unaware of this dramatic effect because
long ago the respected authority Theobald "corrected" the original
by changing *niece* (right along with its sense-giving little comma) to
"near"—and so all the editions read today.

awful — then meant full of awe; *practicing* — plotting; *heir* —
then also meant heiress.

ORIGINAL

2nd OUT. And I from Mantua, for a gentleman
Whom, in my mood, I stabbed unto the heart.
    1st OUT.   And I, for such like petty crimes as
        these.
But to the purpose—for we cite our faults
That they may hold excus'd our lawless lives,
And, partly, seeing you are beautified
With goodly shape; and by your own report
A linguist; and a man of such perfection,
As we do in our quality much want.
    2nd OUT. Indeed, because you are a banish'd man,
Therefore, above the rest, we parley to you:
Are you content to be our general?
To make a virtue of necessity,
And live, as we do, in this wilderness?
    3rd OUT.   What say'st thou? Wilt thou be of our
        consort?
Say, *Ay,* and be the captain of us all:
We'll do thee homage, and be rul'd by thee,
Love thee as our commander, and our king.
    1st OUT.   But if thou scorn our courtesy, thou
        diest.
    2nd OUT.   Thou shalt not live to brag what we have
        offer'd.

VAL.   I take your offer and will live with you,
Provided that you do no outrages
On helpless women or poor travelers.

3rd OUT. No! We detest such vile, base practices.
Come, go with us. We'll bring you to our gangs,
And show you all the treasure we have got—
Which, with ourselves, all rest at your disposal.

Exeunt.

NOTES

mood — here also means sexually in the mood.

stabbed — also sexually as used today; *unto the heart* — in sexual sense, so deeply as to reach.

purpose — also means male organ; *cite* — (1) mention (2) in sense of "'cite"—often used by Shakespeare for incite or excite . . .

faults — as previously.

And partly . . . much want. — the New Cambridge suggests a script cut here since these four lines have no finite verb; for essentially the same reason Theobald "corrected" the original by substituting a dash for the period after *want,* a change most editions have accepted and a change which changes the correct meaning. There is a finite verb here—the line reads *And partly* (cite our faults) *seeing* etc. The trouble of course lay in not recognizing the bawdy as noted above.

quality — specialty (banditry); *want* — need; *consort* — group; *silly* — lamblike, helpless.

crews — so in the original; variously and wrongly "corrected" by scholars to *crew, cave, caves,* and even the far-out *cruives* (Bulloch); cf. scenario offered in notes below.

If *Two Gentlemen* is deemed the least of Shakespeare's plays, the forest scene here is deemed the least of the least. Most commentators consider it so irrelevant and meaningless as to be an embarrassment. Although dispensable in terms of plot exposition, it contributes humorous relief—but then no one ever saw the humor . . . and some may not yet.

A possible scenario is—

The scene opens boisterously with leaping *Outlaws* and a hapless *Valentine* and *Speed.* Almost immediately *Valentine,* ever the naive optimist and certain he can talk his way out of this, pushes

VAL.   I take your offer, and will live with you;
Provided that you do no outrages
On silly women, or poor passengers.
     3rd OUT. No, we detest such vile base practices.
Come, go with us, we'll bring thee to our crews,
And show thee all the treasure we have got,
Which, with ourselves, all rest at thy dispose.

Exeunt.

Speed aside and expansively extends his hand with *My friends—*.
The audience, but not *Valentine*, gets a hint of what is up when one
Outlaw observes *he is a proper man!*

Cocksure of his persuasive powers *Valentine* begins with the
humble appeal of a man of *little wealth* and, alas, *cross'd with
adversity.* Warming to his "pitch" he begins to embellish it with
some sixteen months which would bring a reaction from *Speed*,
which in turn could be noticed by the *Outlaws*; the latter in any
event would recognize a lie when they hear one, and they now
begin to bait *Valentine*.

Trying to win them over by being "one of the boys" he an-
nounces *I killed a man.* The audience hardly has time to catch its
breath before it realizes the *Outlaws*, by their gestures, are taking all
this in the bawdy sense.

Rising to the bait of has he *the tongues*, there is no stopping
him now as he brags about his linguistic skills; the *Outlaws* know
perfectly well that if he knows any language other than Italian it is
Pig Latin. Then, as a bolt from the blue, they decide they will *have
him* and promptly withdraw and go into a huddle.

Scholars have always puzzled over this retreat from stage
center of the *Outlaws*. It seems to be for the dramatic effect of leaving *Valentine* alone stage center in a state of shock as he realizes,
finally, not what he has talked himself out of, but what he has talked
himself into. That he is upset is manifest from his shout at *Speed*.

Upon the *Outlaws'* return he immediately puts his foot in his
mouth again with the bawdy term *fortune*. Then for line after
agonizing line he is silent—more precisely, speechless—as he hears
of a *gentleman* being *stabbed* and the "pettiness" of *such like*
crimes.

Before casting a stone at Elizabethan humor, a question of com-
parative sophistication could be legitimately raised. That sex will

out, even in the absence of sexes, equated in the Elizabethan mind with truth will out. They could have predicted, had today's society been listening, the very prison sex problems that seem to come today as a surprise. But the serious aspect aside, the Elizabethans incorporated the universality of sex into their humor, which universality accounts for much of American humor as well—the cowboy joke: *That's your night in the barrel*; the navy joke: *Never drop your soap*; et al.

And this is the humor behind the subtle humor in *Valentine's* hearing his very own words twisted back upon him— . . . *by your own report a linguist* and *Indeed, because you are a banish'd man.* Finally, with the anguish of a man made an offer he cannot refuse, he agrees . . . provided of course that they *do no outrages.* Who, them? Do outrages? One can almost see their hurt looks at being so misjudged.

But *Valentine's* expression must be the most hurt of all as he is told that somewhere in the deep forests there is not just one or two more outlaws, not just one more crew of them, but——*Exit* ALL.

And so this most "irrelevant" scene comes to a most irreverent end.

MODERN

ACT IV

SCENE 2 — *Milan. Court of the Palace.*

Enter PROTEUS.

PRO.   Already have I been false to Valentine,
And now I must be just as false to Thurio.
Under the pretext of my praising him
I have a chance to further my own love.
But Silvia is too fair, too true, too holy,
For me to influence her with my poor gifts.
When I avow true loyalty to her,
She charges me with falseness to my friend;
And when I hail her beauty with my praise,
She then reminds me of my forsworn pledge
In breaking faith with Julia, whom I loved.
And notwithstanding all her sharp rebuffs—
The least of which would kill a lover's hope—
Yet, like a dog, the more she spurns my love
The more it grows, and fawns upon her still.
But here comes Thurio. Now we'll go to her window
And send some evening music to her ear.

Enter THURIO *and* MUSICIANS.

THU.   Well now, Sir Proteus, did you sneak
            before us?
PRO.   Yes, gentle Thurio, for as you know, love
Will get to where it cannot go.
THU.   Yes, but I hope, sir, that your love's not
            here.
PRO.   Sir, but it is; or else I would be gone.
THU.   Who? Silvia?
PRO.   Yes, Silvia—for your sake.
THU.   I thank you for your own. Now, gentlemen,
Tune up, and play it lustily awhile.

ORIGINAL

ACT IV

SCENE 2 — *Milan. Court of the Palace.*

Enter PROTEUS.

PRO.   Already have I been false to Valentine,
And now I must be as unjust to Thurio.
Under the color of commending him,
I have access my own love to prefer;
But Silvia is too fair, too true, too holy,
To be corrupted with my worthless gifts.
When I protest true loyalty to her,
She twits me with my falsehood to my friend:
When to her beauty I commend my vows,
She bids me think how I have been forsworn
In breaking faith with Julia whom I lov'd:
And, notwithstanding all her sudden quips,
The least whereof would quell a lover's hope,
Yet, spaniel-like, the more she spurns my love,
The more it grows, and fawneth on her still.
But here comes Thurio: now must we to her window,
And give some evening music to her ear.

Enter THURIO *and* MUSICIANS.

THU.   How now, sir Proteus; are you crept before
us?
PRO.   Ay, gentle Thurio; for you know that love
Will creep in service where it cannot go.
THU.   Ay, but I hope, sir, that you love not here.
PRO.   Sir, but I do; or else I would be hence.
THU.   Who? Silvia?
PRO.   Ay, Silvia—for your sake.
THU.   I thank you for your own. Now, gentlemen,
Let's tune, and to it lustily awhile.

NOTES

In the opinion of some the "mini-scenes" within this scene make for such problems of staging as to suggest text cuts, or revisions, etc.; actually, with a little ingenuity several possibilities—all viable—exist.

unjust — dishonest; *color* — false light, pretext; *access* — a way, opportunity; *prefer* — promote; *corrupted* — bribed, influenced; *protest* — attest.

She twits me — because this must have occurred since the time

MODERN

Enter HOST *at a distance, and* JULIA *disguised as a boy.*

HOST.   Now, my young guest! I think you're melancholy. Please tell me, what is it?

JUL.   Indeed, my host, because I cannot be merry.

HOST.   Come, we'll make you merry. I'll bring you where you will hear music and see the gentleman that you asked for.

JUL.   But will I hear him speak?

HOST.   Oh, yes, you will.

JUL.   That will be music.

Music plays.

HOST.   Hark! hark!

JUL.   Is he among these?

HOST.   Yes, but quiet—let's hear 'em.

SONG

Who is Silvia? What is she,
    That all our swains commend her?
Holy, fair, and wise is she,
    The heaven such grace did lend her,
That she might admired be.

that the two were last onstage together, a time compression has been noted here which is, as Arden sees it, "contrary to the time-scheme of the quick-moving plot." It was precisely to keep the plot quick-moving that the playwright compressed the time, using *Proteus'* very own words to effect it.

commend — dedicate; *sudden quips* — rebuffs; *still* — constantly; *crept* — sneaked; *creep . . . go* — crawl . . . walk, from the proverb "love will creep where it cannot go".

ORIGINAL

Enter HOST, *at a distance; and* JULIA,
in boy's clothes.

HOST.   Now, my young guest! methinks you're allycholly; I pray you, why is it?

JUL.   Marry, mine host, because I cannot be merry.

HOST.   Come, we'll have you merry: I'll bring you where you shall hear music, and see the gentleman that you asked for.

JUL.   But shall I hear him speak?

HOST.   Ay, that you shall.

JUL.   That will be music.

Music plays.

HOST.   Hark! hark!

JUL.   Is he among these?

HOST.   Ay: but peace, let's hear 'em.

SONG

Who is Silvia? What is she,
    That all our swains commend her?
Holy, fair, and wise is she,
    The heaven such grace did lend her,
That she might admired be.

Is she kind as she is fair?
　　For beauty lives with kindness:
Love doth to her eyes repair,
　　To help him of his blindness;
And, being helped, inhabits there.

NOTES

allycholly — a fad word for melancholy (not unlike today's fabutastic or fantabulous).

That will be music. — the stage direction *Music plays* has been added to the original script and usually appears just before this line; it should appear right after the line since *Julia* is referring to the

MODERN

Then to Silvia let us sing,
　　That Silvia is excelling;
She excels each mortal thing,
　　Upon the dull earth dwelling:
To her let us garlands bring.

HOST.　What's this? Are you sadder than you were before? How do you feel, man? You do not like the music.

JUL.　You are wrong—the musician does not like me.

HOST.　Why, my pretty youth?

JUL.　He plays false, good sir.

HOST.　How—out of tune on the strings?

JUL.　Not that, and yet so false that he grieves my very heartstrings.

HOST.　You have a keen ear.

JUL.　But I wish I were deaf! It gives me such a heavy heart.

HOST.　I see you don't delight in music.

Is she kind as she is fair?
　　For beauty lives with kindness:
Love doth to her eyes repair,
　　To help him of his blindness;
And, being help'd, inhabits there.

"music" of hearing *Proteus* speak; of course it happens to make an excellent cue for the real music to begin.

　　repair — repair to, go to; *inhabits there* — remains there.

　　Since *Proteus* is undoubtedly the singer here, the impact on *Julia* is enormous because she does not know that he is nominally singing on *Thurio's* behalf.

ORIGINAL

Then to Silvia let us sing,
　　That Silvia is excelling;
She excels each mortal thing,
　　Upon the dull earth dwelling:
To her let us garlands bring.

HOST.　How now? are you sadder than you were before? How do you, man? the music likes you not.

JUL.　　You mistake; the musician likes me not.

HOST.　Why, my pretty youth?

JUL.　　He plays false, father.

HOST.　How? out of tune on the strings?

JUL.　　Not so; but yet so false that he grieves my very heartstrings.

HOST.　You have a quick ear.

JUL.　　Ay, I would I were deaf! it makes me have a slow heart.

HOST.　I perceive you delight not in music.

JUL.　　Not a whit, when it jars so.

HOST.　Hark, what fine change is in the music!

JUL.   Not a bit when it jars so.

HOST.   Hark, what fine change is in the music!

JUL.   Indeed, it is the change that hurts.

HOST.   Would you always have them play but one thing?

JUL.   I would always have one play but one thing. But, host, does this Sir Proteus that we talk of
Often pay visits to this gentlewoman?

HOST.   I'll tell you what Launce, his man, told me; he loves her out of all bounds.

————————

NOTES

likes you not — does not please you; *the musician* — *Proteus*, who plucks the lute and sings by proxy for *Thurio*; *quick* — alert, sharp; *slow heart* — heavy heart; *change* — variation, modulation, with a play on *Proteus'* change to a new love and followed by a similar play on *play*; *talk on* — talk about; *out of all nick* — beyond reckoning (from nicks knifed into wood sticks to keep a tally, especially of drinks imbibed by alehouse clientele).

MODERN

JUL.   Where is Launce?

HOST.   Gone to find his dog, which tomorrow, by his master's command, he must deliver as a present to his lady.

JUL.   Quiet! Stand aside! The group is breaking up.

PRO.   Sir Thurio, do not fear! I'll plead your case, So that you'll say my clever scheme wins all.

THU.   Where shall we meet?

PRO.   At Saint Gregory's well.

THU.   Farewell.

Exit THURIO *and* MUSICIANS.

SILVIA *appears above at her window.*

JUL.   Ay, that change is the spite.

HOST.   You would have them always play but one thing?

JUL.   I would always have one play but one thing.
But, host, doth this sir Proteus, that we talk on,
Often resort unto this gentlewoman?

HOST.   I tell you what Launce, his man, told me;
he loved her out of all nick.

ORIGINAL

JUL.   Where is Launce?

HOST.   Gone to seek his dog; which, tomorrow,
by his master's command, he must carry for a present to
his lady.

JUL.   Peace! stand aside! the company parts.

PRO.   Sir Thurio, fear not you! I will so plead,
That you shall say, my cunning drift excels.

THU.   Where meet we?

PRO.   At Saint Gregory's well.

THU.   Farewell.

            Exeunt THURIO *and* MUSICIANS.

          SILVIA *appears above at her window.*

PRO.   Madam, good evening to your ladyship.

SIL.   I thank you for your music, gentlemen.
Who is that who spoke?

PRO.   Someone who, if you knew his pure heart's
        truth,
You'd quickly learn to know him by his voice.

SIL.   Sir Proteus, as I take it.

PRO.   Sir Proteus, gentle lady, at your service.

SIL.   What's your will?

PRO.   That it be one with yours.

NOTES

Where is Launce? — the Arden edition puzzles over *Julia's* asking about *Launce* since they "have never met in the play". Must they have met "in the play"? Considering that *Proteus* is, or was once, betrothed to her and that *Launce* is his personal servant, one might as well puzzle over whether she has ever seen *Proteus'* shadow since it too is never mentioned in the play. The only question here—since in the *Host's* mind she is not supposed to know *Launce*, a point the commentators have all missed, is whether *Julia's* delivery is a casual *Where is* (this person called) *Launce?* or that of suddenly cupping her mouth for fear of having let a cat out of the bag.

At any rate where is *Launce* indeed? The audience is probably asking that very question, and the dramatist obliges with the *Host's* reply about the dog. The Arden edition criticizes the playwright for

MODERN

SIL.   You have your wish; my will's exactly this—
That now, right now, you hurry home to bed.
You scheming, lying, false, disloyal man!
D'you think I am so simple and so stupid,
To be seduced by all your flattery,
One who's deceived so many with his vows?
Go back, go back, and make up to your love.

PRO.   Madam, good even to your ladyship.

SIL.   I thank you for your music, gentlemen:
Who is that, that spake?

PRO.   One, lady, if you knew his pure heart's
        truth,
You'd quickly learn to know him by his voice.

SIL.   Sir Proteus, as I take it.

PRO.   Sir Proteus, gentle lady, and your servant.

SIL.   What's your will?

PRO.   That I may compass yours.

mentioning this dog event with no explanation and thereby presumably confusing the audience. They comment, "This is, of
course, palpably absurd, and is inexplicable without reference to
what follows."; and they add, ". . . the Host's statement about the
dog is unexplained nonsense until we reach Act IV Scene IV."

Arden, not the bard, is palpably absurd. Why every dog lover
and every *Launce* lover in the theater must have audibly moaned
and sadly "aw"-ed at hearing that *Launce* was going to lose his dog.
Every heart is touched, and what is more, the suspense has risen—
Will *Launce* really lose his dog? In one deft sentence the playwright
has explained *Launce's* absence, aroused sympathy, added to the
suspense, and whetted the appetite for the classic dog episode to
follow.

the company parts — the group parts itself, i.e., breaks up;
drift — scheme; *Saint Gregory's well* — a well really existing out-
side of Milan (per Halliwell); *compass* — encompass, i.e., win.

ORIGINAL

SIL.   You have your wish; my will is even this—
That presently you hie you home to bed.
Thou subtle, perjur'd, false, disloyal man!
Think'st thou, I am so shallow, so conceitless,
To be seduced by thy flattery,
That hast deceiv'd so many with thy vows?
Return, return, and make thy love amends.

For me—by this pale moon above I swear
I am so far from granting your request
That I despise you for your shameful pleas,
And by and by I'll surely hate myself
Even for this time I spend in talking to you.

      PRO.   I grant, sweet love, that I once loved a lady;
But she is dead.

      JUL.   (*Aside*) Had I said so, that's false,
Because I know she is not buried yet.

      SIL.   Say that she is. Yet Valentine, your friend,
Survives—to whom, as you are well aware,
I am betrothed. And are you not ashamed
To wrong him by proposing to his love?

      PRO.   I likewise hear that Valentine is dead.

      SIL.   Then so consider me, for in his grave,
You can be sure, my love is buried too.

NOTES

even — exactly; *presently* — immediately; *thou* — Silvia switches to the familiar form, deprecatory here; *subtle* — crafty; *conceitless* — stupid; *thy love* — i.e., *Julia; pale queen of night* — the moon; *if I should speak it* — even if, etc.; *importunacy* — persistent proposing.

Valentine is dead. — Shakespeare has been nothing short of lambasted for this line. In the New Cambridge edition—"Daniel notes that this lie would lack even the merit of plausibility if the scene took place on the same day as Valentine's banishment." In the Arden edition—"This excuse is so feeble that it reflects from the incompetence of Proteus to that of the dramatist."

The premise of the first complaint is that Shakespeare does not specifically indicate that this scene does *not* take place on the same day as the banishment. Ergo, in some convoluted rationale, it must take place on the same day and therefore lacks "even the merit of plausibility".

Consider: The playwright makes it clear that the day of banishment is past when *Valentine*, in exile, says upon hearing of the proc-

For me—by this pale queen of night I swear,
I am so far from granting thy request,
That I despise thee for thy wrongful suit;
And by and by intend to chide myself,
Even for this time I spend in talking to thee.
    PRO.   I grant, sweet love, that I did love a lady;
But she is dead.
    JUL. (*Aside*) 'T were false, if I should speak it;
For I am sure she is not buried.
    SIL.   Say that she be; yet Valentine, thy friend,
Survives; to whom, thyself art witness,
I am betroth'd: And art thou not asham'd
To wrong him with thy importunacy?
    PRO.   I likewise hear that Valentine is dead.
    SIL.   And so suppose am I; for in his grave
Assure thyself my love is buried.

lamation of banishment—*I have fed upon this woe already, and now excess of it* etc. . . . And again, when he hears that since his banishment *Silvia* has shed tears and wrung her hands in pleading for him . . . And again, when *Thurio* complains that *since his (Valentine's) exile Silvia* has spurned him more than ever . . . And again, when the *Duke* complains that *Silvia persevers* in opposing him.

    Surely the grimiest Elizabethan groundling perceived no time problem with this play. Are the mental limitations of some Shakespearean scholars such that they require a blown-up calendar onstage with a pageboy stage left crossing off the days with crayon "X"'s? And perhaps another page stage right pushing the hands of a huge cardboard clock?

    As to the Arden complaint the terms "feeble" and "incompetency"reflect back not on the dramatist but on Arden. It could not be more obvious that Shakespeare is limning *Proteus* as the consummate cad, the villain to be hissed. If he has betrayed his best friend, abandoned his bethrothed, is now betraying *Thurio*—and, in the process, the *Duke*—and has just lied that *Julia is dead*, why would he not stoop to the lie that *likewise . . . Valentine is dead*? He would be out of character if he told the truth.

MODERN

PRO.   Sweet lady, let me raise it from the earth.

SIL.   Go to your lady's grave and call hers forth;
Or, at the least, in her love bury yours.

JUL.   (*Aside*) He did not hear that.

PRO.   Madame, if your heart be so obdurate,
Yet let me have your picture for my love,
The picture that is hanging in your chamber.
To that I'll speak, to that I'll sigh and weep,
For since the substance of your perfect self
Is elsewhere pledged, then I am but a shadow,
And to your silhouette I'll make true love.

JUL.   (*Aside*) If 't were of substance, you would
            sure deceive it,
And make it but a shadow, as I am.

SIL.   I'm very loathe to be your idol, sir;
But since your falseness makes it fit that you
Should worship shadows and adore false shapes,
Send for it in the morning, and I'll give it—
And so, good night.

PRO.   As good as wretches have,
Who wait all night for morning execution.

Exit PROTEUS *and* SILVIA.

JUL.   Host, shall we go?

HOST.   Ye gods and little fishes, I was fast asleep.

JUL.   Tell me, where does Sir Proteus stay?

HOST.   T' be sure, at my inn. Believe me, I think 't
is almost day.

JUL.   Not yet; but it has been the longest night
I ever spent awake—and saddest, too.

Exeunt.

ORIGINAL

PRO.   Sweet lady, let me rake it from the earth.

SIL.   Go to thy lady's grave, and call hers thence;
Or, at the least, in hers sepulcher thine.

JUL.   (*Aside*) He heard not that.

PRO.   Madame, if your heart be so obdurate,
Vouchsafe me yet your picture for my love,
The picture that is hanging in your chamber;
To that I'll speak, to that I'll sigh and weep:
For, since the substance of your perfect self
Is else devoted, I am but a shadow;
And to your shadow will I make true love.

JUL.   (*Aside*) If 't were a substance, you would,
            sure, deceive it,
And make it but a shadow, as I am.

SIL.   I am very loathe to be your idol, sir;
But, since your falsehood shall become you well
To worship shadows, and adore false shapes,
Send to me in the morning, and I'll send it:
And so, good rest.

PRO.   As wretches have o'er night,
That wait for execution in the morn.

Exeunt PROTEUS; *and* SILVIA, *from above.*

JUL.   Host, will you go?

HOST.   By my halidom, I was fast asleep.

JUL.   Pray you, where lies sir Proteus?

HOST.   Marry, at my house: trust me, I think 't is
almost day.

JUL.   Not so; but it hath been the longest night
That e'er I watch'd, and the most heaviest.

Exeunt.

NOTES

sepulcher — to entomb, bury; *vouchsafe* — grant.

the picture . . . in your chamber — this has raised a question with some anent how *Proteus* knew about the picture. There were so many ways *Proteus* could have come to know about the picture that the question of whether he had been inside her chamber (most unlikely) is not to the point. The request for a picture, repeated and made specific with the one *that is hanging* is simply a device for *Proteus* (and the playwright) to provide for a messenger (*Julia*) to deliver—unbeknownst to *Thurio*—his ring to *Silvia*. For her part, the hope that he will cease to bother her if given a substitute for the real thing is sufficient motivation for giving him the picture.

    else devoted — devoted to someone else; *to your shadow* — to your picture; *shall become you well to worship* — makes it appropriate that you worship; *send to me* — send a messenger to me; *by my halidome* — "holydom", an expletive as mild as "Holy cow!"; *where lies* — where sleeps, stays; *watched* — stayed awake; *most heaviest* — saddest (double superlatives were acceptable then).

MODERN

ACT IV

SCENE 3 — *The same.*

Enter EGLAMOUR.

EGL.   This is the hour that Madame Silvia
Asked me to come, to learn what's on her mind.
There's some great matter she'd engage me in—
Madam, madam!

SILVIA *appears at her window.*

SIL.   Who calls?
EGL.   Your servant, and your friend—
One that awaits your ladyship's command.
SIL.   Sir Eglamour, a thousand times good
            morning.
EGL.   As many, worthy lady, to yourself.
According to your ladyship's request,
I came here early just to learn what service
It is your pleasure to command me in.
SIL.   Oh Eglamour, you are a gentleman—
Don't think I flatter you; I swear I do not—
Valiant, wise, and tender, well accomplished.
You are aware, I'm sure, of all the love
That I hold for the banished Valentine;
And how my father would demand I marry
Fool Thurio, whom my very soul abhorred.
Yourself, you've loved. And I-have heard you say,
No grief did ever come so near your heart
As when your lady, your one true love, died,
Upon whose grave you vowed pure chastity.
Sir Eglamour, I must find Valentine,
In Mantua where, I hear, he makes his home.
And since the roads are dangerous to pass,
I do desire your able company—
It's on your faith and honor I depend.

ORIGINAL

ACT IV

SCENE 3 — *The same.*

Enter EGLAMOUR.

EGL.   This is the hour that madam Silvia
Entreated me to call, and know her mind;
There's some great matter she'd employ me in—
Madam, madam!

SILVIA *appears above, at her window.*

SIL.   Who calls?
EGL.   Your servant, and your friend;
One that attends your ladyship's command.
SIL.   Sir Eglamour, a thousand times good
            morrow.
EGL.   As many, worthy lady, to yourself.
According to your ladyship's impose,
I am thus early come, to know what service
It is your pleasure to command me in.
SIL.   O Eglamour, thou art a gentleman,
(Think not I flatter, for I swear I do not)
Valiant, wise, remorseful, well accomplish'd.
Thou art not ignorant what dear good will
I bear unto the banish'd Valentine;
Nor how my father would enforce me marry
Vain Thurio, whom my very soul abhorr'd.
Thyself hast lov'd; and I have heard thee say,
No grief did ever come so near thy heart
As when thy lady and thy true love died,
Upon whose grave thou vow'dst pure chastity.
Sir Eglamour, I would to Valentine,
To Mantua, where, I hear, he makes abode;
And, for the ways are dangerous to pass,
I do desire thy worthy company,
Upon whose faith and honor I repose.

COMMENTS

The purpose of Scene 3 is to provide the tension of anticipation; the following long Scene 4, thanks to *Silvia's* plans being
revealed here, does not then bog down.

Nevertheless the valid question of "Does the play really need
Eglamour?" arises. Since nobody is a stickler for detail in a comedy
of this type *Silvia* could have enlisted the friar to accompany her, or
perhaps borrowed a monk's habit disguise from him, all in the
space of a half dozen lines. Further, the scene's function of providing anticipation would not have suffered.

But there seems something in Sir Eglamour which does not
meet the reader's eye, yet does not escape the audience. Since he is
probably as young as the other blades in the play, it is likely that he
is as untrustworthy and lecherous as any of them. His indicating
this, easily accomplished given his lines, and with *Silvia* thinking
him a chaste gentleman in mourning, could produce a humorous
suspense over what is going to happen when they are alone in the
forest. Such a dramatist's comment on those who swear everlasting
celibacy upon the death of a loved one would certainly be in the
spirit of this satire on Love.

MODERN

Don't argue that my father will be angry,
But think about my grief, a lady's grief;
And on the rightness of my leaving here,
To keep me from a most unholy match,
Which always Heaven and fate afflict with plagues.
I do so want you, from this very heart,
As full with sorrows as the sea with sands,
To keep me company and go with me—
If not, hold secret what I've said to you,
So I may leave and travel on my own.
    EGL.   Madam, I have great pity for your grief,
And since I know that you are not to blame,
I give my word to go along with you,
As fearless of the consequence to me
As I am hopeful of the benefit to you.
When shall you go?

NOTES

The Sir Eglamour here is not the same as that of Act I; the latter was in a different city, was a suitor to *Julia*, and accordingly hardly a man who had "*vowd'st pure chastity*". Yet as recently as 1957 Munro's edition in a kind of retrogressive scholarship observes, if that is the word for it: "There are two Eglamours, Julia's admirer (I ii 9) and Silvia's escort (or are they the same?)".

know her mind — learn what is on her mind.

a thousand times good morrow — the Arden edition notes: "We have met this language before, at Act II, Scene I, 91 – 4, and again it is difficult to believe that, on the dramatist's part, it is wholly serious." What is difficult to believe is that Arden is serious.

impose — request; *remorseful* — knowing remorse, i.e., emphathetic; *vain* — foolish; *I would to* — I wish to go to; *repose* — depend.

ORIGINAL

Urge not my father's anger, Eglamour,
But think upon my grief, a lady's grief;
And on the justice of my flying hence,
To keep me from a most unholy match,
Which Heaven and fortune still reward with plagues.
I do desire thee, even from a heart
As full of sorrows as the sea of sands,
To bear me company, and go with me:
If not, to hide what I have said to thee,
That I may venture to depart alone.
    EGL.   Madam, I pity much your grievances;
Which since I know they virtuously are plac'd,
I give consent to go along with you;
Recking as little what betideth me
As much I wish all good befortune you.
When will you go?

SIL.   This very evening.

EGL.   Where should I meet you?

SIL.   At Friar Patrick's cell,
Where I intend holy confession.

EGL.   I will not fail your ladyship.
Good day now, gentle lady.

SIL.   Good day now, kind sir Eglamour.

Exeunt.

NOTES

urge not — argue not; *still* — ever; *rewards* — punishes; *even* — especially; *sea of sands* — sea is full of sands; *grievances* — troubles; *virtuously are plac'd* — precisely because you are virtuous they are placed in motion, i.e., virtue has troubles just in maintaining itself; *recking* — caring; *betideth* — befalls; *good befortune you* — be your good fortune.

SIL.   This evening coming.
EGL.   Where shall I meet you?
SIL.   At friar Patrick's cell,
Where I intend holy confession.
EGL.   I will not fail your ladyship:
Good morrow, gentle lady.
SIL.   Good morrow, kind sir Eglamour.

Exeunt.

MODERN

ACT IV

SCENE 4 — *The same.*

Enter LAUNCE *with his* DOG.

LAUN.   When a man's best friend plays the cur with him, mind you, it goes hard. One that I brought up from a puppy; one that I saved from drowning when three or four of his blind brothers and sisters went to it! I have taught him—indeed as one would say with no exaggeration, *Thus I would teach a dog.* I was sent to deliver him as a present to Mistress Silvia from my master; and I no sooner came into the dining chamber but he runs ahead to her plate and steals her capon's leg. Oh, it's a foul thing when a cur cannot contain himself in all groups. I would seem to have, as one might say, one that takes upon himself to be a dog indeed, to be, as it were, a dog at all things. If I had not had more sense than he, to take the blame upon myself for what he did, I think truly he would have been hanged for it; sure as I live he would have suffered for it—but you can judge. He thrusts himself on me into the company of three or four gentlemanlike dogs under the duke's table; he had not been there, pardon the expression, a pissing while when all the chamber smelled him. *Out with the dog*, says one. *What cur is that?* says another. *Whip him out*, says a third. *Hang him up*, says the Duke. I, having been acquainted with the smell before, knew it was Crab, and I go to the fellow who was whipping the dogs. *Friend*, says I, *You mean to whip the dog! I'll say I do*, says he. *You do him the more wrong*, says I; *it was I who did the thing you noticed.*

ORIGINAL

ACT IV

SCENE 4 — *The same.*

Enter LAUNCE *with his* DOG.

LAUN. When a man's servant shall play the cur with him, look you, it goes hard: one that I brought up of a puppy; one that I saved from drowning, when three or four of his blind brothers and sisters went to it! I have taught him—even as one would say precisely, *Thus I would teach a dog.* I was sent to deliver him, as a present to mistress Silvia, from my master; and I came no sooner into the dining chamber, but he steps me to her trencher and steals her capon's leg. O, 't is a foul thing when a cur cannot keep himself in all companies. I would have, as one should say, one that takes upon him to be a dog indeed, to be, as it were, a dog at all things. If I had not had more wit than he, to take a fault upon me that he did, I think verily he had been hanged for 't; sure as I live he had suffer'd for 't: you shall judge. He thrusts me himself into the company of three or four gentlemanlike dogs, under the duke's table: he had not been there (bless the mark!) a pissing while, but all the chamber smelt him. *Out with the dog,* says one; *What cur is that?* says another; *Whip him out,* says a third; *Hang him up,* says the duke. I, having been acquainted with the smell before, knew it was Crab; and goes me to the fellow that whips the dogs: *Friend,* quoth I, *you mean to whip the dog. Ay, marry, do I,* quoth he. *You do him the more wrong,* quoth I; *'t was I did the thing you wot of.*

COMMENTS

The *Launce* episode here is the last interlude. From this point on the play is essentially a rush of events to its climax and denouement.

———————

NOTES

The New Cambridge, here using a stopwatch, is disturbed that several unaccounted-for hours have elapsed between *Eglamour's* departure in the previous scene and *Launce's* entrance. Who cares? Besides, do not *Launce's* lines humorously give account for part of the unaccounted-for time?

But if the New Cambridge sees nothing in the lines, another commentator—J. Vyvyan—sees a great deal between the lines. Indeed, he sees the whole play as one grand allegory where everything takes on a significance which the audience never dreamt of. Thus—

"Crab is little better than 'ingrateful man'—and, incidentally, most undoglike. His resemblance to Proteus is remarkable."

MODERN

He makes no further ado, but whips me out of the chamber. How many masters would do this for his servant? No, I'll swear, I have sat in the stocks for sausages he has stolen, otherwise he had been executed. I have stood on the pillory for geese he has killed, otherwise he had suffered for it. You don't think of this now!—No, I remember the trick you played me when I took my leave of madam Silvia; didn't I tell you to always heed me, and do as I do? When did you see me lift up my leg and make water against a gentlewoman's hoop skirt? Did you ever see me do such a trick?

Enter PROTEUS *and* JULIA.

PRO.   Sebastian is your name. I like you well,
And will employ you in some service very soon.
JUL.   In what you wish. I'll do what I can.

Proteus, too, in his present phase, is being 'a dog in all things', he, too, has thrust himself into the company of gentlemanlike dogs around the duke's table, and misbehaved there; and he would have stolen more from Silvia, had he been able, than a capon's leg."

This is not scholarship so much as it is an attempt to read Shake-speare's subconscious, or at least his mind, and since the subject is deceased it takes on the aspect of an unintendedly amusing literary seance.

   even — truly; *steps me* — outsteps me, runs ahead; *trencher* — plate; *keep himself* — behave himself; *take upon him* — takes upon himself, i.e., presumes; *a dog* — also means an expert; *bless the mark* — common phrase equivalent here to the modern "excuse the expression", although the following *pissing-while* was merely slang for "a short time" and not the vulgarism then that it would be today; *fellow that whips* — probably the *Duke's* kennel keeper; *wot of* — know of.

ORIGINAL

He makes me no more ado, but whips me out of the chamber. How many masters would do this for his ser-vant? Nay, I'll be sworn, I have sat in the stocks for pud-dings he hath stolen, otherwise he had been executed: I have stood on the pillory for geese he hath killed, other-wise he had suffered for 't: thou think'st not of this now! —Nay, I remember the trick you served me when I took my leave of madam Silvia; did not I bid thee still mark me, and do as I do? When didst thou see me heave up my leg, and make water against a gentlewoman's far-thingale? didst thou ever see me do such a trick?

Enter PROTEUS *and* JULIA.

PRO.   Sebastian is thy name. I like thee well,
And will employ thee in some service presently.
   JUL.   In what you please. I'll do what I can.

PRO.   I hope you will.

(*To* LAUNCE) Well now, you whoreson peasant!

Where have you been these two days' loitering?

LAUN.   Indeed, sir, I brought Mistress Silvia the dog as you told me.

PRO.   And what does she say about my little jewel?

LAUN.   The truth is she says your dog was a cur, and tells you currish thanks is good enough for such a present.

PRO.   But she received my dog?

LAUN.   No, indeed, she did not—Here, see, I brought him back again.

PRO.   What! Did you offer her this from me?

NOTES

stocks — locking in of the legs, usually a milder punishment than *pillory* — locking in of the hands and neck; *puddings* — sausages.

took my leave of madam Silvia — one scholar (Warburton)

MODERN

LAUN.   Yes, sir, the other squirrel was stolen from me by the chicken hawker's boys in the marketplace; and then I offered her my own, who is a dog as big as ten of yours—and therefore a gift all the greater.

PRO.   Go, get away and find my dog again,

Or never come again within my sight.

Away, I say. Do you stay out of spite!

Exit LAUNCE.

PRO.   I hope thou wilt.

        (*To* LAUNCE) How now, you whoreson peasant,
Where have you been these two days loitering?

    LAUN.   Marry, sir, I carried mistress Silvia the dog you bade me.

    PRO.   And what says she to my little jewel?

    LAUN.   Marry, she says, your dog was a cur; and tells you, currish thanks is good enough for such a present.

    PRO.   But she received my dog?

    LAUN.   No, indeed, did she not: here have I brought him back again.

    PRO.   What, didst thou offer her this from me?

---

emended this to *Julia*, which change is seconded by the New Cambridge edition—". . . since at any rate on the occasion of which Launce has just been speaking 'the fellow that whips the dogs' allowed him no opportunity for taking formal leave of Silvia." Who ever said that *Launce's* leave-taking was formal? Not Shakespeare.

    still mark me — ever heed me; *farthingale* — hoop skirt; *presently* — shortly.

ORIGINAL

    LAUN.   Ay, sir, the other squirrel was stolen from me by the hangman's boys in the marketplace: and then I offered her mine own; who is a dog as big as ten of yours, and therefore the gift the greater.

    PRO.   Go, get thee hence, and find my dog again,
Or ne'er return again into my sight.
Away, I say: Stay'st thou to vex me here?

                      Exit LAUNCE.

A scamp who without end makes me ashamed . . .
Sebastian, I've engaged your services
Partly since I have need of such as you,
Who can with some discretion do my business,
For there's no trusting of that foolish lout.
But chiefly for your face and your behavior,
Which—if my estimate should be correct—
Bespeaks good bringing up, success, and truth.
So now you know the reason I employ you.
Go right away, and take this ring with you.
Deliver it to Madam Silvia . . .
She loved me well—who gave it once to me.

     JUL.   It seems you loved her not—to leave this
                go.
Is she dead, perhaps?
     PRO.   Not so. I think she lives.
     JUL.   Oh, no!
     PRO.   Why do you cry—*Oh, no!*
     JUL.   I cannot help but pity her.
     PRO.   And why should you pity her?

NOTES

squirrel — *Launce's* appellation for a fancy dog (alluding to a quixotic fancy of some ladies then to make pets of squirrels—cf. Marshall); *hangman* — a term applied then to anyone contemptible, but here it is a taunt which, being such an implausible explanation, amounts to a refusal to explain.

then I offered her my own — it would appear that here, finally, the critics have the "reviser" where they want him (or Shakespeare —out of embarrassment—where they do not want him). The problem—(1) *Launce* earlier told the *Host* that *Proteus* ordered him to give *Crab* to *Silvia* (2) he subsequently told the audience, in his monologue, the very same thing and (3) now it turns out that *Proteus* gave him an altogether different dog to present to *Silvia*. Arden, using its favorite words again, notes that *Launce's* earlier statement in the monologue ". . . is palpably absurd and is contradicted by what we hear later . . ."

A slave, that still an end turns me to shame.
Sebastian, I have entertained thee,
Partly, that I have need of such a youth,
That can with some discretion do my business,
For 't is no trusting to yon foolish lout;
But, chiefly, for thy face and thy behavior;
Which (if my augury deceive me not)
Witness good bringing up, fortune, and truth.
Therefore know thee, for this I entertain thee.
Go presently, and take this ring with thee,
Deliver it to madam Silvia:
She lov'd me well, deliver'd it to me.
       JUL.   It seems you lov'd not her to leave her
                 token:
She is dead, belike?
       PRO.   Not so; I think she lives.
       JUL.   Alas!
       PRO.   Why dost thou cry, *alas!*
       JUL.   I cannot choose but pity her.
       PRO.   Wherefore shouldst thou pity her?

What the critics overlook, and what is the key, is when *Launce* looks *Proteus* right in the eye and tells that self-same bald lie— *Marry, sir, I carried mistress Silvia the dog you bade me*—knowing full well that *Proteus* knows full well that *Crab* was not the dog to be delivered. Moreover, the audience is instantly puzzled because if *Launce* took *Crab* to *Silvia* how could the big mutt be sitting now, as big as life, onstage? And when *Proteus* now refers to his *little jewel*, the puzzlement only increases. But when *Launce* relates *your dog was a cur*, then everyone—including *Proteus*— suspects the worst. Then *Proteus*, fearful now, asks, *But she received MY dog?* With that the audience, if not *Proteus*, knows all; and with *here have I brought him back again*, *Proteus* knows all.

A miniature denouement follows in which the spectators learn of the other dog. But when *Launce* uses the *hangman's boys* as his excuse, they would have caught their breath, for such a bold mock went far beyond the impertinency allowed a servant. They realized that this was *Launce's* swan song from his indenture to *Proteus*.

Also, there was the realization now that *Launce* never intended to deliver the *little jewel*, that all along he intended to embarrass *Proteus* by presenting *Crab*. The action here then did not result from a plot contrivance, such as the alleged theft of the *little jewel*; the action, all of it, flowed from *Launce's* character.

As *Speed* had done earlier, *Launce* here confronted the villain of the piece and won a triumph of sorts. His obviously delayed exit (*Stay'st thou to vex me here?*) could easily have been to accommodate a rousing ovation for him . . . and *Crab*.

MODERN

JUL.   Because, I think that she loved you as well
As you do love your lady, Silvia.
She dreams of him who has forgot her love;
You dote on her who cares not for your love.
What pity, love should be so contrary.
And just the thought—it makes me cry, *Oh, no!*

PRO.   Well, give her that ring and there, with that,
This letter. That's her chamber. Tell my lady
I claim her promise of her heavenly picture.
Your errand done, then speed back to my quarters,
Where you will find me, sad and solitary.

Exit PROTEUS.

JUL.   How many women would run such an
        errand?
Ah you, poor Proteus! You have here employed
A fox to be the shepherd of your lambs.
Ah me, poor fool! Why do I pity him
Who with his very heart despises me?
Because he loves her, he despises me;
Because I love him, I must pity him.
This ring I gave him, when he parted from me,
To keep him from forgetting my deep love—
And here am I—unhappy messenger—
To plead for that which I don't want to get,
To offer that which I hope is refused,

still an end — on without end; *witness good bringing-up* —
serve as witness to good bringing-up; *entertain* — retain, employ;
She . . . me — "who" is understood between *well* and *deliver'd*;
leave her token — leave go with, i.e., part with her ring; *belike* —
perhaps.

ORIGINAL

JUL. Because, methinks, that she lov'd you as
    well
As you do love your lady Silvia:
She dreams on him that has forgot her love;
You dote on her that cares not for your love.
'T is pity, love should be so contrary;
And thinking on it makes me cry, alas!
  PRO. Well, give her that ring, and therewithal
This letter—that's her chamber—Tell my lady,
I claim the promise for her heavenly picture.
Your message done, hie home unto my chamber,
Where thou shalt find me, sad and solitary.

    Exit PROTEUS.

JUL. How many women would do such a
    message?
Alas, poor Proteus! thou hast entertain'd
A fox, to be the shepherd of thy lambs:
Alas, poor fool! why do I pity him
That with his very heart despiseth me?
Because he loves her, he despiseth me;
Because I love him, I must pity him.
This ring I gave him, when he parted from me,
To bind him to remember my good will:
And now am I (unhappy messenger)
To plead for that, which I would not obtain:
To carry that, which I would have refus'd;

To pledge his faith, which I would wish unpledged.
I am my master's true betrothed in love,
But cannot be true servant to my master,
Unless I prove false traitor to myself.
Yet I shall woo for him, but yet so coldly
That, Heaven knows, I hope he won't succeed.

NOTES

dreams on — dotes on; *message* — errand; *poor fool* — *Julia*,
herself; *would . . . would . . . would* — would like to; *true confirmed* — betrothed; *speed* — succeed.

MODERN

Enter SYLVIA *and* ATTENDANTS.

Gentlewoman, good day! I humbly ask you, please,
To let me see and speak with Madam Silvia.

SIL.   What do you want with her, if I am she?

JUL.   If you are she, then I request your patience
To hear me state the errand I've been sent on.

SIL.   From whom?

JUL.   From my master, Sir Proteus, madam.

SIL.   Oh! He sent you for a picture?

JUL.   Yes, madam.

SIL.   Ursula, bring my picture there.

(Picture brought.)

Go, give your master this. Tell him, from me—
One Julia that his changing mind forgets,
Would better fit his quarters than this image.

JUL.   Madam, please would you read this letter—
Pardon me, madam, inadvertently
I've given you a paper that I should not—
This is the letter to your ladyship.

To praise his faith, which I would have disprais'd.
I am my master's true confirmed love;
But cannot be true servant to my master,
Unless I prove false traitor to myself.
Yet will I woo for him; but yet so coldly,
As, Heaven it knows, I would not have him speed.

ORIGINAL

Enter SILVIA *and* ATTENDANTS.

Gentlewoman, good day! I pray you, be my mean
To bring me where to speak with madam Silvia.

SIL.   What would you with her, if that I be she?

JUL.   If you be she, I do entreat your patience
To hear me speak the message I am sent on.

SIL.   From whom?

JUL.   From my master, sir Proteus, madam.

SIL.   O!—he sends you for a picture?

JUL.   Ay, madam.

SIL.   Ursula, bring my picture there.

(*Picture brought*)

Go, give your master this: tell him, from me,
One Julia, that his changing thoughts forget,
Would better fit his chamber, than this shadow.

JUL.   Madam, please you peruse this letter—
Pardon me, madam; I have, unadvis'd
Deliver'd you a paper that I should not:
This is the letter to your ladyship.

SIL.   I beg you, let me look at that again.

JUL.   That I can't do. Good madam, pardon me.

SIL.   There, hold.

I will not look upon your master's words.
I know that they are stuffed with declamations,
And full of thought up vows which he will break
As easily as I now tear his letter.

JUL.   Madam, he sends your ladyship this ring.

SIL.   That much more shame that he sends it to
me;

For I have heard him say a thousand times—
His Julia gave it to him when he left.
Though his false finger has defiled the ring,
Mine will not do his Julia such a wrong.

COMMENTS

The inevitable meeting of *Julia* and *Silvia* draws Act IV to a close and marks the beginning of the end for the villain of the plot. It is the first reversal in *Proteus'* evil scheme. Although his chances for success with *Silvia* were slim all along, *Julia* renders them null and void.

In this exchange it becomes clear that Shakespeare has given all the brains of his comedy to the women. *Julia* is *Proteus'* undoing when she "inadvertently" shows *Silvia* one of her own love letters from him (see *Notes*). It is presumably full of the same old "line" that he has been trying to feed *Silvia*.

It is also here where *Silvia's* suspicion that the "youth" is perhaps in truth *Julia* takes hold, a suspicion which will turn gradually and delightfully into a final recognition. The recognition, however, remains shrewdly tacit between the two.

NOTES

mean — means; *where to speak* — where I may speak; *shadow* — picture; *unadvis'd* — inadvertently.

The "wrong" letter which *Julia* "inadvertently" gives to *Silvia* has become a mystery letter of sorts to Shakespearean authorities.

SIL.   I pray thee, let me look on that again.

JUL.   It may not be; good madam, pardon me.

SIL.   There, hold.

I will not look upon your master's lines:
I know they are stuff'd with protestations,
And full of new-found oaths; which he will break,
As easily as I do tear his paper.

JUL.   Madam, he sends your ladyship this ring.

SIL.   The more shame for him that he sends it me;

For, I have heard him say a thousand times,
His Julia gave it him at his departure:
Though his false finger have profan'd the ring,
Mine shall not do his Julia so much wrong.

Brooks conjectured that it is the same letter *Julia* previously tore up (in Act I) and restored somehow by patching; why she would use that very first letter from *Proteus* when she undoubtedly received many subsequent letters from him Brooks does not explain.

The mystery only deepens when commentators try to explain the sequence of events in the light of *Silvia's, There, hold.* At this point, some (Bond, Capell) say, *Silvia* gives back the first letter; but Arden notes that in view of *Silvia's* previous, *let me look on that again*, "it is difficult to believe that she had it then in her possession." Arden then points out that *Silvia* could have taken it back a second time from *Julia* . . .

"   . . . and give it back again at *There, hold.* But it would be very confusing to an audience to have letters passed over-frequently between the two girls: the words (*There, hold*) seem to indicate rather that Silvia is about to return the second letter, but then decides to tear it (first?)."

. . . And so the commentators haggle on.

No one seems to see a very simple explanation which is obvious the moment one gives the two girls the same credit for intelligence that the dramatist did. *Julia* clearly wants to expose *Proteus* for the fickle, false lover he is by showing *Silvia* one of his flowery, impassioned love letters to her, *Julia*; yet she must do this accidentally on purpose in the role of "Sebastian".

So when *Julia* snatches back the "wrong" letter she is apparently in no great rush to whisk it out of sight. *Silvia*, upon being "denied" the return of the letter, nevertheless sees it still open to view. Understanding, and understanding that *Julia* understands, she says—*There, hold. Julia* obligingly does so—her conscience being "cleared" with the snatching back of the letter she knew she was not supposed to deliver in the first place.

With it now dangling from *Julia's* hand, *Silvia* proceeds to read the whole letter, which is presumably chock full of the same declamatory oaths and platitudes as she has been hearing from *Proteus* all along. Then, knowing without knowing what is in her own letter from *Proteus*, she tears it to shreds; and her rejection of the ring becomes a bygone conclusion.

MODERN

JUL.   She thanks you.

SIL.   What did you say?

JUL.   I thank you that you sympathize with her.
Poor gentlewoman! My master does her wrong.

SIL.   Do you know her?

JUL.   Almost as well as I do know myself.
To think about her woes! I do declare
That I have wept a hundred different times.

SIL.   It seems she thinks that Proteus has
            forsook her.

JUL.   I think she does, and that's her cause for
            sorrow.

SIL.   Is she not beautiful?

JUL.   She once was more so, madam, than she is.
When she believed my master loved her true,
She, in my judgment, was as fair as you.
Since then she has not used her looking-glass,
And threw her sun-protecting mask away;
The wind has blown the roses from her cheeks,
And stippl'd the lily-whiteness of her face,
Till now she has become as dark as I.

SIL.   How tall was she?

One aspect of *Silvia's* rejection of the ring—*For I have heard him say a thousand times/His Julia gave it him at his departure*—troubles some authorities. Arden for one notes—"As Proteus loved Silvia at first sight, it is difficult to believe that he would talk about Julia in Silvia's presence 'a thousand times'."

Instead of concentrating on the hyperbole, Arden could have and should have observed that it is almost a certainty that *Proteus* never even so much as once talked about this ring to *Silvia*. Arden simply does not see what any audience would not fail to see—that this five line speech of *Silvia*, properly delivered, is proof positive that she has begun to suspect *Julia's* true identity. *Julia*, too, understands this and enters into the just-between-us-girls identity game that follows.

ORIGINAL

JUL.   She thanks you.

SIL.   What say'st thou?

JUL.   I thank you, madam, that you tender her:
Poor gentlewoman! my master wrongs her much.

SIL.   Dost thou know her?

JUL.   Almost as well as I do know myself:
To think upon her woes I do protest
That I have wept a hundred several times.

SIL.   Belike, she thinks that Proteus hath
        forsook her.

JUL.   I think she doth, and that's her cause of
        sorrow.

SIL.   Is she not passing fair?

JUL.   She hath been fairer, madam, than she is:
When she did think my master lov'd her well,
She, in my judgment, was as fair as you;
But since she did neglect her looking-glass,
And threw her sun-expelling mask away,
The air hath starv'd the roses in her cheeks,
And pinch'd the lily-tincture of her face,
That now she is become as black as I.

SIL.   How tall was she?

NOTES

tender her — have a tender spot for her; *Dost thou know her?* — that *Silvia* never follows this up with "how" suggests she is "on to" *Julia; protest* — attest; *several* — different; *belike* — seemingly; *passing* — surpassingly; *mask* — sun shade.

MODERN

JUL.   About my own height, for at Pentecost,
When all our gala pageants then were played,
Some there got me to play the woman's part.
And I was dressed in Madam Julia's gown,
Which fitted me as well—they all did say so—
As if the dress had just been made for me.
That's how I know she is about my height.
And, at that time, I made her weep so much,
Because I played a very tragic part.
Madam, 't was that of Ariadne's sobs
For Theseus' treachery and hurting her,
Which I so lifelike acted with my tears
That my poor mistress, moved so by it all
Wept painfully—and strike me dead right now,
If I had not felt all her selfsame sorrow!

SIL.   She is indebted to you, gentle youth!
Oh, that poor lady! Desolate and left!
I weep, myself, just thinking of her words.
Here, youth, there is my purse. I give you this
For your sweet mistress' sake; because you love her.
Farewell.

NOTES

Pentecost — seventh Sunday after Easter, i.e., early summer festival time; *trimm'd* — dressed up; *a-good* — aplenty; *lamentable* — tragic.
Ariadne — the maiden who helped Theseus kill the Minotaur

pinch'd — many interpretations given, but it appears to simply mean windburn, i.e., a reddening not dissimilar from that of being pinched; *black* — dark from sunburn and windburn.

ORIGINAL

JUL.   About my stature: for, at Pentecost,
When all our pageants of delight were play'd,
Our youth got me to play the woman's part,
And I was trimm'd in madam Julia's gown;
Which served me as fit, by all men's judgments,
As if the garment had been made for me:
Therefore, I know she is about my height.
And, at that time, I made her weep a-good,
For I did play a lamentable part;
Madam, 't was Ariadne, passioning
For Theseus' perjury and unjust flight;
Which I so lively acted with my tears,
That my poor mistress, moved therewithal,
Wept bitterly; and would I might be dead,
If I in thought felt not her very sorrow!
SIL.   She is beholding to thee, gentle youth!
Alas, poor lady! desolate and left!
I weep myself to think upon her words.
Here, youth, there is my purse: I give thee this
For thy sweet mistress' sake, because thou lov'st her.
Farewell.

monster and escape from the labyrinth, and whose thanks was to be abandoned by him on an island; *passioning/For* — grieving over; *unjust* — betraying.

my poor mistress — some scholars quibble that nowhere previously did "Sebastian" say he served a mistress; "mistress" is not restricted to someone with servants, and the phrase here merely means the lady in question; in like vein *Silvia*—knowingly—

echoes *sweet mistress*; and again later, when *Julia* is alone and need not pretend she is a servant, she similarly refers to *my mistress*, meaning herself, a lady.

beholding — beholden; *purse* — in Elizabethan times a tip to a messenger was one thing, while a purse of money, purse and all,

MODERN

JUL.   And she will thank you for 't, if e'er you
        meet her.

Exit SILVIA.

A virtuous gentlewoman, mild and beautiful.
I hope my master's efforts will all fail,
For she respects my mistress' love so much.
So sad, how love can trifle with itself!
Here is her picture. Let me see—I think
If my hair were so styled, this face of mine
Were just as lovely as is this of hers . . .
And yet the painter flattered her a little,
Unless I'm flattering myself too much.
Her hair is auburn, mine is fully yellow;
If that makes all the difference in his love
I'll get myself an auburn colored wig.
Her eyes are silv'ry blue—and so are mine.
Yes, but her forehead's low, and mine's as high.
What can it be that he must see in her
That I could not make him to see in me,
If foolish love were not so blind a force?
Come, shadow, come, and take this image on,
For it's your rival. Oh, you senseless form—
You will be worshipped, kissed, loved, and adored!
If there were sense in his idolatry,
I'd carve myself in stone and take your place.
I'll treat you kindly for your mistress' sake,

was unheard of; an expensive gift from one gentlewoman to another, however, would be normal; and *Silvia*—aware now of *Julia's* identity—knowing *Julia* to be away from home and her accustomed comforts, perhaps feels she can use the money, which, since *Julia* accepts the purse, is probably the case.

ORIGINAL

JUL.   And she shall thank you for 't, if e'er you
know her.

Exit SILVIA.

A virtuous gentlewoman, mild, and beautiful.
I hope my master's suit will be but cold,
Since she respects my mistress' love so much.
Alas, how love can trifle with itself!
Here is her picture: let me see; I think,
If I had such a tire this face of mine
Were full as lovely as is this of hers:
And yet the painter flatter'd her a little,
Unless I flatter with myself too much.
Her hair is auburn, mine is perfect yellow:
If that be all the difference in his love,
I'll get me such a color'd periwig.
Her eyes are gray as glass; and so are mine:
Ay, but her forehead's low, and mine's as high.
What should it be, that he respects in her,
But I can make respective in myself,
If this fond love were not a blinded god?
Come, shadow, come, and take this shadow up,
For 't is thy rival. O thou senseless form,
Thou shalt be worshipp'd, kiss'd, lov'd, and ador'd;
And, were there sense in his idolatry,
My substance should be statue in thy stead.
I'll use thee kindly for thy mistress' sake,

As she did me—or else, by heav'n above,
I would have scratched out your unseeing eyes,
To make my master lose his love of you!

Exit.

COMMENTS

The act ends with what in today's theater would be a lighting man's dream—a charming "shadow" metaphor delivered with *Julia* alone on stage, reminiscent of her earlier paper-doll soliloquy.

NOTES

cold — unsuccessful; *tire* — headdress; *flatter with* — flatter; *gray as glass* — blue (cf. Malone, also Knight); *high* — high

That used me so; or else, by Jove I vow,
I should have scratch'd out your unseeing eyes,
To make my master out of love with thee!

Exit.

foreheads were greatly admired then; *respects* — esteems; *respective* — worthy of esteem; *fond Love* — foolish Love.

come, shadow — probably delivered as she looks at her onstage shadow (real or make-believe); *and take this shadow up* — referring to *Silvia's* picture; *O thou senseless form* — again, and in all remaining lines, *Silvia's* portrait.

My substance . . . stead — I would displace this picture by becoming, myself, a lifeless object of worship.

your unseeing eyes — Hanmer suggests *thy* for *your* to be consistent with the animus conveyed by the use of this familiar form in the lines before and after; perhaps *your* was used here so as not to detract form the power of the final word of the act—*thee!*

ACT V

SCENE 1 — *The same. An Abbey.*

Enter EGLAMOUR.

EGL.   The sun begins to gild the western sky;
And now it is about the very hour
That Silvia, at Friar Patrick's cell, should meet me.
She will be here, for lovers don't break dates—
If anything, they come before the time,
So eager are they to speed up their pace.

Enter SILVIA.

See, there she comes . . . Lady, a happy evening!
SIL.   Amen, amen! . . . Move on, good Eglamour,
Out through the back door by the abbey wall—
I fear that I've been followed by some spies.
EGL.   Fear not—the forest is not nine miles off.
If we can reach it, we are safe enough.

Exeunt.

NOTES

hours — appointments; *spur their expedition* — quicken their pace; *amen!* — probably loud, in case someone is listening, followed by hushed tones; *postern* — small door at side or rear; *attended* — followed; *league* — about three miles; *recover* — reach; *sure* — safe.

ORIGINAL

ACT V

SCENE 1 — *The same. An Abbey.*

Enter EGLAMOUR.

EGL.   The sun begins to gild the western sky;
And now it is about the very hour
That Silvia, at friar Patrick's cell, should meet me.
She will not fail; for lovers break not hours,
Unless it be to come before their time;
So much they spur their expedition.

Enter SILVIA.

See where she comes: Lady, a happy evening!
SIL.   Amen, amen! go on, good Eglamour,
Out at the postern by the abbey wall;
I fear I am attended by some spies.
EGL.   Fear not; the forest is not three leagues off:
If we recover that, we are sure enough.

Exeunt.

MODERN

ACT V

SCENE 2 — *The same. A room in the* DUKE'S *Palace.*

Enter THURIO, PROTEUS, *and* JULIA.

THU.   Sir Proteus, what says Silvia to my suit?

PRO.   Oh, sir, I find her milder than she was,
And yet she takes exceptions to your person.

THU.   What, that my leg is too long?

PRO.   No—that your limb is too little.

THU.   I'll wear a boot, to make it somewhat
            rounder.

JUL.   (*Aside*) But love cannot be spurred to
            what it loathes.

THU.   And what about my face?

PRO.   She says it is a fair one.

THU.   Oh, no—the rascal lies—my face is dark.

PRO.   But pearls are light, and the old saying is—
Dark men are pearls in beautiful ladies' eyes.

JUL.   (*Aside*) It's true—such perils as cause a
            lady's sighs;
I'd rather close my lids than look at them.

THU.   How does she like my talk?

PRO.   Ill, when you talk of war.

THU.   But well when I converse of love and peace.

JUL.   (*Aside*) But better, indeed, when you hold
your peace.

THU.   What says she of my valor?

PRO.   Oh, sir, she has no doubt of that.

JUL.   (*Aside*) She need not, when she knows
            it's cowardice.

ORIGINAL

ACT V

SCENE 2 — *The same. A room in the* DUKE'S *Palace.*

Enter THURIO, PROTEUS, *and* JULIA.

THU.   Sir Proteus, what says Silvia to my suit?
PRO.   O, sir, I find her milder than she was;
And yet she takes exceptions at your person.
THU.   What, that my leg is too long?
PRO.   No, that it is too little.
THU.   I'll wear a boot, to make it somewhat
          rounder.
JUL.   (*Aside*) But love will not be spurr'd to
          what it loathes.
THU.   What says she to my face?
PRO.   She says it is a fair one.
THU.   Nay then, the wanton lies, my face is black.
PRO.   But pearls are fair; and the old saying is,
Black men are pearls in beauteous ladies' eyes.
JUL.   (*Aside*) 'T is true, such pearls as put out
          ladies' eyes;
For I had rather wink than look on them.
THU.   How likes she my discourse?
PRO.   Ill, when you talk of war.
THU.   But well, when I discourse of love and
peace.
JUL.   (*Aside*) But better, indeed, when you hold
your peace.
THU.   What says she to my valor?
PRO.   O, sir, she makes no doubt of that.
JUL.   (*Aside*) She needs not, when she knows it
          cowardice.

NOTES

*leg — also means male organ.

But love . . . loathes — this line is attributed to *Thurio* in the original; sensing an error the older editions changed the attribution to *Proteus*; modern editions (after Boswell) usually assign the line to *Julia* as an *Aside*, which this edition prefers.

my face?/ . . . it is a fair one. — the New Cambridge interprets, "i.e. Thurio is 'fair faced', a specious deceiver."; Arden supports Bond in a possible "effeminacy" intended; it seems however merely a word play with the following *black* and *pearls*.

wanton — here in its milder "rascal" sense; *black* — dark or swarthy, as elsewhere in Shakespeare (and cf. Sonnet 131).

MODERN

THU.   What says she of my birth?

PRO.   That you are well descended.

JUL.   (*Aside*) True—from a gentleman to a fool.

THU.   Has she considered my possessions?

PRO.   Oh, yes—and pities them.

THU.   How so?

JUL.   (*Aside*) That such an ass should own them.

PRO.   That they have been let out.

JUL.   Here comes the duke.

Enter DUKE.

DUKE.   Well now, Sir Proteus! And you, Thurio! Which of you saw Eglamour around?

THU.   Not I.

PRO.   Nor I.

DUKE.   Or saw my daughter?

PRO.   Neither.

black men are pearls — again swarthy or dark, not unlike the modern "tall, dark, and handsome"; although moors, "Ethiopes", and other truly "black" men were not unknown to the Elizabethans, they were treated as being exotic; this is to say that had *Thurio* been depicted as truly black, more would have been made of it through the play.

eye(s) — also means female organ (orifice); of course then *wink*, which then meant to close the eyes and keep them closed, takes on a double entendre; the original script assigns this speech to *Thurio*, but Boswell (see above) appears correct to give the lines to *Julia* as an *Aside*, especially since she could then effect the bawdy by pronouncing *pearls* as "perils".

peace — also means male organ (piece).

ORIGINAL

THU.	What says she to my birth?
PRO.	That you are well derived.
JUL.	(*Aside*) True; from a gentleman to a fool.
THU.	Considers she my possessions?
PRO.	O, ay; and pities them.
THU.	Wherefore?
JUL.	(*Aside*) That such an ass should owe them.
PRO.	That they are out by lease.
JUL.	Here comes the duke.

Enter DUKE.

DUKE. How now, sir Proteus? how now, Thurio?
Which of you saw Eglamour of late?

THU.   Not I.

PRO.   Nor I.

DUKE.   Saw you my daughter?

PRO.   Neither.

NOTES

derived — descended; *possessions* — allusive to his codpiece.

pities them — Arden sees a double entendre here—"(1) is sorry for them; (2) considers them 'pitiful', of no account"; New Cambridge sees a pun on *possessions* by the devil; actually it seems to have no elaborate meaning at all, being merely a vehicle to the humorous retorts of *Julia* and *Proteus*; *owe* — own.

out by lease — past explanations have been inordinately involved: (Signet) "Because Thurio is such a fool he will surely only hold onto his possessions temporarily."; (Staunton, quoting Lord Hailes) "By Thurio's *possessions* he himself understands his *lands*. But Proteus chooses to take the word likewise in a figurative sense, as signifying his *mental endowments*; and whence he says they *are out by lease*, he means that they are no longer enjoyed by their master, (who is a fool,) but are *leased out* to another."; (Arden) "The obvious meaning here, as indicated by Mason, is that Thurio's estates are not 'in his own dear hands' and therefore (ironically) Proteus says that Silvia 'pities them' . . . But the laboured mockery of this scene hardly repays investigation."

MODERN

DUKE.   Why, then, she's run off to that scoundrel
          Valentine.
And Eglamour has gone along with her.
It's true, for Friar Lawrence met them both
While wandering in penance through the forest.
He's sure 't was him, and guessed that it was she.
Since she was masked, he was not sure of it.
Besides, she was to make confession
At Patrick's cell tonight, and never showed up.
These circumstances mean she's run away.
I beg you, then, don't stand around and talk,
But mount your horse right now, and then we'll meet
Upon the foothill of the mountain ridge
That leads toward Mantua, where I think they've fled.
Make haste, good gentlemen, and follow me.

The "mockery" is far less labored than Arden's interpretation. Indeed, if the meaning were as labored as any of the above explanations not one soul in the Elizabethan audience would have caught it. For correct meaning it has only need be known that *lease* was then pronounced "leash", and that both words meant, respectively, renting or letting out and a cord to walk a dog; the bawdy play on *Thurio's possessions* is then obvious.

How now etc. — the New Cambridge notes that prior to this line the scene has been a mixture of prose and verse and that the remaining lines are all verse; if they had also noted that this line demarcates the end of the bawdy, the change to all verse would have been self-explanatory.

saw Eglamour — the Fourth Folio changed this to *saw* SIR *Eglamour*; the bafflement lies not so much in the change as in the acceptance of it by virtually all commentators. Why? Because of meter? The meter of the *Duke's* opening lines seems deliberately rough to point up his agitation over his missing daughter; also, he is no more bound by the polite form of address here than a few lines later—*And Eglamour is in her company.*

ORIGINAL

DUKE. Why, then, she's fled unto that peasant
           Valentine;
And Eglamour is in her company.
'T is true; for friar Lawrence met them both,
As he in penance wander'd through the forest:
Him he knew well, and guess'd that it was she;
But, being mask'd, he was not sure of it:
Besides, she did intend confession
At Patrick's cell this even; and there she was not:
These likelihoods confirm her flight from hence.
Therefore, I pray you, stand not to discourse,
But mount you presently, and meet with me
Upon the rising of the mountain-foot
That leads toward Mantua, whither they are fled.
Dispatch, sweet gentlemen, and follow me.

THU.   Well, this is what befalls a stubborn girl
Who does not know when she is so well off.
I'll follow—more to take revenge on Eglamour
Than for the love of reckless Silvia.

PRO.   And I will follow, more for Silvia's love
Than hate of Eglamour who's gone with her.

JUL.   And I will follow, more to thwart that love
Than hate for Silvia, who has found her love.

Exeunt.

NOTES

friar Lawrence — "I" dotters see an error here and "correct" the line to read *friar Patrick*, but they never address the question of why *friar Patrick*, the name of a small monastery in this play, must be the same as *friar Lawrence*, the name of a particular friar in this play.

likelihoods — circumstances; *stand not* — don't stand around; *presently* — immediately; *foot* — foothill.

rising of the mountain-foot that leads toward Mantua — this pinpointing surmise of the *Duke* is presumably based on what *friar*

THU.   Why, this it is to be a peevish girl,
That flies her fortune when it follows her:
I'll after; more to be reveng'd on Eglamour,
Than for the love of reckless Silvia.
        PRO.   And I will follow, more for Silvia's love,
Than hate of Eglamour that goes with her.
        JUL.   And I will follow, more to cross that love,
Than hate for Silvia, that is gone for love.

Exeunt.

Lawrence told him and helps explain their finding *Silvia* so easily; *dispatch* — make haste; *peevish* — stubborn; *flies her fortune* — does not know when she is well off; *cross* — cross up.

The bing-bang-bing-bang exits at the end of this scene as found in modern editions were added by commentators. Unless the four characters are going to be shot off stage, one by one, out of a cannon, it were best to follow the original final *Exeunt.* Each character probably made some move to exit at the end of each speech, but what could be more effective than a mass exit, with the *Duke* leading, in an Elizabethan equivalent of a conga line?

MODERN

ACT V

SCENE 3 — *Frontiers of Mantua. The forest.*

Enter SILVIA *and* OUTLAWS.

1st OUT.   Come, come, be patient.
We must bring you to our captain.

SIL.   A thousand more misfortunes than this one
Have taught me how to bear this patiently.

2nd OUT. Come, bring her along.

1st OUT.   Where is the gentleman who was with her?

3rd OUT.   Being nimble-footed he has outrun us.
But Moses and Valerius follow him.
Go now with her to the west end of the wood.
Our captain's there, and we'll chase him who's fled.
We've sealed the thicket off; he can't escape.

1st OUT.   Come, I must bring you to our captain's cave.
Fear not—he is an honorable man,
And will not use a woman lawlessly.

SIL.   Oh, Valentine, this I endure for you!

Exeunt.

NOTES

learn'd me — taught me; *brook* — endure; *Moyses* — common spelling of Moses then; *beset* — surrounded.

Arden comments—"Why more than Moyses and Valerius were needed to pursue Eglamour is obscure." So is someone in a forest.

Arden again—"Eglamour's quick abandoning of Silvia has caused a good deal of comment, especially in view of the picture of him given in Act IV, Scene 3;" and they add—"We may say the character has been sacrificed to the plotting, but surely egregiously so." The New Cambridge notes that *Eglamour's* desertion from his

ORIGINAL

ACT V

SCENE 3 — *Frontiers of Mantua. The forest.*

Enter SILVIA *and* OUTLAWS.

1st OUT.   Come, come, be patient:
We must bring you to our captain.
   SIL.   A thousand more mischances than this
            one
Have learn'd me how to brook this patiently.
   2nd OUT.   Come, bring her away.
   1st OUT.   Where is the gentleman that was with
            her?
   3rd OUT.   Being nimble-footed, he hath outrun us,
But Moyses and Valerius follow him.
Go thou with her to the west end of the wood,
There is our captain: we'll follow him that's fled,
The thicket is beset, he cannot 'scape.
   1st OUT.   Come, I must bring you to our captain's
            cave;
Fear not; he bears an honorable mind,
And will not use a woman lawlessly.
   SIL.   O Valentine, this I endure for thee!

Exeunt.

promise to help Silvia "without warning or excuse" indicates "the adapter" at work. A minority of commentators come to Eglamour's (and the bard's) defense, saying that he realized he was out-numbered and, logically, ran to get help.

Neither view seems adequate. Earlier conjecture of this edition that *Eglamour* is just as lecherous as the best and rest of the male principals would not make his desertion less cowardly; but far from the character being egregiously sacrificed to the plotting, his action would be fully in character.

Some editions have adopted the "improvement" (by Capell) of having the second and third *Outlaws* exit four lines before the scene's end, whereas the original has only one exit for all at the end.

Even though the "falling curtain" had not been yet invented the
original final "exit all"—although surely with a split exit to rear left
and right—is preferable to the "improved" ping-pong exits suggested.

For one thing the urgency of chasing the *nimble-footed gentle-*

man is mitigated by other *Outlaws* already giving chase, which is why these *Outlaws* are still dawdling onstage. For another thing the commotion of an earlier exit would require either a delay of or a drowning out of *Silvia's* last line since *Outlaws* are not expected to depart on mincing tiptoes.

MODERN

ACT V

SCENE 4 — *Another part of the forest.*

Enter VALENTINE.

VAL.   How use does breed a habit in a man!
This shadowy wild place, unfrequented woods,
I better bear than flourishing peopled towns.
Here I can sit alone, unseen by any,
And to the nightingale's lamenting notes
Sing my distresses, and repeat my woes.
Oh you who dwells and lives inside my breast,
Leave not the mansion so long tenantless,
Lest it, becoming ruins, the building fall,
And leave no memory of what it was!
Restore me with your presence, Silvia—
You gentle nymph, cherish your lovelorn swain!—
What yelling and commotion is all this?
These are my mates, who make their wills their law,
They must have some poor traveler in chase.
They love me well, yet I've all I can do
To keep them from uncivil outrages.
You'd best hide, Valentine . . . Who's this comes here?

———————

NOTES

use — getting used to something, repetition; *breed a habit in a man* — produce a man of habit; *desert* — then meant any deserted place; *brook* — tolerate; *tune* — express musically, sing; *record* — repeat musically, especially as do birds; *inhabit* — live, dwell.

And to . . . it was! — these six lines have been admired for their sheer poetry; *repair* — restore; *have* — and have, now have (he deduces from the shouting that they have a traveler in chase).

ORIGINAL

ACT V

SCENE 4 — *Another part of the forest.*

Enter VALENTINE.

VAL.   How use doth breed a habit in a man!
This shadowy desert, unfrequented woods,
I better brook than flourishing peopled towns:
Here can I sit alone, unseen of any,
And to the nightingale's complaining notes
Tune my distresses, and record my woes.
O thou that dost inhabit in my breast,
Leave not the mansion so long tenantless;
Lest, growing ruinous, the building fall,
And leave no memory of what it was!
Repair me with thy presence, Silvia;
Thou gentle nymph, cherish thy forlorn swain!
What hallooing, and what stir, is this today?
These are my mates, that make their wills their law,
Have some unhappy passenger in chase:
They love me well; yet I have much to do,
To keep them from uncivil outrages.
Withdraw thee, Valentine; who's this comes here?

MODERN

Enter PROTEUS, SILVIA *and* JULIA.

PRO.   Madam, this good deed I have done for
          you—
Though you've no gratitude for what I do—
To risk my life, and rescue you from him
Who would have forced your honor and your love.
Allow me, as reward, but one kind look.
A smaller gift than this I could not ask,
And less than this I'm sure you would not give.

VAL.   (*Aside*) How like a dream is this! I see, and
          hear.
Love, lend me patience to hold back awhile.

SIL.   Oh miserable, unhappy that I am!

PRO.   You were unhappy long before I came,
But by my coming I have made you happy.

SIL.   By your approach you made me most
          unhappy.

JUL.   (*Aside*) And me, when he approaches
          close to you.

SIL.   Had I been seized by any hungry lion,
I would have been a breakfast to the beast
Rather than have false Proteus rescue me.
Oh, Heaven be judge—how I love Valentine,
Whose life's as precious to me as my soul;
And full as much—for more it cannot be—
I do detest false lying Proteus—
Therefore be gone; solicit me no more.

NOTES

respect not aught — are not grateful for.
would have forc'd your honor — would have raped you. It has
been argued (Tannenbaum) that the outlaws, being sworn by
Valentine to be honorable, would not have attempted rape. It could
be better argued that *Valentine* only thinks he has sworn his men to

ORIGINAL

Enter PROTEUS, SILVIA, *and* JULIA.

PRO.   Madam, this service I have done for you,
(though you respect not aught your servant doth)
To hazard life, and rescue you from him
That would have forc'd your honor and your love.
Vouchsafe me, for my meed, but one fair look;
A smaller boon than this I cannot beg,
And less than this, I am sure, you cannot give.

VAL.   (*Aside*) How like a dream is this? I see, and
        hear?
Love, lend me patience to forbear awhile.

SIL.   O miserable, unhappy that I am!

PRO.   Unhappy were you, madam, ere I came;
But by my coming, I have made you happy.

SIL.   By thy approach thou mak'st me most
        unhappy.

JUL.   (*Aside*) And me, when he approacheth to
        your presence.

SIL.   Had I been seized by a hungry lion,
I would have been a breakfast to the beast,
Rather than have false Proteus rescue me.
O, Heaven be judge how I love Valentine,
Whose life's as tender to me as my soul;
And full as much (for more there cannot be)
I do detest false perjur'd Proteus:
Therefore be gone, solicit me no more.

honor. Arden has a point—"However, all we need to deduce is that Proteus here found it useful to assume that the outlaw had rape in mind;" but this does not square with *Silvia* herself using the word *rescue* in her *hungry lion* retort.

meed — just due, reward; *cannot beg/ . . . cannot give* — could not beg/ . . . would not give.

a dream is this? I see, and hear? — most editions have "corrected" this to *a dream is this I see and hear!* or some variant thereof; the original calls for a different delivery—a pause after *this?*—making it more effective.

   patience to forbear — much conjecture here about why *Valentine*, if he is a manly lover at all, does not jump out at this point to rescue *Silvia*; Collier even theorized that *Valentine* exited and re-entered later; Arden explains it well—"We can understand Valentine not immediately breaking silence, for Proteus' words would

MODERN

PRO.   What dangerous hazard, though I risked
        my life,
Would I not undertake for one kind look.
Oh, it's the curse of love—will always be—
When women cannot love where they're beloved.

SIL.   When Proteus cannot love where he's
        beloved.
Look into Julia's heart, your first best love,
For whose dear sake you did once split your love
Into a thousand vows; and all those vows
You let degenerate to lies, to love me.
You've no true love left now, unless you've two,
And that's far worse than none—better have none
Than double love, which is too much by one—
You traitor, you, to your true friend!

PRO.   In love
Who cares of friend?

SIL.   All men but Proteus.

PRO.   Then, if the gentle spirit of moving words
Can no way make you more agreeable,
I'll woo you like a soldier does in war,
And love you must unlovingly—I'll force you.

SIL.   Oh Heaven!

PRO.   I'll make you yield to
        my desire.

amaze him; but simple curiosity, allied of course with his love, would keep him within earshot." The only point this edition might add is that *Valentine* would not be *Valentine* if some time were not required for events to "sink in"; to have had him grasp the situation immediately would have been to throw him out of character.

    approach — amorous advances; *tender* — precious, dear.

ORIGINAL

    PRO.   What dangerous action, stood it next to death,
Would I not undergo for one calm look?
O, 't is the curse in love, and still approv'd,
When women cannot love where they're belov'd.
    SIL.   When Proteus cannot love where he's belov'd.
Read over Julia's heart, thy first best love,
For whose dear sake thou didst then rend thy faith
Into a thousand oaths; and all those oaths
Descended into perjury, to love me.
Thou hast no faith left now, unless thou'dst two,
And that's far worse than none; better have none
Than plural faith, which is too much by one:
Thou counterfeit to thy true friend!
    PRO.   In love,
Who respects friend?
    SIL.   All men but Proteus.
    PRO.   Nay, if the gentle spirit of moving words
Can no way change you to a milder form,
I'll woo you like a soldier, at arms' end;
And love you 'gainst the nature of love, force you.
    SIL.   O Heaven!
    PRO.   I'll force thee yield to my desire.

NOTES

calm look — kind look or glance; *still approv'd* — ever proved, i.e., reaffirmed repeatedly.

For whose dear sake . . . to love me. — these three lines pose a problem for many. The preparers of the Second Folio changed *love me* to *deceive me*, thereby touching off a debate that continues. The New Cambridge believes the passage to be "clearly corrupt". Daniel suggested "discandied" (thawed, melted) for *descended*, for which same word Bond proposed "re-rented" (re-torn). Arden has doubts about the word *rend* being the correct one. Sisson, however, appears correct in noting that if the comma after the second *oaths* is ignored the original passage makes perfect sense; This

MODERN

VAL.   Ruffian, let go that rude uncivil hold;
You untrustworthy friend, you!

PRO.   Valentine!

VAL.   You common friend, who's without trust
        or love—
To me now *friend* means that—treacherous man!
You have betrayed my hopes; I would not have
Believed what I see here. Now I can't say
I have one friend alive; you're proof I don't.
Who can be trusted when one's best friend
Is rotten to the core? Oh, Proteus,
I'm sorry—I can't trust you any more.
I'll see all men as strangers, thanks to you.
My inner wound is deepest—this day most accursed!
Of all one's foes, a friend who's false is worst.

PRO.   My shame, and guilt, o'ercome me—
Forgive me, Valentine. If heartfelt sorrow
Be price enough to pay for my offense,
I offer it here. My suffering's as great
As what I did commit.

VAL.   Then I feel paid—

edition omits the comma and suggests reading . . . *all those oaths descended into perjury,* (when you decided) *to love me.*

faith — true love; *counterfeit* — traitor, i.e., false friend; *respects* — cares about.

arms' end — many interpretations offered, including a quibble and/or bawdy meaning; the problem here is that the usual meaning then was "at a distance", i.e., at arms' length; a quibble or, worse, bawdy effect is out of the question on purely dramaturgic grounds—a laugh at this point would be a jarring clash of moods; therefore, Bond could be right in suggesting a meaning of "at sword's point", which in turn suggests a rapacious "conquering" soldier.

ORIGINAL

VAL.   Ruffian, let go that rude uncivil touch;
Thou friend of an ill fashion!

PRO.   Valentine!

VAL.   Thou common friend, that's without faith
           or love;
(For such is a friend now); treacherous man!
Thou hast beguil'd my hopes; nought but mine eye
Could have persuaded me: now I dare not say
I have one friend alive; thou wouldst disprove me.
Who should be trusted when one's right hand
Is perjur'd to the bosom? Proteus,
I am sorry I must never trust thee more,
But count the world a stranger for thy sake.
The private wound is deepest: O time most accurs'd!
'Mongst all foes, that a friend should be the worst.

PRO.   My shame, and guilt, confounds me—
Forgive me, Valentine: if hearty sorrow
Be a sufficient ransom for offense,
I tender it here; I do as truly suffer
As e'er I did commit.

VAL.   Then I am paid;

And once again regard you to be honest.
Who won't forgive another who repents
Is not of heaven, or earth—these both forgive;
By penitence the Eternal's wrath is calmed—
And that my love may show both great and true,
All that was mine in Silvia, I give you.

NOTES

touch — hold; *ill fashion* — bad sort (a friend fashioned in an ill way); *common* — vulgar, cheap; *beguil'd* — deceived, betrayed; *disprove me* — prove me wrong; *right hand* — closest friend; *perjur'd* — false; *a stranger for thy sake* — never make another friend because of your betrayal; *private* — personal. Several lines of this speech are emended in most editions to "improve" Shakespeare's meter; they are not so here.

confounds — overcomes; *hearty* — heartfelt; *ransom* — price to pay, restitution; *as e'er I did commit* — as much as I have sinned; *paid* — satisfied; *receive thee honest* — accept you as honest; *love* — friendship; *plain and free* — evident and generous.

All that was mine, in Silvia, I give thee — this is the climax both of the play and of the criticism heaped upon the play. Indeed, of all the bard's lines in all his plays, this has become the most notorious. Why in the world would *Valentine* be so unworldly as to offer *Silvia* to *Proteus*?

This climax has occasioned a literary free-for-all that has lasted centuries. Those kind to Shakespeare blame it all on a "ghost writer"; those unkind simply condemn him for it; and those in-between have stood on their heads to explain it away—with transpositions of words, with changes of punctuation, with deletions and even additions of words and whole lines, adding stage directions, changing events, giving *Julia's* line to *Silvia*, having *Silvia* faint instead of *Julia*, citing the sonnets for meaning, etc., etc., etc. (The renowned Mr.Collier even argued that *Valentine*, believing that *Silvia* had already been unfaithful, offers her up because she has thereby lost her desirability; that conclusion in the face of the text can only suggest that Mr. Collier's mind, not *Valentine's*, was in the gutter.) In all the standard literature hardly a com-

And once again I do receive thee honest:
Who by repentance is not satisfied
Is nor of heaven, nor earth; for these are pleas'd;
By penitence the Eternal's wrath's appeas'd—
And, that my love may appear plain and free,
All that was mine, in Silvia, I give thee.

mentator shows support here for the dramatist. But then the dramatist hardly needs any support.

Firstly, if the critics are so right that this climax is so wrong, then it follows as night does day that the play "bombed", or at best had a very short run. A play may hobble along with many defects, but not with a wrong climax—the audience would not tolerate the letdown. Regarding the *Two Gentlemen* the evidence points the other way.

There is of course the extrinsic evidence: (1) the specific evidence of a favorable reaction to the play found in Francis Meres' *Palladis Tamia* in 1598 (2) the speculative evidence (in and of this edition, cf. *Induction*) that the play had a remarkably long performance life (3) the general evidence of public esteem for Shakespeare from the earliest of his plays, which hardly suggests "turkeys", and (4) the common horse sense that had the climax been egregious to the audience the playwright—any playwright—would have changed it early in the tryouts.

The intrinsic evidence is staring one in the face. *Valentine* was exactly that—a "Valentine". Not a greeting card—those did not then exist—but a personification of the Valentine Day sentiments—which did exist. He was meant to be noble . . . and pure . . . and loving in his thoughts, which is one way of saying he was meant to be naive. And Shakespeare dubbed him what he dubbed him lest anyone miss the point.

And lest any American miss the point, this play is pure satire—a satire that happens to be set in Verona but could as well have been set in Dogpatch. An American need only ask himself—would *Li'l Abner* have held a grudge against *Proteus*? Of course not! Would *Li'l Abner* have offered to share *Daisy Mae* with his best friend? He sho 'nuff would!

Or again, lest *Valentine* be considered a cartoon, *Valentine's All that was mine, in Silvia, I give thee* is no less credible than Will

Rogers' *I never met a man I didn't like.* Or yet again, the response of one wag that Will Rogers was either *an angel or an ass . . . or both . . .* applies equally well to *Valentine.* Between the two, the true character was stranger than the fictional one for *Valentine* managed to meet one man he did not like—*Thurio.*

But *Thurio's* lust for *Silvia,* like that of *Proteus,* was a minor evil to *Valentine.* Indeed, if only *Thurio* had had the humbleness to say, as did *Proteus,* that he was sorry for what he had done *Valentine* surely would have forgiven him on the spot.

And it is just the very lack of this lustful thinking in *Valentine* that makes this climax the last and greatest laugh of the play. While *Valentine* monogamously, and therefore permissibly, lusts after his own *Silvia,* he would never so lust after any other woman. And so it was that when he "gave" his beloved *Silvia* to *Proteus* he had no carnal thoughts. His gift was purely Platonic. It is this that was the crowning humor of the comedy. Laughter there must have been,

MODERN

JUL.   (*Faints.*) Unhappy me!

PRO.   Look to the boy.

VAL.   Why, boy!

There, friend! Hey there—what's the matter?
Look up. Speak

JUL.   Oh good sir, my master sent me to deliver a ring to Madam Silvia which, out of my neglect, was never done.

PRO.   Where is that ring, boy?

JUL.   It's here—this is it.

PRO.   Well! Let me see—
Why this is the ring I gave to Julia.

JUL.   I beg your pardon, sir, but I am wrong.
This is the ring you sent to Silvia.

PRO.   How did you come to have this ring?
On leaving her, I gave this ring to Julia.

JUL.   And Julia herself gave it to me.
And Julia herself has brought it to you.

PRO.   Ho! Julia!

for *Silvia* and *Julia* and *Proteus* and every last soul in the audience knew that in offering to "share" *Silvia* the last thing *Valentine* had on his mind—and the first thing on everyone else's—was sex.

It was and is only the Shakespearean "scholars" who, with sex on "their" collective mind, assumed it was on *Valentine's* too; and it is those selfsame scholars who, for nigh onto four centuries now, have derisively contemned Mr. Shakespeare for this climax. But in all fairness let the condemnation of the respected Shakespearean authority E. M. W. Tillyard be admitted in evidence here:

> "It has been pretty well agreed that this scene is morally and dramatically monstrous: that a proposal to hand over a girl to the man who has just proposed to rape her revolts our moral sense and that the perfunctory speed with which these staggering events are recounted can only provoke our laughter."

You're the one who said it, E. M. W. T.

ORIGINAL

JUL.   (*Faints.*) O me, unhappy!
PRO.   Look to the boy.
VAL.   Why, boy!
Why, wag! how now? what's the matter? Look up;
Speak.
JUL.   O good sir, my master charged me to deliver a ring to madam Silvia; which, out of my neglect, was never done.
PRO.   Where is that ring, boy?
JUL.   Her 't is: this is it.
PRO.   How! let me see:
Why, this is the ring I gave to Julia.
JUL.   O, cry you mercy, sir, I have mistook;
This is the ring you sent to Silvia.
PRO.   But how cam'st thou by this ring?
At my depart, I gave this unto Julia.
JUL.   And Julia herself did give it me;
And Julia herself hath brought it hither.
PRO.   How! Julia!

NOTES

Silvia's silence when she is offered on a platter to *Proteus*—indeed she is silent for the rest of the play—has been puzzled over and widely criticized as being unrealistic. This certainly presented no problem in performance. The climax has just occurred and is itself so "unrealistic" that no one expects her to say something realistic.

She could of course nod in disbelief, but since she knows her *Valentine* there is no disbelief. She is far more apt to have shrugged her shoulders and shaken her head in resignation.

MODERN

JUL.   Behold her who has guided all your vows,
And held them closely deep inside her heart,
Where with your lies you pierced me to the quick.
Oh, Proteus, let my clothing make you blush!
Be much ashamed that I have had to wear
Such poor and common clothing . . . if there's shame
In wearing these for love.
It is a lesser evil that one finds
When women change their looks, than men their minds.
PRO.   Than men their minds! It's true—
Oh, Heaven! If man
Were faithful, he'd be perfect—that one defect
Fills him with faults; makes him run through all th' sins;
Unfaithfulness deludes ere it begins—
For what's in Silvia's face that I can't spy
More sweet in Julia's with a faithful eye.
VAL.   Come, come, hold hands together.
I'm glad to help—How this warm union glows.
A pity if such friends should long be foes.
PRO.   Bear witness, I have my wish forever.
JUL.   And I mine.
Enter OUTLAWS *with* DUKE *and* THURIO.
OUTS.   A prize, a prize, a prize!

It is therefore not surprising—although it appears so to many commentators—that *Julia* is the one who reacts to *Valentine's* give-away. Now that *Valentine* has effectively neutralized *Proteus*, what more propitious timing for *Julia* to make her own bid for him? She accordingly does what women traditionally did to get attention—feints a faint. Then, through the ploy of the betrothal ring she effects a recognition scene.

   wag — a friendly term akin to pal, chum; *deliver a ring* — this "fib" and the following lines are *Julia's* playful way of evoking *Proteus'* recognition of her; *cry you mercy* — beg your pardon.

ORIGINAL

JUL.   Behold her that gave aim to all thy oaths,
And entertain'd them deeply in her heart:
How oft hast thou with perjury cleft the root?
O Proteus, let this habit make thee blush!
Be thou asham'd, that I have took upon me
Such an immodest raiment; if shame live
In a disguise of love:
It is the lesser blot, modesty finds,
Women to change their shapes, than men their minds.
PRO.   Than men their minds! 't is true; O Heaven!
            were man
But constant, he were perfect: that one error
Fills him with faults; makes him run through all th' sins:
Inconstancy falls off ere it begins:
What is in Silvia's face, but I may spy
More fresh in Julia's with a constant eye?
VAL.   Come, come, a hand from either:
Let me be bless'd to make this happy close;
'T were pity two such friends should be long foes.
PRO.   Bear witness, I have my wish forever.
JUL.   And I mine.

   Enter OUTLAWS *with* DUKE *and* THURIO.

OUTS.   A prize, a prize, a prize!

NOTES

gave aim to — gave direction to all of his vows, to her own and —as messenger—to *Silvia* (an archery term); *entertain'd* — kept; *cleft the root* — i.e., pierced her heart to its very root (another allusion to archery); *habit* — clothes (of a boy); *asham'd* — "for my sake" is understood; *if shame live in a disguise of love* — if there is anything wrong with disguising myself for the sake of love; *shapes* — appearances; *constant* — faithful; *Inconstancy . . . begins* —

MODERN

VAL. Hold on, hold on, I say—it is my lord the Duke.
Your grace is welcome to a man disgraced,
Banished Valentine.

  DUKE.   Sir Valentine!

  THU. And there is Silvia—and Silvia's mine!

  VAL. Thurio, back up, or else prepare to die!
Don't come where I can reach you in my wrath.
Do not claim Silvia's yours—If once again,
I'll have Verona ban you. Here she stands—
And if you make the slightest move to touch her!—
I dare you even breathe toward my love.

  THU. Sir Valentine, I don't want her, not I.
A man is but a fool if he will risk
His body for a girl who does not love him.
I do not want her, therefore she's all yours.

  DUKE. It proves you all the more degenerate
To have professed such love, as you have done,
And then to drop her on the slightest grounds—
Now, by the honor of my ancestry,
I do applaud your spirit, Valentine,
And I think you're worthy of an empress' love!
Hear then, I here erase all grievances,
Remove all grudges, allow you back again,
Your proven merit changes everything;

"the inconstant man proves false even before he begins to love"
(Signet); *What is in Silvia's face . . . constant eye* — if I were
faithful to *Julia* I could see that she is even prettier than *Silvia; close*
— coming together.

    Enter OUTLAWS — if anyone has been wondering (and all the
scholars have) whatever happened to *Speed*, most certainly he appears here, knife in mouth, out outlawing the outlaws.

ORIGINAL

VAL.   Forbear, forbear, I say; it is my lord the
        duke.
Your grace is welcome to a man disgrac'd,
Banished Valentine.
    DUKE   Sir Valentine!
    THU.   Yonder is Silvia; and Silvia's mine.
    VAL.   Thurio, give back, or else embrace thy
        death;
Come not within the measure of my wrath:
Do not name Silvia thine; if once again,
Verona shall not hold thee. Here she stands;
Take but possession of her with a touch—
I dare thee but to breathe upon my love.
    THU.   Sir Valentine, I care not for her, I;
I hold him but a fool, that will endanger
His body for a girl that loves him not:
I claim her not, and therefore she is thine.
    DUKE.   The more degenerate and base art thou,
To make such means for her as thou hast done,
And leave her on such slight conditions—
Now, by the honor of my ancestry,
I do applaud thy spirit,Valentine,
And I think thee worthy of an empress' love!
Know then, I here forget all former griefs,
Cancel all grudge, repeal thee home again,
Plead a new state in thy unrival'd merit,

You have my full support. Sir Valentine,
You are a gentleman, of good descent—
Take you your Silvia, for you well deserve her.

———————

NOTES

give back — back off, back up; *measure* — reach.

Verona shall not hold thee — Many editors make a mountain out of this foothill. Some change this to *Milan* since the foothill is far closer thereto than Verona. Some substitute *behold* or *'hold* for *hold* to effect yet another correction. R. G. White argues—"To *Valentine's* apprehension, the whole party were on their way from Milan to Verona, as he was when the Outlaws stayed him; and therefore his threat to *Thurio* that he shall never reach his destination".

Valentine here is not looking at a road map; he does not, nor does the script's printer, intend "behold" for *hold*; and he knows

MODERN

VAL.   I thank your grace. This gift has made me happy.
And now, I beg you for your daughter's sake,
To grant one wish that I will ask of you.

DUKE.   I grant it, for your sake, whate'er it be.

VAL.   These banished men, with whom I've lately lived,
Are men endowed with worthy qualities;
Forgive them for what they've committed here,
And let them be recalled from their exile—
They are reformed men, peaceful, full of good,
And fit for great employment, worthy lord.

DUKE.   You have prevailed—I pardon them, and you.
Take charge of them, you know what they deserve.
Come, let us go; we'll bury all our woes
With celebrations and most joyous times.

To which I thus subscribe, Sir Valentine,
Thou art a gentleman, and well deriv'd;
Take thou thy Silvia, for thou hast deserv'd her.

without knowing that the *Duke* is looking for his daughter, not making a business trip to Verona with such an entourage. All that *Valentine* is doing here is making a young man's macho threat, partly to impress *Silvia*, telling *Thurio* that he had better never ever set foot in his, *Valentine's* home town—or else!

    means for her — effort to win her; *leave her on such slight conditions* — i.e., grounds, drop her at the first sign of difficulty; *forget* — forgive; *griefs* — grievances; *repeal thee home again* — repeal your exile, i.e., regard my home as yours again.

    Plead a new state in thy unrival'd merit. — many interpretations of this, but most are substantially "I plead (in defense of my repealing your exile) a new state of affairs wherein you have proved your unrivaled merit."; *well deriv'd* — of good family.

ORIGINAL

VAL.   I thank your grace; the gift hath made me
        happy.
I now beseech you, for your daughter's sake,
To grant one boon that I shall ask of you.
    DUKE.   I grant it, for thine own, whate'er it be.
    VAL.   These banish'd men, that I have kept
        withal,
Are men endued with worthy qualities;
Forgive them what they have committed here,
And let them be recall'd from their exile:
They are reformed, civil, full of good,
And fit for great employment, worthy lord.
    DUKE.   Thou hast prevail'd; I pardon them, and
        thee;
Dispose of them, as thou know'st their deserts.
Come, let us go; we will include all jars
With triumphs, mirth, and rare solemnity.

VAL.   And as we walk along, I'll be so bold
Your grace will smile with what I have to tell.
How do you like this page, my lord?

    DUKE.   I think the boy is somewhat shy; he
            blushes.

    VAL.   I promise you, my lord, more shy than
            boy.

    DUKE.   What do you mean by that?

    VAL.   Please sir, I'll tell you as we go along,
And you will wonder at what's happened.
Come, Proteus—it's your only punishment
To have your secret love life all exposed.
That done, our wedding day will be yours too—
One feast, one house, one mutual happiness.

Exeunt.

NOTES

kept withal — kept myself (lived) with; *endued* — endowed.

DUKE. I grant it . . . whate'er it be — the *Duke* may have slightly regretted *whate'er it be* since this edition senses that at this point *Valentine* made a signal . . . and every available member of the performing company, complete in outlaw regalia, trooped onstage.

include — virtually all editions gloss "conclude"; Malone suggested "shut in" based on Cowdrey's *Alphabetical Table of Head English Words* (1604); in an even closer year to this play, 1592, Greene, a contemporary of Shakespeare, has in his play *James IV* the line—*O, that I were included in my grave*; also cf. O.E.D.; "bury" is interpreted here and fits well.

jars — troubles, misfortunes; *triumphs, mirth, and rare solemnity* — the more particular meanings here add up to "joyous celebrations".

grace in him; he blushes. — *grace* then incorporated internal as well as external "graciousness", and one attribute was considered to be the feminine quality of blushing (cf. Tilley's Proverbs).

fortuned — happened; *your penance . . . discovered* — your only punishment will be that of hearing your secret love life exposed; *shall be yours* — shall be yours as well.

VAL.   And, as we walk along, I dare be bold
With our discourse to make your grace to smile:
What think you of this page, my lord?
        DUKE.   I think the boy hath grace in him; he
                blushes.
        VAL.   I warrant you, my lord; more grace than
                boy.
        DUKE.   What mean you by that saying?
        VAL.   Please you, I'll tell you as we pass along,
That you will wonder what hath fortuned—
Come, Proteus; 't is your penance, but to hear
The story of your loves discovered:
That done, our day of marriage shall be yours;
One feast, one house, one mutual happiness.

                Exeunt.

    Arden notes that Shakespeare uses the as-we-walk-along ending in five other plays and adds—"In the present play the formula awkwardly appears both in this line and in l. 166 [*as we pass along*]." If only the original complement of three *Outlaws* is onstage Arden may have a point. If on the other hand the alluded to "*crews*" of *Outlaws* materialize to receive their *pardon* the "walk-along" would assume the proportions of a triumphal march going to an offstage double wedding—

    One feast, one house, one mutual happiness.
                                EXEUNT.

Satire? If humorous fiction is more difficult to write successfully than serious fiction—and it is— then satire is the most difficult to write of all forms of fiction. The rarity of successful satire is testimony to this. Even when successful satire is almost never great; it is almost always diminished by limiting itself to local institutions and customs (Gilbert and Sullivan, Lewis Carroll, Mark Twain), or to a social class (Guy de Maupassant, Anton Chekhov), or by gimmicks (the Lilliputions of Swift, the "shmoo" of Al Capp, the Tin Woodman et al of the Wizard of Oz and, again, Alice in Wonderland), or to an ephemeral "hot" issue of the day as in movie and television fare.

Satire in its purest form holds a mirror in which all men everywhere, in laughing at the laughing reflection, only gradually realize they are laughing at themselves. Such satire is as universal as it is timeless. Although judgment is in the mind of the beholder, only three great satires in all literature come to mind here—where the characters could be reborn at any time, any place, and be believable, recognizable as a friend or relative or the neighbor next door. Those are Voltaire's optimistic *Candide*, Cervantes' noble *Don Quixote*, and Shakespeare's heart-in-the-right-place *Valentine*.

Valentine is perhaps the classic case of a young man growing up and doing exactly what society—any society— preaches while being blind to what society is in reality doing —any society. At the play's outset he believes in what society has told him is noble love and accordingly chides *Proteus* for succumbing to lowly physical love. He is next seen writing himself a love letter, not recognizing *Silvia's* deception because the same is beyond his ken. He has been taught that it is better to give than to receive so he offers *Silvia* to *Proteus*, once in the palace and again after the attempted rape. He is a trusting soul, and confides in *Proteus* his plan for elopement. His only attempt at deception—if elopement in this case is deception—is undone by his inculcated anxiousness to be helpful when he suggests a cord ladder to the *Duke*. His only attempt at lying—however justified by the circumstances—

backfires when the *Outlaws* make him an offer he cannot refuse; then, only momentarily daunted, he characteristically resolves to reform them from their *uncivil outrages.* At the end he forgives *Proteus* for trying to rape *Silvia;* he forgives the *Duke* before the latter forgives him; and he gets jobs for all his "reformed" *Outlaws.* And at the very, very end he even includes *Julia* in a kind of *menage a quatre.* In short, he is the quintessential Elizabethan nice guy.

There seems to be a timeless timeliness here: Modern society still gives lip service to a noble versus a physical love, still teaches honesty as the best policy, still professes it is better to give than to receive, still swears on a bible to tell nothing but the truth. Even on somewhat subtler levels it is still examining friendship (the "buddy" system of the Army, and of police patrol cars), still exploring the reform of outlaws, still praying for the forgiving of others, still experimenting with utopian communes—*one feast, one house*—and still seeking universal brotherhood—*one mutual happiness.* Still looking for a *Valentine*, always finding a *Proteus.*

And here, with *Proteus*, is where Shakespeare's satire is unique. Great satire of the past is in the form of a hero fighting the windmills of established society; but Shakespeare being a dramatist personifies the establishment—it is *Proteus.* More than just a villain, he is the little villain inside everyman's heart. He is a protean opportunist, a servant beater, a betrayer of his betrothed, of his best friend, of his rival, of his possible father-in-law, a rapist and, at least in *Speed's* opinion, a poor tipper. He does everything that is not nice for a nice young man to do —the ultimate bad guy. And his just reward?—to end up every bit as successful and happy as the good guy. Here is a timeless timeliness too.

Here then is a satire whose point is made as much by the villain as the hero. Indeed, each is intensified by contrast with the other, for white is never whiter nor black more black than when the two are side by side. It is just such mutual reinforcement which gives the satire its power. And hence the official title of not *One* but *The Two Gentlemen of Verona.*

And so the final curtain falls on . . .

William Shakespeare's least appreciated, ugly duckling comedy.

Good night, sweet swan . . .

. . . good night.

GLOSSARY

All asterisked words in the *Notes* will be found below; all other words are a part of the running glossary in the *Notes* section. Abbreviations for the plays given below are not overly abbreviated and should not require a companion spelling out of the complete title. All scene and line designations are based on the *Globe* edition. *The Two Gentlemen of Verona* of course is not cited.

Antony	3rd Henry VI	Othello
All's Well	Henry VIII	Pericles
As You Like	King John	Richard II
Coriolanus	Caesar	Richard III
Errors	Lear	Romeo
Cymbeline	Love's Labor	Tempest
Hamlet	Macbeth	Titus
1st Henry IV	Much Ado	Troilus
2nd Henry IV	Measure	Timon
Henry V	Midsummer	Twelfth
1st Henry VI	Merchant	Shrew
2nd Henry VI	Wives	Winter's

---

answer — sexual response of the male to a female, or (usually in jest or mockery) to another male or beast; cf. Antony II-7-107; Hamlet III-2-333; Ado III-3-50; et al.

bear(er) — the "underneath" sexual partner; cf. 2nd Henry IV II-4-65; Henry V III-7-48; et al; also cf. Partridge.

break — devirginate; cf. As You Like V-4-59; cf. Lover's Complaint 254-5; also cf. Partridge.

burden — the weight of the male body in coitus; cf. Winter's IV-4-195; As You Like III-2-261; et al; also cf. Partridge.

burn — contract or inflict a venereal disease; cf. Errors IV-3-58; 2nd Henry VI IV-2-67; also cf. Partridge.

come — orgasm and/or resulting emission; cf. Merchant III-5-68; Love's Labor V-2-112; et al; also cf. Partridge; cf. *welcome*.

condition — male or female organ; cf. 2nd Henry IV IV-3-90; Henry V V-2-314 & 326; et al; perhaps from the common connotation then of "a prerequisite, something indispensable."

cover — mount sexually; cf. Merchant III-5-58; Othello I-1-111; also cf. Partridge.

deform(ed) — (1) to erect; cf. Love's Labor V-2-767 (2) erected; Much Ado III-3-131; from bawdy of *form*, q.v.

eye — male or female organ (orifice); cf. Troilus V-10-49; Measure I-2-113; et al; also cf. Partridge.

fault — male or female organ; cf. Wives I-4-13 and V-5-9; 1st Henry IV III-1-245; et al.

favor — male or female organ; cf. Much Ado II-1- 97; Twelfth II-4-25; Measure IV-2-34; et al; also cf. Partridge.

fight — contend sexually; cf. Wives II-1-19; Troilus III-2-54.

figure — male or female organ; cf. Love's Labor V-1-67; Shrew I-2-114; et al.

folly — male or female organ; cf. As You Like V-4-111; Twelfth III-1-75; et al.

form — male or female organ; cf. Love's Labor I-1-209; Measure II-4-12; cf. *deformed.*

fortune — male or female organ; cf. Timon I-1-55; All's Well V-2-5; et al; also cf. Partridge at "fortunate".

go — reach orgasm; cf. 2nd Henry IV I-2-190; Troilus IV-2-23; et al; also cf. Partridge.

grace — male organ; cf. Love's Labor II-1-104 and V-1-148; Much Ado II-1-128; et al.

hang — cause to go limp (usually penis), trans. and intrans. verb; cf. Twelfth I-5-5 & 20; All's Well I-1-150; et al; also cf. Partridge.

hard — erection of penis or clitoris; cf. Much Ado V-2-38; As You Like III-2-331; et al; also cf. Partridge.

hard-favored — cf. *favored.*

hole — female organ (sometimes female or male anus); cf. Romeo II-4-97; 2nd Henry IV III-2-165; et al; also cf. Partridge.

horn — (1) male erection; Love's Labor IV-1-113 ff. and V-2-252; Much Ado V-2-38; et al; also cf. Partridge (2) cuckoldry; 2nd Henry IV I-2-52; Wives II-2-293 and V-5-4; et al; also cf. Partridge.

horse — whores; cf. Much Ado I-1-70; 1st Henry IV III-3-210; et al; also cf. Kökeritz.

kill — (1) the male role (insertion) in coitus; perhaps from "keel"; cf. Much Ado I-1-44; 2nd Henry IV Epilogue 147; et al (2) cause to go limp ("die"); cf. Henry V III-7-100; Love's Labor IV-1-113; et al.

knave — male organ (from knife?); Wives III-1-14 & 91; Twelfth II-3-69 ff.; et al.

knot — virgin knot; cf. Pericles IV-2-160; Tempest IV-1-15; also cf. Partridge; also cf. *not*.

know — to know carnally; cf. Merchant V-229; Measure V-1-186, 203, 230, 426; et al; also cf. Partridge.

leg — male organ; cf. 2nd Henry IV II-4-265; Love's Labor V-2-644; et al.

letter — female organ; cf. Love's Labor V-1-48 and V-2-44; Romeo I-2-64 and II-4-220; et al.

lose (lost), or *loss* — to lose, or loss of, semen; cf. All's Well III-2-44 and III-6-51; et al; also cf. Partridge.

matter — flesh of genitalia; cf. Caesar I-1-25; Tempest III-1-3; et al.

mind — male organ (cf. *wit*); Errors II-1-48; Pericles I-2-34; et al.

mood — sexually in the mood; cf. Romeo III-1-13; Merchant IV-1-51; et al.

mutton — male or female flesh; Measure III-2-192 (also cited by Partridge); not so much a bawdy term as slang.

not — virgin *knot*, q.v., maidenhead; cf. All's Well III-2-24 and V-3-248; also cf. Kökeritz.

note — (1) male organ; cf. Love's Labor III-1-14; Much Ado III-3-29; et al (2) fornicate (male role); cf. Much Ado I-1-165; Troilus V-2-11; et al.

nothing — female pudend; cf. Hamlet III-2-128; Cymbeline II-4-112; et al.

often — "offing" sexually; the Elizabethan "t" was silent (cf. Kökeritz); Timon III-1-25; As You Like IV-1-19.

pasture — female pubic hair; cf. Love's Labor II-221; also cf. Partridge at "bottom-grass" and "park".

peace — male or female organ (piece); cf. Measure I-2-4; Twelfth II-3-74; et al; also cf. Partridge at "piece".

post — male organ; cf. Much Ado II-1-207; Merchant II-9-100; et al.

purpose — male organ; cf. Wives IV-4-77; Troilus I-3-323-330; Timon III-1-26; et al.

repent — weep (sexually, "tears" of orgasm); All's Well IV-3-272; 1st Henry IV III-3-5; Troilus III-2-139.

scour — skewer, with probable sexual implication in this play; not in itself a bawdy term (cf. Henry V II-1-60; 2nd Henry VI III-2-199).

set — the state of or to cause erection (usually in the male); cf. 1st Henry IV II-4-482; Macbeth II-3-36; et al; also cf. Partridge.

shoot — male or female orgasm; cf. As You Like V-4-112; Love's Labor IV-1-11; also cf. Partridge; cf. *shot*.

shot — male or female emission; cf. Henry V III-7-131; Love's Labor IV-1-138 (upshot or upshoot); also cf. *shoot*.

sing — fellatio; cf. Troilus V-2-9; Love's Labor III-1-14 & 15; As You Like III-2-261 (very similar passage to that in this play); et al.

sleep — common euphemism, still extant, for sexual intercourse; also cf. Partridge at "lie" and "sleep".

son — usually female organ ("sun") sometimes male organ ("son"); cf. 2nd Henry IV III-2-139; Midsummer I-2-80; Hamlet III-2-340; et al; also cf. Kökeritz and Partridge.

speak — (1) sexually emit (intrans.); cf. As You Like IV-1-73; Love's Labor I-1-212; et al (2) cause sexual emission, usually by fellatio (trans.); cf. Twelfth I-3-27; Much Ado II-1-343; et al.

stab — male role in coition; cf. Caesar I-2-277; 2nd Henry IV II-1-15; also cf. Partridge.

stale — (1) urine; cf. Wives II-3-30; Antony I-4-62 (2) prostitute; cf. Shrew I-1-58; Much Ado II-2-26; also cf. Partridge.

stand — to reach erection; cf. Much Ado III-3-28 ff.; 1st Henry IV II-4-483 ff.; et al; also cf. Partridge.

stones — testicles; cf. Romeo I-3-53; 2nd Henry IV III-2-355; et al; also cf. Partridge.

tail — (1) male organ (appendage); cf. Othello III-1-8; Romeo II-4-101 (2) sometimes podex (rear) Shrew II-1-215; also cf. *tell.*

take it — submit sexually, always refers to the passive partner; cf. Romeo I-1-32; Richard III III-7-51; et al; also cf. Partridge.

tell — verb form of "tail" (often sodomy); cf. 1st Henry IV II-1-43; Errors III-1-53; et al; also cf. Partridge.

tongue — penis or clitoris; cf. Much Ado V-1-170; Troilus III-2-137; Shrew II-219; et al.

undo (undone) — cause another's orgasm (sometimes in context of devirginating or making pregnant); cf. All's Well V-3-147; Titus IV-2-75; et al; also cf. Partridge at "do" and "undo".

welcome — well "come" (q.v.); cf. Errors III-1-21 ff.; Troilus V-1-84; et al.

whip — movement of penis (trans. & intrans.); cf. Love's Labor V-1-69; Winter's IV-3-97; All's Well II-2-56.

wit — male or female organ; cf. Much Ado V-1-128 & 161; Romeo IV-5-124; et al.

word(s) — sexual emission; cf. Wives I-4-109; Twelfth III-4-209; Cymbeline IV-2-240.

The facsimile First Folio used is that of the Yale library prepared under H. Kökeritz (Yale University Press, New Haven, 1954).

Non-Shakespearean plays cited are listed under name of playwright or "Anon.".

Abbott, E. A. — *A Shakespearian Grammar*; London, 1877; reprinted N.Y., 1961.

Alexander, Peter — ed. *William Shakespeare The Complete Works* (Tudor edn.); N.Y., 1952; cf. Sampson, M. W.

———— *Restoring Shakespeare*; an article in Shakespeare Survey #5; Cambridge, 1952.

Annotated Shakespeare — cf. Rowse.

Anon. — *Everie Woman in Her Humor*, a play; Old English Plays (Old Series, Vol. IV), ed. A. H. Bullen; N.Y., 1882-9 (Reissued 1964).

(New) *Arden Shakespeare* — *The Two Gentlemen of Verona*, ed. Clifford Leech; London, 1969.

(Old) *Arden Shakespeare* — herein cited under Bond, R. W., q.v.

Bond, R. Warwick — ed. *The Two Gentlemen of Verona* ("Old" Arden); London, 1906.

Borinski, Ludwig — *Shakespeare's Comic Prose*; an article in Shakespeare Survey #8; Cambridge, 1955.

Boswell, James — ed. (—with E. Malone) *The Plays and Poems*; Rivington, London, 1821.

Brooks, Harold F. — *Two Clowns in a Comedy*; an article in Essays & Studies—1963, gen. ed. S. Gorley Putt; London, 1963.

Brown, John Russell — *Shakespeare and His Comedies*; London, 1957.

Bulloch, John — *Studies on the Text of Shakespeare*; Hamilton-Adams, London, 1878.

Bullough, Geoffrey — ed. *Narrative and Dramatic Sources of Shakespeare*, Vol. I; London, 1957-73.

(New) *Cambridge Shakespeare* — *The Two Gentlemen of Verona*, eds. Sir Arthur Quiller-Couch and J. Dover Wilson; Cambridge, 1921 (also cf. Neilson, W. A.).

(Old) *Cambridge Shakespeare — Works*, eds. W. G. Clark and J. Glover; London, 1863-6.

Capell, Edward — ed. *Mr. William Shakespeare: Comedies, Histories, and Tragedies*; London, 1767-8.

Chambers, Sir Edmund Kerchever — ed. *Works of Shakespeare* (The Red Letter Edition); Gresham, London, undated.

_____ *The Elizabethan Stage*; London, 1923.

Charlton, Henry Buckley — *Shakespearian Comedy*; London, Revised edn. 1955.

Clark, W. G. — cf. (Old) *Cambridge Shakespeare*.

Collier, J. Payne — *Notes and Emendations to the Text of Shakespeare's Plays*; Redfield, N.Y. 1853.

Craig, Hardin — ed. *The Complete Works of Shakespeare*; Scott-Forsman, 1961 (orig. 1891).

Craig, W. J. — ed. *The Complete Works* (The Oxford Edition); Oxford, 1936 (orig. 1904).

Danby, John F. — *Shakespeare Criticism and 'Two Gentlemen of Verona'*; an article in Critical Quarterly Vol. II, #4; Oxford, 1960.

Daniel, P. A. — *Notes and Conjectural Emendations*; London, 1870.

Davenport, Robert — *The City-Night-Cap*, a play; Old English Plays (New Series, Vol. III), ed. A. H. Bullen; Blom, N.Y., 1882-9, Reissued 1964.

Dobson, E. J. — *English Pronunciation 1500-1700*, 2 vols., Second edn.; Oxford, 1968.

Dyce, Rev. Alexander — ed. *The Complete Works of William Shakespeare* (Stratford-on-Avon Edition), Fourth edn.; London, 1880.

Evans, Bertram — ed. *The Two Gentlemen of Verona* (The Signet Classic Edition); N.Y., 1964.

Evans, G. Blakemore — cf. *Riverside Shakespeare*.

Ewbank, Inga-Stina — *Constancy and Consistency in The Two Gentlemen of Verona*; an essay in Stratford-Upon-Avon Studies, Series #14; London, 1972.

Farmer, J. S. — (and Henley, W. E.) *Slang and Its Analogues*; Private printing, 1890.

Fleay, F. G. — *Shakespeare Manual*; London, 1878.

Foakes, R. A. — cf. *Henslowe's Diary*.

Folger Library Shakespeare — *The Two Gentlemen of Verona*, eds. L. B. Wright and V. A. LaMar; N.Y., 1964.

French, Marilyn — *Shakespeare's Division of Experience*; N.Y., 1981.

Glover, J. — cf. (Old) *Cambridge Shakespeare*.

Gordon, George — *Shakespearian Comedy*; Oxford, 1944.

Greene, Robert — *James The Fourth*, a play; Everyman's Library: Minor Elizabethan Drama, Vol. II; N.Y., 1958.

Greg, Sir Walter W. — *The Editorial Problem in Shakespeare*, Third edn.; Oxford, 1954.

———— cf. *Henslowe's Diary*.

———— *The Shakespeare First Folio*; Oxford, 1955.

Halliwell—Phillipps, J. O. — *Memoranda on All's Well . . . The Two Gentlemen of Verona . . .* et al; Brighton, 1879.

Hanmer, Sir Thomas — ed. *The Works of Mr. William Shakespear*; Oxford, 1743-4.

Harrison, G. B. — ed. *Shakespeare the Complete Works*; N.Y., 1968.

Harrison, T. P. Jr. — *Concerning 'Two Gentlemen of Verona' and Montemayor's 'Diana'*; Modern Language Notes, Vol. 41, 1926.

Hazlitt, W. Carew — *Shakespeare Jest-Books*, 3 vols.; N.Y., 1964 (Reprint of 1864 edn.)

———— *Shakespeare's Library*, Second edn; N.Y., 1965 (Reprint of 1844 edn.).

Henley, W. E. — cf. Farmer, J.S.

Henslowe's Diary — (1) ed. Sir Walter W. Greg, 2 vols.; Bullen, London, 1904 (2) ed. R. A. Foakes and R. T. Rickert, Cambridge, 1961.

Hill, Charles Jarvis — cf. Neilson, W. A.

Hinman, Charlton — *The Printing and Proof-reading of the First Folio of Shakespeare*, 2 vols.; London, 1963.

Hulme, Hilda — *Explorations in Shakespeare's Language*; Aberdeen, 1962.

Irvine, T. U. — *How To Pronounce the Names in Shakespeare*; N.Y., 1919.

Irving, Henry and Marshall, Frank A. — *The Works of William Shakespeare*; Blackie, London, 1897.

Jackson, Berners A. W. — cf. *Pelican Shakespeare*.

Johnson, Samuel — ed. *The Plays of William Shakespeare*; Tonson, London, 1765.

_____ ed. (—with George Steevens) *The Plays of William Shakespeare*; Longman, London, 1793.

Jonson, Ben — *Every Man in His Humour*, a play; World Drama, Vol. I, ed. B. H. Clark; N.Y., 1960.

Keightley, Thomas — ed. *Plays of William Shakespeare*; London, 1864.

Kellner, Leon — *Restoring Shakespeare*; N.Y., 1969 (Reprint of 1925 edn.)

Kittredge, George Lyman — ed. *The Complete Works of Shakespeare*; Boston, 1936.

Knight, Charles — ed. *The Pictorial Edition of the Works of Shakspere*; London, 1838-43.

Kökeritz, Helge — *Shakespeare's Pronunciation*; New Haven, 1953.

_____ *Shakespeare's Names* (cf. list of CHARACTERS).

LaMar, Virginia A. — cf. *Folger Library Shakespeare*.

Lee, Sidney — *Shakespeare Facsimile of The First Folio Edition of the Chatsworth Copy*; Oxford, 1902.

Leech, Clifford — cf. (New) *Arden Shakespeare*.

London Shakespeare — The Two Gentlemen of Verona, ed. John Munro; N.Y., 1957.

Long, John H. — *Shakespeare's Use of Music*; Gainesville, Fla., 1955.

Mahood, Molly Maureen — *Shakespeare's Wordplay*; London, 1957.

Malone, Edmond — *The Plays and Poems of William Shakespeare*; Dublin, 1794.

Marshall, Frank A. — cf. Irving, Henry.

Mason, John Monck — *Comments on . . . Shakespeare's Plays*; 1785.

McKerrow, Ronald B. — *Prolegomena for the Oxford Shakespeare*; Oxford, 1939.

Miriam Joseph, Sister — *Shakespeare's Use of the Arts of Language*; N.Y., 1947.

Muir, Kenneth — ed. *Shakespeare The Comedies* (Essays); New Jersey, 1965.

Munro, John — cf. *London Shakespeare*.

Nares, Robert — *A Glossary* (of English Authors), 2 vols.; Reeves-Turner, London, 1888.

Neilson, William Allan and Hill, Charles Jarvis — eds. *The Complete Plays and Poems of William Shakespeare*; N.Y., 1942.

Nemerov, Howard — *A Commentary on The Two Gentlemen of Verona*; an essay in Poetry & Fiction; New Jersey (Rutgers), 1963.

New Cambridge — cf. *Cambridge*; NOTE: All text references to the "New" Cambridge are to the 1921 edn. (eds. Quiller-Couch and Wilson), and are not to be confused with any reissue or with the 1942 edn. (eds. Neilson and Hill), which latter is cited herein only once.

New Temple Shakespeare — ed. M. R. Ridley, 1935-6.

Onions, C. T. — *A Shakespeare Glossary*, Revised second edn. (of orig. 1911); Oxford, 1958.

Oxford Shakespeare — cf. Craig, W. J.

Parrott, Thomas Marc — *Shakespearean Comedy*; N.Y., 1949.

Partridge, Eric — *A Dictionary of Slang and Unconventional English*; N.Y., 1961. (Consulted but not cited herein.)

_____ *Shakespeare's Bawdy*, Revised edn.; N.Y., 1969.

Pelican Shakespeare — *The Two Gentlemen of Verona*, ed. Berners A. W. Jackson; Baltimore, 1964.

Pettet, E. C. — *Shakespeare and the Romance Tradition*; N.Y., 1949.

Pope, Alexander — ed. *The Works of Shakespear*; Tonson, London, 1723-5.

Quiller-Couch, A. — cf. (New) *Cambridge Shakespeare*.

Rickert, R. T. — cf. *Henslowe's Diary*.

Riverside Shakespeare — ed. G. Blakemore Evans; Boston, 1974.

Rolfe, William J. — ed. *Shakespeare's Comedy of The Two Gentlemen of Verona*; English Classics Series; N.Y., 1890.

Rowe, Nicholas — ed. *The Works of Mr. William Shakespear*; Tonson, 1709.

Rowse, A. L. — (The) *Annotated Shakespeare*; N.Y., 1978.

Sampson, M. W. — cf. *Tudor Shakespeare*.

Schmidt, Alexander — *Shakespeare Lexicon*, 2 vols; Third edn., Berlin, 1902.

Signet Classic Shakespeare — cf. Evans, B.

Singer, Samuel Weller — ed. *The Dramatic Works of William Shakespeare*; London, 1826.

Sisson, Charles Jasper — *New Readings in Shakespeare*, 2 vols; London, 1961.

———— ed. *William Shakespeare: The Complete Works*; N.Y., 1954.

Small, Samuel Asa — *The Ending of the Two Gentlemen of Verona*; an essay in Modern Language Publns. Vol. #48, 1933.

Staunton, Howard — ed. *The Plays of Shakespeare*; London, 1858-61.

Steevens, George — cf. Johnson, Samuel.

Stratman, F. H. — *Middle English Dictionary*; Oxford, 1891.

Tannenbaum, Samuel A. — *The New Cambridge Shakespeare and The Two Gentlemen of Verona* (A critique); N.Y., 1939.

Theobald, Lewis — ed. *The Works of Shakespeare*; Bettesworth-Hitch, Tonson, London, 1733.

Tilley, Morris Palmer — *A Dictionary of the Proverbs of England in the Sixteenth and Seventeenth Centuries*; Ann Arbor, 1950.

Tillyard, E. M. W. — *Shakespeare's Early Comedies*; London, 1965.

Tudor Shakespeare — The Two Gentlemen of Verona, ed. Martin W. Sampson; N.Y., 1931.

Udall, Nicholas — *Ralph Roister Doister*, a play; Everyman's Library: Minor Elizabethan Drama, Vol. II; N.Y., 1958.

Warburton, William — ed. (—with Alexander Pope) *The Works of Shakespear*; London, 1747.

Webster, John — *The White Devil*, a play; An Anthology of Jacobean Drama, Vol. I; N.Y., 1963.

White, Richard Grant — ed. *The Works of William Shakespeare*; Boston, 1865.

Wilson, Frank Percy — *Shakespeare and the New Bibliography* (Revised and ed. Helen Gardner); Oxford, 1970.

Wilson, J. Dover — cf. (New) *Cambridge Shakespeare*.

Wright, L. B. — cf. *Folger Library Shakespeare*.

Yale Shakespeare — The Two Gentlemen of Verona, ed. Karl Young; New Haven, 1924.

Young, Karl — cf. *Yale Shakespeare*.